G000091326

Seize the day

Seize
the day

The Story of Seven years
on the Seven Seas

Shirley Billing

Bosun-Publications

Published by Bosun-Publications
The Ferry Point
Ferry Lane
Shepperton on Thames
TW17 9LQ
Email: book@bosun-press.demon.co.uk

ISBN: 0-9546932-2-1

Seize The Day - The Story of Seven Years on the Seven Seas
Copyright © 2005 Shirley Billing

All rights reserved. No part of this publication may be reproduced, stored in a retrieval system, or transmitted in any form or by any means, electronic, mechanical, photocopy, recording, or otherwise, without the prior written permission of the copyright owner.

A CIP catalogue record for this book is available from the British Library.

Printed in England

CONTENTS

Seize the day

**For Peter
and
Paul, Noel, Andrea and their families**

Also by Shirley Billing
Red Sea Peril

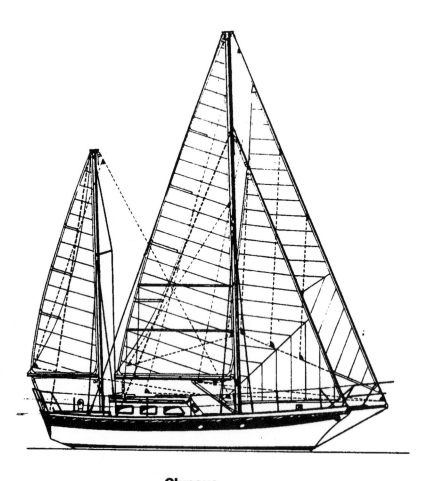

Clypeus

Introduction

CARPE DIEM - SEIZE THE DAY.   Horace 65-8 BC. *Odes*

Seize the Day, before it's too late. There's a wonderful world out there waiting to be explored. Today many forty and fifty-year-olds look with dismay at their future prospects – perhaps it would be better to seize the day and enjoy twenty active years of happy freedom in charge of your own destiny. If you are healthy and enjoy travel – go for it. As Tchekov wrote 'Life does not come again.' Most of us are lucky enough to now have an extra ten years to enjoy life. In 1982, in our late forties we sold the house and cars, cashed insurance policies; invested two thirds, then spent the remaining £30,000 on our boat to sail away. We haven't regretted it for a single day.

We have never looked upon ourselves as real sailors, but here we are, Peter and I, twenty years later, on the verge of completing a 60,000 mile circumnavigation by ourselves, in our own boat. There has been so much more to sailing-around-the-world than sailing. In spite of being an ordinary couple with no introductions to auspicious personages, no rally guide to pave the way and little money, we have been welcomed into grand houses and native huts, enjoyed the world and relished our freedom.

This book is a brief account of the preparations, the voyaging, and of the remote Pacific Islands where, in previous times, the only visitors were missionaries, government officials, traders or slavers. Traditional sailors shunned the perils of swirling currents, hidden coral reefs and the hot, humid mists. Thanks to advances in electronic navigation, we were among the privileged first visitors to arrive just as friends and be welcomed into island life. It also tells of robbery, shipwreck and the self-discovery of ourselves and our relationship.

Why did we go? Like many others we wanted to escape to a wilderness, a frontier, to test ourselves and live with nature before we died. Life was passing us by as we rushed to work. Our three children had left home, it was time to change down, perhaps we would blue-water-cruise one day. Suddenly fate pushed us into a decision when a car accident made us realise our time was running out, if we were going to fulfill our dream of returning to the South Pacific, now was the time to seize the day.

A three-year circumnavigation was planned. The kids encouraged us: 'The sooner you go the sooner you will be back'. None of us imagined that once 'we had drunk the milk of paradise' it would take twenty years to return.

Now we have a home beside Milford Haven estuary and spend our summers in the Mediterranean slowly sailing west until we cross our outward track at Ibiza. But for the first seven years, the compass of this book, we had no other home than our boat and no other income than the interest on our house sale money – we managed not to eat into our capital, but the stock market did. Then, while in Asia, we cheated a bit, as six years were spent on land while Peter took the opportunity to take up three two-year contracts with his previous American employers, in Taiwan, Singapore and later in Shanghai, where we lived the expatriate life and refilled our cruising kitty and retirement coffers. In these places too we seized the day and were able to explore much of Asia and I found easy friendships with local ladies as well as the expatriate wives. The Company included home-leave flights that enabled me to visit family and be there when grand-children arrived. In fact that is one of the astounding spin-offs, never dreamed of when planning our voyage – we have now flown around the world and visited Australia and the USA, more times than I can remember

As a child who wasn't clever or beautiful, I knew that it was up to me to make the first efforts towards friendship in each of the eleven schools I attended during WW2. Those experiences have stood me in good stead when rowing ashore alone to a remote island, armed with the knowledge that they don't eat women (we are unclean; and hoping the islanders think the same way). Sometimes the question is asked 'but where is your husband?' To which I usually reply that he has mainte-nance work to do on Clypeus, but really, he is a shy man who doesn't enjoy making new friends.

The sea has always charmed and fascinated me. My mother often told the story of her screaming baby sitting in the water's edge when an angry matron strode up and admonished her: 'How dare you frighten that poor child by putting her in the sea.' My mother abjectly replied 'I'm not putting her in, I'm trying to get her out.' I love the sea. I love being on it, in it, under it and writing about it. Snorkelling in the aquamarine water of a lagoon is my idea of heaven, the warm water caressing and cleansing my body and my soul. I love being on shore and watching the break-ers crash against cliffs; or waves sweeping the beach clean, the froth rolling back like suds in a car wash, or paddling with wavelets plopping on my toes. I love being on the ocean when the sun sparkles on each faceted deep blue ripple like undulating sapphires. Peter enjoys the solitude, being in charge of his own destiny and the chal-lenge of keeping all our life support systems functioning efficiently as if in a slow spaceship.

The forces of nature give a kind of security as there is no purpose in fighting them. You have to endure and have patience until they are in accord with your plans, as when having to linger in frustrating calms, or when the wind billows the sails so that our boat skims through the sea surface and fills our hearts with joy and the thrill of speed. I love being behind the wheel in light airs, barefoot and scantily clad with the spinnaker flying, trying to encourage our staid old boat to pick up her skirts and dance for me. The power of a gale excites me when clutching the wheel, feet braced on deck, trying to control our skid down an angry breaking wave. There is a peace and trust in a higher being during heavy weather when we furl the sails, close the hatches and cower in the cabin. I'm not sure I could accept fate as easily if I was younger and hadn't had the joy of children and grandchildren.

I feel privileged to have had the opportunity to sail to remote corners of our planet and meet people still unaffected by material wealth, television or tourists. To enjoy the simple life, close to nature, eating the food available to the local community. I like entering a new country by the back door of a commercial harbour, rather than the crush of bodies waiting behind the white line for the Immigration officer's silent curt nod, the grim inspection of passports and faces, his power in stamping and handing back your identity. We have to anchor, row ashore, scour the shoreline for Harbour Control, Police, Immigration and Customs office, to present ourselves and our papers. Perhaps stopping for an ice cream or beer between offices, then walking to buy fresh bread, fruit and vegetables from the real people. It isn't always a good experience but we are usually welcomed with courtesy and friendliness. Now, efficient clean marinas greet blue-water sailors, but we were lucky enough to cruise at a time when we were part of the general shipping world, before electricity, radio or TV sullied the waters and clouded national characteristics.

I enjoy cruising yachtsmen and women. I admire their courage, determination and resourcefulness. Most are humble, knowing they could be zapped at any time. Nature is capricious and the sea pitiless.

Some of the joys of growing old are that you haven't got to worry about dying young, nor, as a traveler, are you a threatening person. A young man arriving at a lonely island is approached with caution - he may be after food, a woman, possessions or even your land, and a young woman could have come to seduce your man, take your child or even just eat more than her fair share of food.

There is so much more to a voyage around the world than just sailing. We discovered that the poorer the people, the more generous they are. We didn't think it would happen to us, but we did meet people who considered it an honour to welcome a guest from a foreign land. Seize The Day tells of the first seven years of our circumnavigation and affords some glimpses of island life we were privileged to share. This book is dedicated to islanders everywhere.

The more I have, the more I want
The more I want, the less I have,
The less I have, the less I want
The less I want, the more I have.

Babylonian Philosophy

Burton Ferry
April 2005

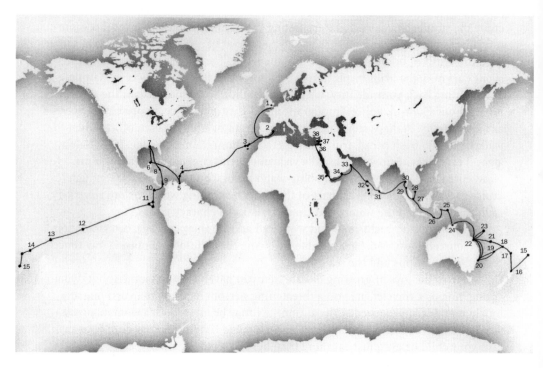

**WORLD MAP
SHOWING ROUTE**

1. London 1982/3
2. Ibiza
3. Santa Cruz Teneriffe
4. Antigua 1984
5. Carupano (Venezuala)
6. Cozumel (Mexico)
7. Gulfport (Mississippi)
8. Isla Providencia 1985
9. Panama Canal
10. Cocos
11. Galapagos
12. Hiva Oa Marquesa
13. Tahiti

14. Raratonga
15. Vavua (Tonga)
16. Bay of Islands 1986
17. Fiji
18. Port Vila (Vanuatu)
19. Noumea (New Caledonia)
20. Coffs Harbour 1987
21. Chesterfield Reef
22. Townsville 1988
23. Louisiades Papua New Guinea
24. Darwin 1989
25. Ambon
26. Bali
27. Singapore 1989/94
28. Tioman 1994
29. Langkawi 1995

30 Phuket
31 Galle (Sri Lanka)1996
32 Maldives
33 Salalah (Oman)
34 Aden
35 Barasoile Bay, Eritrea
36 Suez Canal
37 Ashkelon 1996
38 Cyprus 1996-2000

The final part of the journey will cover Cyprus to Milford Haven

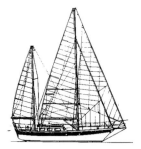

CHAPTER ONE

CLYPEUS

I sit in the cockpit, freezing cold and scared stiff. My ears pricked, listening out for the slightest noise. The cold damp fog wraps itself around me like a soggy blanket. Is that sound of a gourmet licking his lips actually waves slurping against the rocks off Cap Barfleur? Is that thump, thump, thump, my heart beating, or the throb of the engine of one of the four hundred merchant ships that pass this way every day and could mow us down without trace?

A couple of hours ago Peter, my husband and captain, (assuming I have the title of Admiral) sank, exhausted, onto the saloon settee after wrestling unsuccessfully with a seized-up engine, groaning as he dropped, "If the echo sounder shows less than thirty feet, head north."

Did we really sell up our home and cars, abandon our family and friends; give up our careers to do this? We must be mad. What insane, romantic, idea of cruising around the world in our own boat, addled our brains and dumped me here, in fog in the English Channel, the world's busiest shipping lane, at midnight, with no wind and no engine?

Head north! I can't head anywhere. We're completely at the mercy of the tide as the limp sails hang, dripping onto the deck of our home, our all. We haven't even reached our fitting-out destination yet. Crisis has followed crisis since we left St. Katherine's Dock and sailed down the Thames into the cold, stormy, North Sea.

Most of the blue water sailing books we had read, gave the impression that the voyagers jumped into their boats, waved a cheery goodbye, and sailed off into the sunset. They hadn't prepared us for the trauma of selling up and the heart-rending good-byes to family and friends. So far, in spite of our brave faces, we aren't doing very well.

'It's all my fault', I thought. 'Will we ever be able to buy ourselves back into a comfortable home and find new jobs without severe loss of face and money?' I recalled when we made our life-changing decision. We were a typical, almost fifty, 'empty nest' couple faced with what were we going to do with the rest of our lives now that our three children Paul, Noel and Andrea, had left home.

I remembered gliding along under a billowing spinnaker, barefoot and scantily clad. I thought of the sun-soaked islands, pale blue skies and deep-blue sea of last year's Greek flotilla charter, and the happy times sailing to France for summer holidays and weekend racing in the Solent. Those were the only times we really talked to each other now. At home, Peter was totally absorbed in his job and communications to me were on a 'need to know' basis. I no longer said much to him because he didn't listen anyway. What were we going to achieve working for the next fifteen years? A bigger pension? If we sold up and invested half the money for an income, surely we could manage to sail away? Who would suffer if we pushed off?

Peter trudged up the stairs after working another sixteen-hour day. We had married young while he was still studying. At 25, when he qualified as an Electrical Engineer, he was whipped straight into National Service. In the sixties, his company sent him to Sydney and after two happy years there with the three children, we returned to England on the liner Ellinis. The six-week voyage had taken us to New Zealand, Tahiti, Acapulco and New York. In Tahiti we had said "Wouldn't it be wonderful to come back in our own boat in our own time?" It was beyond our dreams - and means - to think it might ever happen.

My imagination raced. Next day I plotted and planned as the snowflakes fell.

The car slid on the black ice and landed upside down in the ditch

Suddenly Fate pushed us into a decision. Peter was late, very late home from a meeting in Leeds. At 11 p.m. the doorbell rang, before me was a white and shaken husband being held up on either side by kindly policemen. He had driven the 400 miles to his meeting and back in continuous snow. About two miles from home the car slid on black ice and landed upside down in a ditch. As I tucked him into bed he said, "The car doors wouldn't open, they were trapped by the ditch. I crawled out through the tailgate". His teeth chattered as he warmed his hands around a mug of hot soup,

"What if it had caught fire? I shuddered at the appalling thoughts that kept

red velvet upholstery. CLYPEUS' cabin felt like a country cottage in the calm marina. One cheeky visitor asked "When are you going to have her thatched?"

Some friends were envious, others thought us mad, and told us so. We did have doubts: could we actually live in such a small space? I worried about our emotional suitability for this life of 'forsaking all others'. We would only have each other for company for months on end, not being able to go for a walk when quarrelling. We are opposites: Peter is a shy, patient, methodical engineer. I'm an impatient, energetic, outgoing, people person. Before we left, we made a pact that, no matter how angry we were with each other, our 'happy hour' each evening would be a social time to talk and share thoughts, even if we reverted to 'not speaking' again afterwards. (We've never had to call our pact. Not because we haven't quarreled, but because both of us realise that if we let bad feeling fester, the results could be disastrous.)

The London Boat Show was especially exciting, for once we bought things instead of 'just looking': a new Perkins 4108 diesel engine, electronic equipment and an extra set of sails, triple stitched.

Many hours were spent in the Cruising Association library planning our route to coincide with the most suitable weather patterns using Ocean Passages for the World. Our forward-address list was sent off to family and friends so that they would have no doubt where to send letters. We realised we would only be a small part of their busy lives but I knew keeping the ties strong would be very important to us.

THE FIRST PLANNED ITINERARY OF CLYPEUS's ROUTE AROUND THE WORLD.

May-June 1983	- Leave Guernsey for France, Spain, Portugal.
July-Sept.	- Gibraltar, Balearics, Gibraltar
Oct	- Canary Islands
Nov-Dec	- Cross Atlantic to English Harbour, Antigua.
Jan-March 1984	- Cruise Caribbean and on to Panama
March	- Transit Panama Canal
March - April	- Galapagos Islands, then the longest hop across the Pacific to Marquesa Islands.
Jun-July	- Tahiti to be there for Bastille Day Celebrations - two weeks of dancing and singing and competitions.
Dec	- Bay of Islands, New Zealand
Mar 1985	- Sydney, East coast Australia and round "The Top End."
	- S. Africa, Cape Verde Islands, Azores and home by Sept. 1986.

Aahh! "The best laid schemes o' mice an' men, gang aft a-gley" - our scheme didn't 'gang' even to our first scheduled port. Our plan was to leave London in March, finish our fitting out in Guernsey, and then in June head down to Spain, Portugal and the Mediterranean and get some long voyages under our belts before venturing across the Atlantic. However it didn't quite happen that way....

CHAPTER TWO

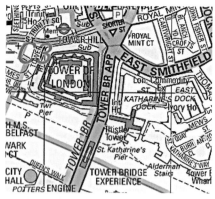

St Katherine's Dock London
Lat 50° 50' Long 00°
March - October 1983

W e set sail too early. Common sense should have prevailed and delayed our start for another month. But, we wanted to go, go, go. All the new gear should be waiting for us in Guernsey.

We motored out into the Thames from St Katherine's Dock

Early on 19th March 1983, the day of our Sailaway Party in St. Katherine's Dock, the Vicar of All Hallows by the Tower came on board and gave a short service blessing our boat, our family, and our voyage, as he had done for Sir Francis Chichester. It was sincere and made us feel we had taken every possible precaution, 'including celestial insurance', Peter said.

CLYPEUS looked spanking smart dressed overall with flags. Friends flowed on and off, marvelling that we were putting our lives into such a small container. After a lunch party in the Yacht Club our families stepped on board to join us for the first couple of miles. At high tide we waited for the lock gates to open. The Harbour Master brought a cable from my father in Australia, which I read out to those standing looking down at us:-

Farewell down the Thames

"Peter and Shirley have now set their sails,
To cruise round the world but dodging the gales,
After farewells to friends in old London Town,
They'll be seeing their 'Aussie Mates'
Who are all upside down."

In the feeble spring sunshine we motored out into the Thames under popping streamers and a chorus of *"Rule Britannia"* and *"Land of Hope and Glory"*. The love and affection voiced as they sang, floated across the water and comforted us in the cold and lonely days ahead. At Greenwich Pier we said our family good-byes and, except for Andrea, they caught a water taxi back up river to Tower Bridge.

Motoring down river the unusually shaped bastions of the, then unfinished, Thames Barrier reminded us of Sydney Opera House. Would we ever see it? It too was unfinished when we left Australia in 1968.

Anchoring just below the Barrier, we had supper and turned in early, still wrapped in our rosy glow. On Sunday morning a cold north easterly wind blew up the grey deserted river. Derelict abandoned warehouse ruins etched a black and bleak horizon against the ominous clouds. As the grey dawn lightened, we motored on and anchored for lunch off Shellhaven. I forgot to pull in the trailing log, which tells us how far we have gone and our speed through the water. Re-starting, Peter shouted "Anchor's off the bottom," as I put the engine into gear the propeller shaft whined and 'twang'. Yes, the log cable had caught around the propeller and snapped it off. Damn! Already one expensive piece of equipment destroyed, and I'd thrown money down the drain.

Late afternoon, in howling rain and squalls, we anchored in Queenborough and managed to row Andrea ashore to start her train journey back to Bristol where she was on nursing duty on Monday morning. We promised we would be in Guernsey to smother her in tender loving care after her impending tonsillectomy. How lucky we are that our children have given us every encouragement and never complained, (not even at being landed in the middle of a cold, wet and windy no-where to make their own way back right across the country).

The freezing north-easterly gale continued all week as we huddled in the harbour. We couldn't even row ashore as the seas were so rough. The Avon inflatable dinghy was sometimes airborne, flying horizontally on its steel painter above the waves.

Five days later we crept up the river valley to a vacant mooring at Medway Sailing Club alongside a south-facing wood. The sun broke through and I rowed ashore and found primroses and violets in peaceful dappled woodland. To sail out of the Thames should have taken nine hours, but it took us nine days... we weren't doing too well so far. Our Accountant had advised it would save paperwork if we were non-resident by the start of the new tax year in April and would make life easier - but for him, not us! We knew it was going to be rough and cold but, after all, we were only going to familiar old Guernsey to fit out and wait for the sun.

Midst a squall and snow flurry we hung outside the eastern entrance to Dover Harbour waiting for better visibility in case a Channel ferry steamed out. "As soon as this snow flurry is over we'll call and ask for permission to enter," Peter promised as we huddled in the cockpit.

"Now?"

"Not yet."

Ten minutes later: "Now?"

"OK." he grudgingly conceded and picked up the VHF microphone. "Dover Harbour Control, Dover Harbour Control this is sailing yacht CLYPEUS."

"Go ahead CLYPEUS this is Dover Harbour Control."

"Good afternoon. I request permission to enter through the eastern entrance. Please."

"Good. Come on in. I thought you'd never ask," chuckled the Officer. "Hasn't it been snowing out there?"

"Thanks. Yes, it has. We will be very pleased to come in. CLYPEUS standing by."

That night Peter had his last pint of "warm and cloudy" (as we heard some Dutch

Ferry Captains order their beer) at the Royal Cinque Ports Yacht Club. On Tuesday at dawn we gave in our customs forms, filled in with: 'Port of embarkation? Dover. Port of re-entry? "Dover.' Would we ever make it?

Cowes was to be the first port, but the wind was westerly and against us so Bolougne became our destination. CLYPEUS flew across the Channel, sliding and rolling over the grey choppy waves as spray broke over the starboard dodgers blasted by the westerly Atlantic wind. We tied up in the small marina in time to buy wine, baguettes and pate before the shops closed.

The BBC issued gale warnings on Tuesday, Wednesday, Thursday, but by Thursday the wind was abating and we had to get to Guernsey in time for Andrea's arrival. We left for Dieppe in huge following seas. It was exhilerating sailing, reefed right down, but shivering within thermal underwear, sweaters, balaclava helmet, fur mittens and hugging a hot water bottle between our knees.

After seven hours, sure that we should be nearing Dieppe, we hove-to to study the chart. CLYPEUS poppled up and down comfortably on the spot with the jib backed out one side and the mainsail balancing it on the other.

"Look! A merchant ship coming out of the mist. There must be a port there somewhere." Peter pointed.

"There's another cargo boat coming from the same place. See the white cliffs behind it. Have a look through the binoculars." I thrust them at him.

Shivering within thermal underwear and a hot water bottle between our knees

"Must be Dieppe" we both said.

The trailing log (Peter had replaced the cable and fitted a spare impeller) said we still had five miles to go, but with such pushy following seas, surely we were there already.

"This must be it." I said. It didn't need much to convince me it was Dieppe. I just wanted to get warm and still somewhere.

"Agreed. Turn the engine on. Take the wheel. Steer for the entrance lights and I'll lower the staysail and main." Peter went forward lowered and stowed the sails, leaving up just the working jib. As we approached the entrance the waves behind us got higher, white tops curled over and began to gurgle and crash menacingly.

"It doesn't look like the chartlet in the Channel Pilot, but we can't go back now. You take it." I handed the wheel over to him.

Fighting with the wheel to keep CLYPEUS from broaching we surfed down a narrow channel between iron latticework jetties into the harbour. There was no room for error, as we could broach and be rolled over at any moment. Terror mounted. The scend was terrific. In the harbour the water resembled a swirling, boiling, cauldron.

"This doesn't look anything like the chartlet." I gasped. "Are you sure this is

Dieppe?"

"No. But where else could it be? Where's the Basin a Flot? It's supposed to be here on the right," but we could see no opening or steel gates in the harbour wall.

Frantically I flicked through the Handbook. "This could be it. It shows a lattice-work entrance. Oh dear it's Le Treport. There's no hope of getting back out to sea is there?"

"Read me what it says," Peter demanded.

"A small commercial harbour.. blah... blah....outer harbour dries out. Oh No! "

"Does WHAT?"

"Dries out. Oh God! But look, over to the left there's the entrance to the inner dock. There's big ships in there."

We circled round between moored motor boats to the control tower. I shouted to the face behind the glass. "Bonjour. A quelle heure ouvert il, s'il vous plait?"

"Douze heure" a voice shouted.

"Ah! deux heure." Peter breathed a sigh of relief. "It will open at two; must be that now."

"No. No. He means douze, twelve o'clock. Another ten hours away."

"Bloody Hell!"

We continued circling around the heaving harbour between the moored fishing boats trying to find a free mooring, somewhere to anchor, or tie up. If I could have seen through his gloves, Peter's knuckles would have shone white as he gripped the steering wheel. "Read me some more."

"The gates to the inner basin open one hour before high water and close one hour after high water. Oh my God!"

Some wet-suited French divers in a red inflatable dinghy zoomed around us like an angry wasp trying to be helpful. They tied us fore and aft between two moored fishing boats, but too close. CLYPEUS's eleven tons of concrete thrashed up and down in the ten-foot swell. We hit the front one and our bowsprit crashed into a cabin window and broke it. Our arms and legs came perilously close to being crushed or broken as we fended off.

As the tide receded, gradually the harbour became less agitated because the shallow entrance dried out first. We managed to tie up alongside the quay and, sitting on the deck, easing the lines, kept our feet against the wall until the water went right out, leaving CLYPEUS sitting nose down in soft yellow mud. Shivering with fright and cold we grabbed a hot drink and three hours sleep and were up again at ten to fend ourselves off, while the tide rose its customary twenty or so feet. We were eventually allowed into the sanctuary of the inner harbour at 2 am. What bliss to be cold, wet and bruised but STILL and SAFE.

The gales went on for another week. We tried to find the owner of the boat with the broken window, but were eventually told "Pas de probleme." The boat was being held by the Harbour Authority for non-payment of fees, and nobody knew where the owner was.

Le Treport is a delightful resort and fishing harbour. We walked along cliff tops and analysed supermarket prices. The Poissonerie Municipale had a wide variety of fish for sale and we were interested to see what the French consider edible.

After a week we left for Dieppe. However, the weather resumed being cold, grey and windy as we tacked through big seas. Salt water came in around the hatch and soaked the bed, duvet, pillows and carpet. New hatches became an urgent priority.

No problems entering Dieppe - we were looking at the right chart this time. The yacht pontoons were in the Basin a Flot with the trawlers and wholesale fish market. It stank of oil, fish and flotsam. Stepping off the boat onto the oily, slippery walkways, was revolting. I tried not to breathe in the fetid smell. Our lovely clean white topsides became covered in black slime.

Dieppe is a pleasant ancient French town with a good street market on Saturdays. Bright striped awnings over stalls displaying glistening fish, red, green and orange fruit and vegetables. Old ladies dressed in black sat on stools with perhaps a bunch of leeks, a few eggs and a jug of cream to sell. Live ducks and chickens, like untidy feather dusters, hung by their feet or peered, bright eyed, out of their cages.

In the cabin, listening to Edith Piaf's laments while the freezing rain drummed on deck, I wrote letters to family and friends trying to convince them we were enjoying our adventure as 'this MUST be the worst bit. When we reach the sun, you'll wish you were with us.'

The paraffin heater caused prodigious condensation so there were trickles of water running down the inside, as well as the outside of the misted windows. Peter sat mending the Stowe log which had been doused. As he drew the circuit of the electronics he muttered: "Ridiculous making cockpit electronic equipment which isn't waterproof."

It was so cold he was sitting at the table wearing his fleecy-lined jacket and the Greek fisherman's black serge cap that a pilot friend had given him. He hardly took it off for three weeks and even kept it on indoors. He did take it off to go to bed though! We were both wearing our thermal underwear, socks and taking the hot water bottle to bed. On some nights we should have worn oilskins as well since the hatch still leaked. It's a fact that you don't catch cold by being damp and shivering all night. We tried to convince ourselves that soon we would be sailing south to the sun and then most of our problems would be over.

An uneventful sail to Fecamp restored our confidence. In the Laundromat opposite the fine cathedral, I was trying to fold the clean sheets on my own. A tall teenage French boy - all arms, legs and spiky hair - who sat slouching watching his washing go round, stood up and offered to help me fold. He was polite and charming and chatted in broken English. I was delighted by his friendly gesture. We phoned our family and reported progress - and as the machine appeared to work without money, we phoned a few friends as well.

After a promising midnight weather forecast we left Fecamp. It took us a while to pluck up courage, hoist the sails and push off in the dark. Letting go the dock lines from each port was becoming increasingly traumatic.

Motor-sailing out of the harbour into a clear starry night the sea was calm wiith no moon. A beautiful crisp, sunny day's sailing took us across Le Baie du Seine. On sighting Isle de Marcouf we turned north and beat hard into the wind to keep our offing. As dusk fell, a thick grey bank of fog rolled towards us and the wind died. Surrounded by grey mist, with eyes fixed on the compass we motored blindly, parallel with the coast towards Cape Barfleur, one of the most notorious and dangerous headlands in the English Channel. Suddenly silence... the engine stopped. Peter urgently pulled up the cabin floor, lay down and peered into the gaping hole. While I studied the tidal flow charts, he worked desperately for five hours as we drifted with the tide, but to no avail, the engine had completely seized up. At midnight, he gave up and left me on watch alone. The silent sea swirled around us. The tide turned and we were being swept... which way? We floated like a ghost ship, our small dark world surrounded by a thick black blanket of fog. The smell of my wet sheepskin mitten as I wiped it across the freezing drip on the end of my nose, reminded me of the dreams of returning to Australia's sunshine. The woolly odour conjured up the pungent smell of gum leaves and wet sheep, their wool steaming as they emerged into the burning sun.

Cold and apprehensive, I huddled in the damp cockpit clutching the wheel and worrying, I wasn't conscious of praying, what happened to us would be inevitable. I considered: 'If we survive tonight, we know God is with us and our voyage has His blessing.' The picture and inscription from my Welsh childhood church in Milford Haven, which I had contemplated seriously during interminable sermons because there wasn't an 's' on 'alway' came to mind. A kindly Christ blessing the children saying "Lo I am with you alway."

Suddenly peace descended upon me; it felt as if a great weight had been lifted from my shoulders. We would do our best, but the final decision was up to Him. Since then, even in the most dire situations, I'm aware of a comforting presence.

At 3 am the fog lifted and, waking Peter, we realised the tide was sweeping us west. The lights, which we identified as Cherbourg, glowed a few miles to port. However, with no engine and no wind we couldn't steer ourselves into the harbour. We tried lying on the deck near the bow and paddling with the dinghy oars, but couldn't make any headway. The tide was sweeping us past the entrances to the Grand Rade, out into the Atlantic.

A shallow patch of 30 feet was marked on the chart. Peter lowered the CQR anchor and as the echo-sounder showed the shallow patch so the anchor grabbed. He let out 60 feet more chain and we swung out of the shipping lanes and slept, exhausted. In the morning we awoke to a fresh northerly wind which allowed us to sail into Cherbourg Marina dropping the sails as we slid gracefully and gratefully into a berth.

After breakfast we made for the Hypermarket for our usual Cherbourg treats:.St. Vaast oysters, pate, baguettes, and from the Charcuterie in the Square, luscious pizzas dripping with tomatoes, anchovies, cheese and black olives, and duty free wine from Henri Ryst. Humour was restored upon remembering our boys' holiday adage "Get pissed on Ryst". We recovered our composure within 24 hours and were ready to sail again.

We left Cherbourg apprehensively knowing that as we had no engine, we would have to rely on our sailing skills to make our landfall in St. Peter Port through the eight knot tidal flows of the Alderney Race. No problems. When approaching the harbour entrance, St. Peter Port Harbour Control launch came and towed us into the marina where we tied up on the 19th April - having spent a whole month for a journey we expected to take no more than a week.

The next morning, after clearing Customs, we telephoned old friends, who had let us use their postal address. They arrived with a lovely stack of letters and parcels and the news that Andrea and her friend had come and gone having spent a week waiting 'for the ship that never came.'

Of the new equipment Peter had ordered, only the Perkins 4108 diesel engine waited in Customs, the Walker Satnav, Aries windvane self-steering, new hatches, etc. were still waiting to be shipped from London.

Throughout the month the BBC had kept us informed of the bomb in Harrods, whether Mrs. Thatcher would make up her mind about an election, and I 'Fought the Flab' with Terry Wogan. We were also very well up on "Farming Today" which we heard most mornings whilst waiting for the weather forecast. "Sailing By", the tune the BBC play after Radio Four shuts down until the forecast at 00.20 was our 'top of the pops'

St. Peter Port seemed prosperous with money being spent on properties, harbour and town improvements. It was all so fresh and clean. The traumas of the first lap of our voyage soon faded. Our friends gave us a home away from home. They lent us their Land Rover and The Royal Channel Islands Yacht Club was friendly and welcoming.

My parents came and spent two weeks in local hotels nearby before returning to Australia. My mother helped me to prepare my stores. One major task was to make sure labels from canned food could never block the bilge pumps. We sat on deck in the sun, stripping the labels from the cans, varnished them, and with a felt tip pen, marked the contents and date of purchase. They were stowed in neat, but boring, rows in the under-settee locker. I

My mother helped me strip of the labels and varnish the tins

overstocked, and five years later we were still digging into the original hoard - steamed treacle pud not being typical tropical fare. (Heinz treacle puddings were still good after eight years.) I also over-stocked on foot powder - well, I thought our feet would get so hot in our wellies in the tropics. I'd forgotten about being barefoot and scantily clad.

When my parents left, friends towed us to St. Sampsons Dock where Peter fitted the new Perkins engine. Alone, he juggled with pulley block and tackle, sheer legs, chocks of wood and planks to slide the old engine out and the new one in. I hadn't seen him so happy for years. He organised it so efficiently that when the crane lorry arrived to take the old engine away and lower the new one down, it only took 15 minutes and the driver never asked for payment.

As the other new equipment arrived Peter fitted it - the SatNav, wind self-steering gear and new hatches. He designed and made a new larger rudder of steel, coated with fibre glass and epoxy. "Now she won't steer like a pig." he promised. April showers and cold winds couldn't dispel our excitement about our coming voyage of 800 miles to Lisbon.

We thundered around the island in the old 'workhorse' Land Rover, looking for spares, getting bits machined, welded and fibreglassed. We also used it as a taxi for meeting our friends at airport and ferry and gave lifts to anyone prepared to sit in the open back

Going out to dinner and the odd dance was exciting. One night, as I slid across the bench seat to get out of the driver's door (wire and string kept the permanently closed passenger's door together), I ripped the seat of my tights and spent each dance wondering if one or both legs would descend around my ankles. They didn't, and apprehension added a little spice to the Hotel's staid dinner dance.

For four weeks CLYPEUS rested against the wall amongst the fishing boats, regularly showered with black dust from unloading coal vessels, or soot from the Power Station chimneys. We became part of the local scene, the fishermen gave us crabs and we suffered a surfeit of tomatoes. The old engine was bought by a tomato grower for £25 plus bags of tomatoes. He kept coming back for spares, each time with another large plastic bag of green tomatoes. The jars of tomato chutney lasted well across the Atlantic. We learned that growers consider tomatoes at their best, and eat them, when they are still green. His wife and daughters befriended us and showed us around the warm, humid greenhouses

The local fishermen gave us crabs

which they had just scrubbed with disinfectant before planting the new crop.

The smell of hot tomatoes under glass reminded me of the lengths to which my mother went during World War II to feed her family. She tended her tomatoes with loving care. Fertilisers were not readily available. Sheep roamed the local golf course to keep the grass short in those economy days. To my Father's embarrassment he was often followed around the course by my Mother spooning up sheep droppings into a small sack to fertilise her prized tomatoes.

We took the ferry to Herm for a celebration lunch at The White House, and were enchanted. In May, flowers bloomed everywhere, the ground was covered with buttercups, daisies, and dog roses you couldn't avoid stepping on them. Tiny pink cowries and smooth rounded yellow and brown nerites nestled in the sand and I realised I could happily spend the next few years beach-combing for shells. It has proved to be an absorbing hobby and given excitement and interest on every beach we have visited. Even if there are no shells - why? It's a good reason for going ashore and each shell in my collection now brings back a happy memory.

"Buy what you will of arts and crafts
In that exotic store,
It will look paltry by the shell
I found upon the shore."
Genevieve Smith Whitford. USA

One of my jobs was to give the hull a final scrub

Back in St. Sampsons, lying alongside the harbour wall, it was a constant struggle to get on board as the tide rose and fell thirty to forty feet. Mooring lines to the jetty from the bow, stern and mast, needed attention every three hours night and day. Going into town needed fore-thought or we would return to find the ladder lying on deck and we were twelve feet above it. To get on board at low tide meant climbing down the slippery steps at the end of the jetty and trudging through the mud. I would climb on Peter's knee, slipping off my muddy boots, then on to his back and shoulders to reach the swimming ladder. He would try to steady himself and keep from sinking deeper and deeper into the mud, gasping unkind words about my weight.

Once at 3 a.m. when it was my turn to tighten the mast line as the tide went out, so that we didn't fall away from the well-lit quay. I stood on deck wearing oilskins over my nightie and my long blonde hair blowing in the wind and rain. As I slackened the ropes, I looked down and noticed my wellington boots were on the wrong feet. I felt like a happy three year old.

When we were getting near June 1st, our proposed leaving date, one of my jobs was to give the hull a final scrub. I noticed many little holes and white eruptions popping through the recently painted hull. It didn't look healthy.

We wrote and eventually it was agreed the work would be completely redone, free of charge, if we brought CLYPEUS back to the Hamble. It was really depressing to have to sail back. It had been such agony to get this far. However, the weather was fine and we had a glorious sail back to the Solent. We gave ourselves one long sunny day on the beach in Alderney, then spent six weeks getting the job done. So all the time we should have been swanning down the Spanish and Portuguese coasts in the lovely June/July weather, CLYPEUS rested in a dark and dirty paint shed in a boat yard near Southampton.

We made good use of the time but kept our heads down. It was so embarrassing to be back after our lovely send off. Our sea legs and courage waned a little. However, England looked SO lovely that early summer of '83 when the weather was hot and dry. The Boat yard loaned us a caravan usually used by one the Admiral's Cup crews, which was much bigger than CLYPEUS'S interior and the showers were good, so it wasn't too bad.

CLYPEUS was eventually refloated on 21st July and we left next morning. Three hours out, and for the first time in my life, I was so angry, I almost threw something precious away. I never lose my temper - my mother didn't allow it. We were making for the Needles in a turbulent, gunmetal sea and found ourselves in the shallow Shambles turmoil. After two hours at the helm steering carefully through the confused tumbling grey and white water I handed the wheel to Peter and picked up the new and expensive Tamaya binoculars.

"Don't drop them," he cautioned once too often.

"Of course I won't drop them. You trust me with your life and then admonish me in case I drop the binoculars. I'm not a six year old. If you ever say 'don't drop them' again I'll throw them into the sea. Here, have your blasted binoculars." I thrust them at him and retired below to fume and feel unappreciated. This was supposed to be a partnership, not a parent/naughty child relationship and we now only had each other. Later I realised we both say thoughtless things in times of stress and we now try hard not to offend.

We sailed directly to Guernsey, picked up our guns and foreign currency, and struck out next day into the Atlantic to cross the Bay of Biscay well offshore before turning south to Lisbon. Many hours had been spent deliberating whether to take guns or not. In the end we decided to be prepared. Our gun licence was for a pump action shotgun with solid slugs that could be fired at an approaching pirate vessel to pierce holes below their waterline. Hopefully it would divert them from attacking. Also a Smith and Wesson .38 service revolver kept in a neat holder above the bed with the bullets hidden in a nearby drawer so that an intruder wouldn't easily find them to put both together. We didn't realise that in a crisis, we wouldn't find them either. Now we know that pirates are sophisticated and have better guns and are better trained to use them than we would ever be.

Biscay was very confused. Huge ocean swells going all ways and bouncing off each other. In the deep, dark water, great sloping hills of navy-blue sea advanced, passed beneath and continued on their way. We just slid across them and down the other side. Some of the sailing was exhilarating and some was awful. In spite of taking Stugeron, Quells or Dramamine we discovered that 'Togetherness is' - being seasick holding hands.

Gradually the sun warmed and soothed us and we adjusted to three hours on watch and three hours off, through the 24 hours, and found the rhythm of our boat and ourselves. There was much shipping about and by the time we had caught up on sleep, changed sails, prepared and eaten food, cleared up, and plotted our course, we were ready for sleep again. CLYPEUS was proving to be able to take all weathers. The rolling was dreadful at times - each side rail going under alternately.

At 40° North off the Portuguese coast we realised that - at last, our dream was coming true. We were sailing on a smooth blue sea, under a clear sky, in warm sunshine, with the wind behind us... perfect. Our bow cut through the sparkling sea, lifting a pearly curve to bubble and tumble back along the hull. Our days fell into a regular routine. At night with the sea an inch from my ear, the water sighed, like the rhythm of the world breathing. After seven days we arrived at Cascais near Lisbon on 5th August, my 49th birthday. Sailing into Cascais Bay we could see a group of people on the quay jumping up and down and waving their arms.

"Quick, quick pass me the binoculars, and don't say it," I warned. "It's Sheila," I crowed with delight. My sister and children had driven across Portugal on their way to their Spanish vacation to meet us and had managed to be at exactly the right place at the right time. They were staying with a mutual childhood friend who now lived in Estoril. For a whole week CLYPEUS nodded safely at her anchor except for odd jaunts and picnics. Only one hour's easy train ride took us to the ancient and modern white stone city of Lisbon. It was a pleasant excursion to explore the romantic castle which stands high on the hill overlooking the ancient red-tiled roofs of the city.

Coastal hopping south in the sun we visited golden beaches and quaint fishing harbours. Walking to market to buy our food was fun especially when trying to make myself understood in Portuguese. Vegetables were displayed on the ground and dogs lifted their legs indiscriminately which was a little disconcerting. Road workers barbecued fresh sardines on braziers by the roadside. They broke hunks of crusty bread from hot loaves and swigged down red wine from dusty green bottles. The sight and smell were irresistible.

"We must have a barbecue. My mouth waters every time we pass them." Peter said as he bought a small cast-iron BBQ. Grilled fresh sardines, together with tomato salad, crusty bread and wine became our daily fare too.

The nude beaches surprised us and I still think it bizarre to see a young man walking along the beach sun-pink and starkers; especially when carrying a little handbag.

Sandstone cliffs, arches and stacks glowed orange in the rays of the setting sun as we glided by, but thick fog came down as we approached Cape St. Vincent, the most southerly corner of Europe. When the sun came out again bottle-nosed dolphins welcomed us into the Mediterranean and escorted CLYPEUS to Gibraltar. They cavorted and played ahead of us, twisting to look up and make eye to eye contact as they sped beneath the bowsprit. We grew to recognise individuals by the white scratches and scars on their backs and fins. If they were in the offing we would sail towards them. Sometimes I stood on the bow clapping and singing "My Bonnie Lies Over the Ocean" it's amazing how often they came to join in and show off their acrobatic skills.

Entering Gibraltar, Peter declared our guns to the Customs Officer who demanded to impound them at once. Peter came to collect them and took them into the office only to be sent back for the ammunition. It was the first of many disagreeable incidents with officials over guns. We had all the correct paperwork, but carrying guns caused endless official trouble.

In Gibraltar we enjoyed being able to speak English and use sterling. It was more Spanish and Morrocan than expected and nothing seemed particularly cheap. Friends who lived high on The Peak gave us a pleasant day around their swimming pool. The views were stunning over the harbour, airport and Spain. They took us to see the Apes of the Rock: mangy, evil looking creatures, not the smiley primates we were used to seeing in the television tea ads.

At Puerto Duquesa we sailed friends back to Gibraltar for a day out and quite forgot that we were entering another country. The British Immigration Officials verbally smacked our wrists and didn't allow us ashore. On the way back, Bill hooked a 9" brown, ordinary looking, leathery little fish. As I helped him remove it from the hook, it suddenly jabbed the spine on the side of its gills into the ball of my thumb. Within a few seconds my heart started racing and the pain was excruciating. I immediately swallowed three Piriton (antihistamine tablets) and suggested we make for a doctor quickly. On arrival at the Duquesa jetty a cab rushed us to a Doctor, who administered an injection, pills and potion. It was a weaver fish and its painful sting is capable of killing a person.

Along the Spanish coast we called at Cadiz - Estapona - Duquesa - Malaga - Motril - Garrachu - Cartegena - Torrevieja and- Alicante on the way to Ibiza, and many others on the way back. At Granada we stood in the room where Queen Isabella had given Columbus the casket of jewels to fund his voyage to the Americas. How brave and foolhardy were those early explorers to set off with no charts and not knowing whether they would fall off the edge of the flat earth.

The other yacht crews we met were friendly and sociable. Boat names were used rather than family names. We became known as Mr. and Mrs. CLYPEUS or the 'Clypetians'.

Andrea joined us for a holiday. From Alicante we sailed her to Formentera, and Ibiza. We loved Ibiza's ancient hill city with its white sun-soaked walled alleys and arches. The sea was clear and warm, and the beaches golden. In one deserted bay, Andrea and I prepared to snorkel. We tied the dinghy to some rocks and stood waist deep putting on our masks. I felt a light touch on my foot, then something slithering gently around my ankle. I looked down. "Yeeeow!" I leapt into the air like a Polaris missile. It was an octopus curling itself around my leg. I nearly died of a heart attack. It probably did too. Back in the dinghy I poked him with the oar and he hung on, in fact, started to undulate up towards my hand. Thoroughly unnerved, I splashed and banged the oar on the water until the poor thing dropped off. It did bring home to me - how do you actually kill these denizens of the deep if you do manage to catch them?

It was August and some beaches thronged with people. The smell of suntan oil wafted across the water. From the dinghy to get to

Andrea and I prepared to snorkel

the shops meant stepping over the bare-breasted bodies packed close together - the thought of tripping up and putting out a hand to save yourself was un-nerving.

After Andrea had flown home, apprehensive about crossing the Atlantic we hurried back to Gibraltar to start our preparations. We anticipated leaving for Lanzarote in October, spending a few weeks in the Canaries, and preparing to set off for the Caribbean around 14th November so that we should be in Antigua in good time for Christmas. Could we, just Peter and I, actually sail ourselves across the Atlantic? Well, there was only one way to find out.

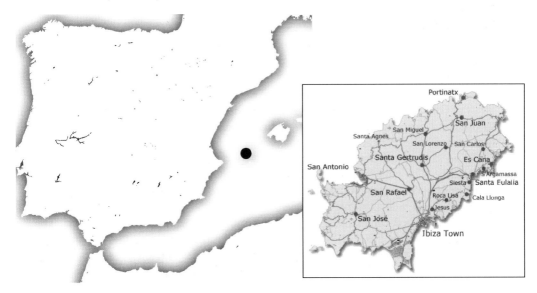

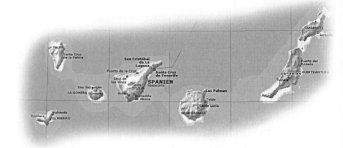

The Atlantic
Lat 10°- 60°W. 25°N-18°N
October - December 1983

CHAPTER THREE

The 5.30 alarm woke us. With excitement mounting and after a hot drink, it was time to leave Gibraltar. The motor purred into action. As I went to let go the lines, Larry of OCEAN WIND strolled up. After a quick hug he encouraged "You hop on board, I'll let go here. Ann apologises for not getting up, she just awoke sufficiently to mumble about sending you her love."

As CLYPEUS slid away from the pontoon I pulled the lines in.

Time to leave Gibraltar

"Bon voyage," he whispered. "Let us know when you get to the Canaries." His solitary figure grew smaller under the lamplight. We really appreciated his gesture - he might have been the last person we ever saw. This wasn't going to be a coastal voyage. This was the real thing across an ocean. I trembled with apprehension as I coiled the ropes and stowed them in the cockpit locker. They wouldn't be needed for a week or so.

The lights of Algecerias on the Spanish coast sparkled and hung in space in that moment before the pink dawn, which blossomed into a lovely sunny day. A good North Easterly breeze gave us courage as we swooped through the rough narrow Strait of Gibraltar. As the brown sandy hills of Morocco fell behind an orange shroud, so the wind dropped and CLYPEUS rolled abominably in the swell. Peter hoisted the mizzen but it didn't help much

Land sank below the horizon, now we were really on our own, actually crossing the Atlantic. The next morning brought a spectacular red and pink dawn with Venus rising huge and luscious. A big lumpy sea made us feel queasy and we just slept alternately all day as well as all night.

Peter switched on the SatNav to check our position. Nothing happened. The screen stayed blank. No comforting numbers of latitude or longitude. "Bloody hell! The SatNav has packed up. What a way to start a voyage!" He diagnosed flat batteries and after motoring for ten hours to charge them, numbers again appeared on the screen but it needed complete reprogramming. The incident shocked us into taking sights again and Peter's dawn sights on Sirius, Venus and the Moon proved accurate.

On the sixth day, 700 miles west of Africa, when daylight emerged, we sighted the mountains of Lanzarote and headed for Ariceffe on the east coast, the main town and port of entry - our first real ocean landfall. Our excitement faltered as the anchor refused to hold in the thin layer of sand over the rocky bottom of the attractive recommended anchorage. As it grew dark, we motored round to the mucky fishing harbour. It was smelly but safe.

Ariceffe town market is entered through stone arches. It was alive with black-clothed women and sun-wrinkled men proffering avocados, onions and oranges. In a cave bodega as we sampled the slightly sulphurous local wine we decided to take an island tour. My mother had once written enthusiastically of the contrasts of Lanzarote: high, hot, mountains; deep cool caverns with sightless fish and crabs.

Never have we seen so much in one day. Lanzarote still has active volcanoes. We lolloped to the crater rim on camels up a sand trail between queer shaped eroded rocks. It resembled a moonscape. On the summit, guides demonstrated the heat beneath our feet, by pouring a shovelful of sand into our outstretched hands. "Oooh! Ouch! It's hot!" We exclaimed in turn as we let it go. A forkful of hay was held into a metre deep hole where, after a few seconds, it ignited spontaneously. A Ranger poured a bucket of water down a 6" pipe set in the ground. Poof! A cloud of steam exploded into the air.

The coach driver pointed out the cliffs where the last of the original inhabitants, the Guanches, committed suicide to avoid being slaves of the Spanish Conquistadors. These mysterious ancient people were thought to be the inhabitants of lost Atlantis. Research shows they were blonde, blue-eyed Cro-Magnon people, probably of Berber and Celtic descent. Their language syntax resembled Basque, Welsh and Gaelic. It's a shame, but the romantic Atlantis theory is faulted on technical grounds. The Canary islands rise directly from the 3,000 metre deep ocean floor and form part of the Mid-Atlantic Ridge, geologically dated around 2.5million years ago.

In the sun's glare, squat white houses quivered like radiators. Each growing plant is still tenderly nourished by hand and surrounded by a little wall of cinders into which seaweed is carefully placed then covered by volcanic ash to retain any moisture. No animals or tractors can be driven over the earth as they would disturb the soil lay-ers of ash and seaweed. Little bent, men and women, with black scarves beneath their straw hats, dotted the fields of this ashy landscape.

At the Cuevas Verdas, we followed our guide down through miles of cool, dim, smooth-walled fumaroles, into great caverns, and felt insignificant in space and time beside the towering stalagmites. Blow-holes led us to wide openings high up in the cliff face where we looked out over the ocean and watched the swell break ferociously against the rocks.

Back in the harbour, CHERETA, a catamaran, was anchored near CLYPEUS. Mary and Bob invited us on board for coffee and later showed us a film of their first Atlantic crossing which they had made with their children. It looked fun and gave us confi-dence and some idea of what it would be like. They were the first real ocean voyagers we had met and they inspired us.

However, the following day of sailing to Teneriffe did not inspire us. The sea was confused, and sick-making, with little wind. Although we could see Teneriffe all day, a strong current swept us north, making us fight every inch of the way south again in the dark. The brilliant lights of Santa Cruz teased us in the distance.

I was woken with the call, "Shirley come up and help me find the harbour lights. There are so many street lights I can't decide where the entrance is." Forcing myself out of my cosy bunk I was delighted to see the shimmering fairy-tale city lights nestled beneath craggy mountains silhouetted against the moon's glow. Eventually we sorted out the flashing green and red lights flanking the harbour entrance from the red, green and orange street traffic lights, and entered calm water, quietly tying up beside a yacht of similar size.

When we awoke to bright sunshine we found the harbour was filthy and full of yachts, over 80, waiting for the NE trade winds to start blowing. Dead rats, globs of tar, oil, plastic bags, wood and garbage floated on the surface. Climbing the iron ladder up to the quay covered our hands and clothes with black oily smudges.

It was exciting to be back on Teneriffe where I had often visited my parents in Puerto de la Cruz. Happy years of their lives during which my father was officially honoured with the title of Don for the pioneer work he had done bringing tourism to the Canary Islands. He had organised and chartered the first tourist flight to Teneriffe in 1957 via Madrid, Casablanca and Las Palmas. Their friends, in Puerto were holding our mail.

The market glowed with fresh smelling, colourful vegetables: tomatoes, cauliflowers, red and yellow capsicums, spinach, carrots, avocados, oranges and coconuts. A stupendous variety of flowers: spiky orange and purple estralitza, red and white carnations, roses of all shades, white feathery gypsophila. The fishermen's section had an ozone of tar and fish. Strung across the stalls were nets, lines, hooks, rope, buoys. We bought twine and hooks, weights and lures and imagined pulling in delicious fish.

We telephoned our friends. "Yes, there are stacks of letters waiting for you. Come and stay." The local bus to Puerto, wheezed up into the mountains where we passed through the narrow streets of the high university town of La Laguna. Morning mist hung over the grey stone halls and ornate Catholic churches. Students and office workers scurried along the damp pavements. The bus slowly trundled down through the hills, the moist red earth contrasting with the verdant growth. Passing the ill-fated Los Rodeos Airport we remembered the devastating crash in 1977 when two taxiing DC10s had collided in fog. A new airport had now been built on the sunny lowlands in the south.

Our friends spoilt us and after a year of living within the confines of our small boat we luxuriated in hot baths, iced drinks and soft four-poster beds. Sophie took me to the market to ensure we were sold the best quality vegetables and fruit for our crossing which included a stick of bananas which unfortunately all ripened before the wind was favourable for us to leave. We ate bananas for breakfast, lunch and snacks. I made banana bread, banana pancakes, fritters, sandwiches. We had them sliced with rum and demerara sugar, I even made banana jam. It tastes good but looks disgusting - a grey-brown paste with short white threads through it.

Back on board in Santa Cruz someone was knocking on the cabin top. A big surprise: friends from Bracknell on holiday. They stayed on board for a few days and sailed with us in the rain to Candelaria. We damply explored the quieter, cleaner, small fishing harbour with a cave chapel on the beach. Always a burning candle and fresh flowers were set before the alabaster feet of the Virgin. The vast cathedral square was surrounded by statues immortalising the tall Guanches. A tourist coach had seats to take our friends back to Los Americos. Tearfully I hugged Terry goodbye as she clutched letters for our children. This really was our last link with home, safety and familiar people.

The trade winds still didn't blow. We spent another ten days waiting in the rain behind the harbour wall watching the ebb and flow of the small fishing town. At all hours a few fishermen would be sitting on the beach smoking and talking beside the chapel. As soon as one of their heavy wooden fleet came into sight, its bright paraffin pressure lamp glowing in the dark, they strolled down to the water's edge flexing their muscles. As the big swell carried the heavy boat forward, so they would lift together and carry it up the black-pebbled beach out of danger from the crashing waves.

At last on 25th November we motored out into a rising north easterly, and made for Los Christianos our port of departure. Hoisting the high-cut jib and reefed main, CLYPEUS roared south and by late afternoon, we anchored in the undulating bay. In the morning, Peter topped up our fuel tanks while I posted last letters, then we both booked out at Customs and Immigration.

It's a hard life, Peter said 'It can't be this easy'
It wasn't

At last, on 26th November 1983, we cautiously left the harbour following the Gomera Ferry. Apprehensively we wondered, was this really what we wanted to do? Would we ever see land or our family again? Our plan was to follow the old sailing ships' route: 'sail south until the butter melts, then turn right.' Not as casual as it sounds because at 17°N the sea warms up to 25°C and any butter stored in the bilges does melt.

For the first eight days' sailing we had fantastic weather. Trade Wind clouds gathered on the horizon like grazing sheep. Peter had the jib boomed out on one side and mainsail on the other, running before a fresh wind. Sun, blue sea, blue sky, averaging over a hundred miles a day. Our wake bubbled behind us white and frothy by day, luminous by night, like long tresses of stars. Water running along the hull rumbled and tumbled, sang and swished or gently rustled. Peter kept saying "It can't be this easy." - it wasn't!

The next nine days were cloudy, hot and humid with little or no wind and we only made between 35 and 75 miles per 24 hours. Every evening at dusk he shortened sail. The boat rolled continuously and even though taking seasick pills, we felt queasy. We kept up our three hours on, three hours off, watches and looked right around the horizon every 15 minutes. The galley belt proved a blessing. I could lean against it no matter which

The galley belt proved a blessing

way CLYPEUS was tipping while the fiddles firmly held the half-filled saucepans.

We kept busy trimming sails. Every six hours our position was entered in the log and every twelve hours plotted on the chart, we also read (about 8-12 novels each). I had prepared to read the Bible, Shakespeare, Proust, but didn't have the staying power - the small print and required concentration, was just too much.

The night watches were a joy for me, holding on with one hand to exercise to pop music, while the floor tipped and rolled. Sometimes I sat behind the wheel and thought, just the ocean and me, the moon and Beethoven's symphonies thundering across the waves. Fragile violin melodies soaring to the stars on calm moonlit nights. This was something I hadn't anticipated - time. Time to think, time to remember my life, my family. Time to decide life's priorities.

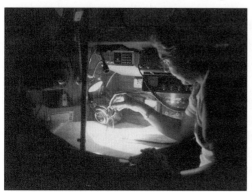

Night navigation position, speed, distance travelled was entered every hour

At night, after having a good look around the horizon with the binoculars, entering in the log book our position, speed, distance travelled and the weather conditions, I would put the kettle on the gas, pop up for another quick look round for any ships. Three minutes before changeover, I would come down into the sleeping cabin and study Peter's calm and peaceful face snuggled up between those inviting sheets. Counting down the seconds before I kissed him awake (he never changed into a frog - just remained my handsome prince!) and would say, "Wake up, your turn, no ships, no problems, the kettle's on. Move over." After a few moments, when the kettle started singing he would crawl out of bed, I'd snuggle into the lovely warm nest and be asleep before he had staggered up the steps to take the kettle off.

However, an acrimonious argument gradually emerged. At night when he had to go on deck, Peter wouldn't bother to wear a harness and clip onto the lifelines. I couldn't sleep in case he fell overboard and I wouldn't know where to start looking for him. At that time he hated the night watches and resented having to be awake. I was just adding extra hassle. My argument: "the Pardeys always wear their harnesses." was countered with: "but the Hiscocks never do, they always hang on carefully, like me."

There were thunderstorms each evening culminating in six or seven storms crashing around us at the same time. Lightning flashed and thunder rolled from lowering clouds with torrential rain. Would we be struck by lightning? Our aluminium masts looked so vulnerable sticking up out there like two hairs standing on the skin of the world. Peter detached the Satnav and radio aerials.

One night I was woken by a loud crash and the sound of splintering wood, the boat rolled wildly and tipped me on to the floor. "Come quickly the self-steering vane has snapped." Peter called. "Come and take the helm while I undo the ropes. Don't bother about oilskins, it isn't cold."

I came out to see him hanging over the stern (without a harness on) undoing the nuts that held what was left of the blade. I gripped the wheel and headed into the strengthening wind and gathering sea. CLYPEUS stayed there, in irons, while he went forward, dropped the mainsail and folded in onto the boom. The deck rolled and dipped.

"Hang on tight," I screamed at him. It took ages for him to tie each reef knot as he clung onto the boom with his elbows.

"Keep her there. Into wind," he shouted back. Spume whipped off the tops of the white horses. White suds gurgled as they rolled down the steep wave-fronts towards us. The rigging started to moan. Our plastic-impregnated Norselay rigging seldom shrieks, but in violent weather sounds like a celestial choir throbbing above the noise of wind and water. "Got to take the Yankee down. Get me the storm jib." It was stacked behind me and had to be untied before I could pass it to him.

He disappeared forward into the dark, dragging the sail bag.

"You haven't got your harness on." My shout was carried behind me in the wind. He didn't hear. At the mast he let go the jib, it flogged, then crumpled like a corpse onto the deck. Now I was really afraid. I couldn't see him. Walls of water were breaking over the bow rails and swishing down the side decks. I could hear the jib being dragged down and saw a faint shape disappearing. The bow dipped, white water crashed onto the cabin top.

"Oh God where is he?' I muttered as the rain beat against my face and stung my eyes. 'He must be kneeling to hank on the storm jib. That wave must have broken right over him. He still has to undo the jib sheet knots and retie them into the storm sail before he can hoist it.' The long-drawn minutes seemed endless. My hands clenched the wheel, as I tried to keep our bow into wind, he certainly would be washed overboard if I let it go. 'What to do if he is? Throw the life belt with its attached automatic light. Help? I don't know after that. I can't turn the boat across these seas to go back for him, we'd be rolled over. Please Peter, hang on.'

At last, a dim shape appeared outlined beside the mast, pulling the halyard. "Pull in the port jib sheet," he shouted.

"Yes, yes," I called to the wind. 'Oh thank you God. Here he comes, dragging the jib behind him.' His hair and clothes plastered to his body.

"Let me take the wheel while you get our oilskins." Slowly I peeled my white and wrinkled fingers from the wheel and moved to let him takeover.

The cabin was chaos: books, cushions, onions and carrots, Scrabble pieces, all slithered across the floor with each roll. 'No time for that now. Getting and keeping us warm is my task.'

"You OK for a minute?" I asked, handing him his oilskin jacket and harness. I talked myself through 'Fill the kettle, light the gas, and clamp it between the fiddles. Thank goodness I don't have to mess with meths and pump a spirit stove.'

After donning my oilskins, I carefully took two mugs of beef and veg Cuppa-Soups into the cockpit. Things had quietened down, the wind and waves were still screaming but CLYPEUS rode before them.

Peter gratefully took the hot mug. "One of us will have to be steering all night. We'll do two hour watches. You go below now and drink your soup and rest."

"OK, thanks, but I'll be out in an hour to see how you're doing."

"OK." A comforting touch on his hand and a fleeting kiss across the wheel, "Love you. You were so brave and strong just now and I was so frightened. I hate it when you go forward and I can't see you, especially if you haven't got your harness on. That's the only time I'm really scared. Thank you for putting it on now."

He grinned "Yes, now that it's dark and rough it's worthwhile. Make sure you clip yours to both hooks when you come out.."

For two days and two nights we took two-hour watches, which seemed the sensible limit of our concentration. We clutched the steering wheel and, with just a tiny storm sail, careered down mountainous seas with the crests breaking above and behind us. To look up behind was to see a wave as high as a double-decker bus rearing up with its white foam tip curling over like a vindictive lip. I was terrified we were going to pitch-pole (go head-over-heels). But we didn't and CLYPEUS handled well.

The wind gradually dropped, and although the seas were still horrendous we were getting used to them. The warmth of the water was comforting when it invaded the cockpit, sloshing around our knees and ankles until it found its way down the cockpit drains. During the hours at the wheel, once, as I looked forward, speeding down a wave I could see two sharks lazily swimming under the surface. How could they be so calm with the turmoil above them? Were we going to be their next meal? Storm petrels grazed the wave tops, swooping and fluttering in the valleys. How do they sleep? Where do they sleep? My thoughts were shattered by the wheel suddenly seeming free in my hands. "Peter, Peter come up, the steering's gone."

"Now what? O heck! a steering cable must have parted again. Move over. Hold up the cockpit seat." His head disappeared down into the bowels of the stern. In minutes he had fitted the emergency tiller. "I can't replace the steering wires in these seas, but let's heave-to and have a rest while I think about it."

When dawn came, the wind had lessened and he replaced the self-steering vane and devised a jury rig to the tiller. My admiration of Peter's practical capabilities grew every day as he coped with each new technical crisis.

Next day as he was coming back into the cabin from checking the jury rig, a huge wave coming up behind us broke, and crashed down into the cockpit and hurled him into the cabin. Tons of water flowed in. Quickly he recovered, closed the door and bent to lift the cabin floor where the water was almost up to the engine's starter motor.

"Quick, quick, buckets. The bilge pumps can't cope with all this. We must bale as well." I rushed for buckets as he climbed down into the bilge. Head down, he scooped up buckets of water and handed them to me to throw out through the open top-half of the stable door. "If it gets as high as the batteries we're lost." he grunted. "The electric bilge pump will stop." CLYPEUS wallowed sluggishly. Lifting and throwing, lifting and throwing, my arms were not strong enough to lift the bucket quite high enough over the bottom door. At every lift some water sloshed over onto Peter's unprotected head.

Where was the Herculean strength one is supposed to acquire in times of crisis? I had been a keen Girl Guide and recalled: 'A Guide smiles and sings under all difficulties' - Perhaps singing in rhythm to each heave would help? "My bonny lies over the ocean" I hummed. "My bonny lies over the sea." Yes, it did help…"My bonny…"

Suddenly, Peter shouted: "For God's sake woman. Here we are sinking in mid-Atlantic and you're singing!"

"I'd rather die singing than swearing." I sanctimoniously replied, then whimpered "I thought it would help me lift" and shut up, hurt to the core.

"If the electric bilge pump stops we've had it. Another wave like that and we won't survive. Can't you lift the bucket higher?"

"No. I can't," I sniffed, "singing helped my rhythm and it didn't seem so awful."

"Oh! All right. Sing then."

"Can't now."

With frenzy he scooped, lifted and passed up the bucket. I lifted, tipped and passed it back. Peter: scoop and up; me: lift and tip, pass back down. On and on.

"I think we're winning." he gasped.

CRASH. Another wave broke into the cockpit. Water squirted in around the bottom of the door, then trickled, the cockpit drains were working well.

"Touching the bottom now. At least the water's warm," he said as he climbed up on the floor and then pushed past me to pour the water out of his wellies over the stable door. "Yup. It's OK now, the electric pump can handle the rest." Looking at me, he pulled me towards him and put his arms around me. "I'm sorry I shouted, but the water slopping on my head every time you lifted the bucket, really got on my nerves."

"I'm sorry too, but I was only trying to help," I said, "to let you know that I wasn't too afraid and to be a comfort and helpmate." My ear against his chest heard his heart beating beneath his oilskins and I knew, in spite of everything, this was where I wanted to be.

"What about some soup?" he suggested.

I put the kettle on. In a few minutes it whistled and we were sitting on the floor in our oilskins hugging warm mugs. With our feet jammed against the far bunk to keep steady, so our home continued to toss, roll and dip. Comforted by the hot drink I crawled over to put the mugs in the sink, then laid down in sodden clothes on the wet floor. Peter curled himself around me and instantly fell asleep. I thought. 'There's nothing we can do. We are in God's hands and He has promised to be with us always."

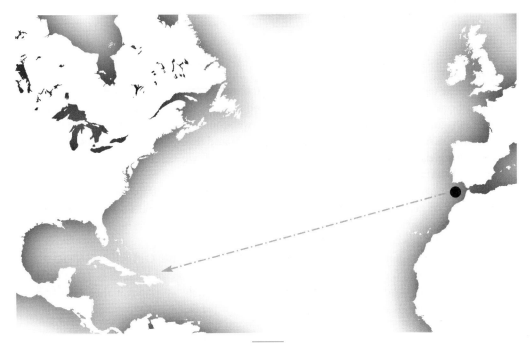

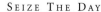

CHAPTER FOUR

The Caribbean Islands
Lat 21°- 32'N Long 24° 47'W. 25°N-18°N
December 1983 - 19th March 1984

The isolation when crossing the ocean was incredible. We listened to BBC World Service and audio tapes when the static was too bad to receive BBC or Voice of America. The whines and squeaks as Peter twiddled the knobs, seldom homing on a station for long, often drove me into my cabin. Having separate rooms proved a blessing. I could jamb myself in to listen to music, poetry or comedy tapes while embroidering Christmas stockings for next year.

I needed voices. Each evening while Peter tried to find a radio weather forecast and wrote up the log I prepared dinner. On fine nights we sat on deck awaiting the green flash as the crimson sun sank below the horizon ahead. (We never saw it.) After dinner we played Scrabble or Canasta, the pinger reminding us every fifteen minutes to go on deck to scan the horizon.

One moonless night, 600 miles out, a ghostly glow lit the south western horizon. Brilliant lights slowly came closer. It looked too high and disorderly for a ship. What could it be? A space ship? Through the binoculars Peter decided it was an oil rig being towed east.

By the tenth day the wind had become fickle and Peter resisted my pleas to motor for just one hour in every four. "We may need all our fuel for an emergency." I knew he was right, but it was frustrating to know we wouldn't be in English Harbour for Christmas. We saw one merchant ship in daylight and the lights of five others. During those long days when we weren't getting anywhere, we gazed across the timeless ocean. What a little speck we were.

My journal notes:- 'Making half a knot. Rattle, rattle, flap, bang, snap. The boomed out genoa and main make a noise like argumentative children. After three hours of concentrated steering and making only one mile, we took the mainsail down and both went to bed.'

A well-wrapped gift parcel proclaimed "NOT TO BE OPENED UNTIL 40 DEGREES WEST". As we crossed the magic line on December 12th it revealed a tinned Fortnum and Mason rich fruit cake. Immediately we tasted it then rationed ourselves to one slice each afternoon with a cup of tea.

One day I shouted, "Peter, come and see. I can't decide what's on the horizon." He took the binoculars from me.

"Looks like huge black and yellow things jumping."

"That's what I think. But what can they be? Whales?"

"I've never heard of black and yellow whales; or any black and yellow sea creatures."

"Can we go closer and see?"

"No. Don't let's look for trouble. We've still got over a thousand miles to go." Researching later, we found they were probably Blue Whales, also known as 'sulphur bottoms' because yellow diatoms (microscopic unicellular algae impregnated with silica) flourish on their skin after they have been in Polar waters.)

A huge bird with a six foot wing span soared and dipped around us. Was it an albatross? It didn't quite fit the illustrations in Tucker's Ocean Bird book and was probably a great shearwater. Six red-billed tropic birds, looking soft and white with long thin tails streaming behind them, hovered above us and inspected our world.

Hundreds of miles from land, how did they sleep? They looked too delicate and

I started daily exercises on deck hanging on to the mast

pretty to be serious pelagic creatures. Twittering storm petrels swooped and fluttered between waves, so small and fragile to be completely at the mercy of the capricious ocean.

A peculiar smell seeped into the cabin. I sniffed around and found in a low locker: an Edam cheese. Its red wax coating had split and the rancid inside was bubbling out. On the eighteenth day I wrote:- 'Most of the fresh food has gone except for some melons which still look good. We also have Lemons, an apple, onions, potatoes and eggs (which I had coated with Vaseline to exclude the air and turned every couple of days). There are still loads of tins of assorted meat, fish, vegetables and fruit, rice and pasta. My bread making is improving. We won't starve!' In fact I was putting on weight and started daily exercising on deck hanging onto the mast.

Flying fish skimmed like silver darts across the waves. We counted out how many seconds they stayed airborne before going 'splat' into an on-coming wave. Each morning a walk on deck revealed a number who gave themselves up for breakfast but they were very boney; hardly worth the bother of cooking. Nothing took our trailing lures.

On the 19th December we had sailed 2,094 miles but with 678 miles to go. Unless the weather picked up we were not going to be on land for Christmas. By the 21st we were both miserable as we knew our family would worry as they expected to hear from us at Christmas. "Perhaps we could ask a passing ship to send a message or telegram." I suggested. "What passing ship?"

"Let's compose what we would say, just in case."

Peter pondered. "They might send a telex to Paul as he works in the shipping world."

"OK let's do it."

Our spirits rose as we did something positive:

23RD DECEMBER 1983.
To: PAUL BILLING,
ALL WELL, FICKLE WINDS. ESTIMATED ETA ANTIGUA 27TH
DECEMBER. PLEASE INFORM FAMILY. HAPPY CHRISTMAS
LOVE PETER AND SHIRLEY, CLYPEUS.

At noon on the 23rd of December a merchant ship steamed towards us on a parallel course. "Call it. Please call it." I pleaded.

Slowly and deliberately Peter lifted the microphone: "Merchant ship heading east, this is British sailing yacht CLYPEUS, CLYPEUS."

"Good morning CLYPEUS. This is British merchant ship ARTHUR. What can I do for you? Over."

"Good morning. We are going to be late arriving in Antigua. Our family will be worrying. Please could you send a short telex to our son in New Orleans. Over."

"Sure. What do you want to say. Over"

Peter read our prepared message and gave Paul's office telex number.

"Right, got it. Is that all you want to say. Over."

"Yes thank you. We are very grateful. Over."

"No problem. I'll telex it off straight away. Over."

"Thank you very much. Happy Christmas! Over and out."

"Happy Christmas! ARTHUR out."

What a relief. What a joy. "Let's have a celebration drink." We both felt so much happier to know nobody would be worrying. We toasted "God bless all Radio Officers, especially the one on the ARTHUR " as we watched her gradually disappear east towards her registered port of London.

I will never complain about Christmas being a rush and scramble again. It was so lonely, I was homesick for my children, our happy family and friends. Putting up, and decorating the little gold Christmas tree in the cabin helped. Only three lonely Christmas cards hung on the tinsel. We knew there would be many waiting for us in Antigua when we got to the Barclays Bank who would be holding our mail and money. Tuning into the local Antigua Radio we could hear shoppers being exhorted to go and buy last minute gifts between the calypso carols.

However, there were compensations. I will always remember sitting alone in the cockpit on a calm sea watching Christmas Day dawn: orange, pink, and gold, while on the BBC World Service the voices of Kings College Choir soared and hung in the still air. It was solitary magic.

It was interesting to think about the rush and bustle of previous Decembers, when every moment around working hours was filled with excitement, present buying, partying, planning and cooking. How many people did I usually talk to in December? Five hundred? A thousand? But this year, Peter was the only person to whom I had spoken, and all I had seen in the past twenty seven days was a combination of ever changing waves and clouds, a few birds, six ships, one yacht, the sun, moon and a million stars.

At breakfast we exchanged presents and opened a huge tin of Roses Chocolate Toffees. That last day we flew along in a good wind. The swell bouncing back from the island made the sea very lumpy. I sat on the bowsprit waiting for land to appear. At last, the smudge on the horizon wasn't moving, it was land.

"Land, land," I called. Peter came on deck and hand in hand we watched the faint grey hills of Antigua gradually firm up into a tropical island. The day was spent with the binoculars scanning the palm covered hills and shoreline. In the evening as I cooked, we pulled our crackers and put on the paper hats. Peter went out into the cockpit to check that all was well, while I dished up our Christmas dinner: baked ham, roast potatoes, tinned carrots, peas, and celery hearts in white sauce. Oops! it slid off the table - "quick spoon it up before he sees" I muttered, as, with my paper crown falling over my eyes, I chased lumps of sauce-coated celery across the varnished floor.

We sat on the cabin roof with our coffee and Drambuie, watching the quivering lights ashore, anticipating our arrival. We were too scared to enter unfamiliar English Harbour in the dark so stood back out to sea for the night.

Too excited to sleep, before dawn we made for English Harbour. Full of expectation we approached the wide entrance between the arms of cliffs. The sweet smell of land, vegetation and blossom wafted out to meet us. Many international yachts were anchored in the enormous calm natural harbour. Splendid classic craft for charterers; modern millionaire motor yachts; smaller and more modest go-it-aloners like us, all nodded peacefully. Yellow sand beaches with palm trees, high green hills and brilliant flowering bushes were a feast for our eyes.

With a rattle and splash Peter let go the anchor. I reversed on it to make sure it had dug in properly then turned the engine off and sat on the cabin top enjoying the cheerful scene. The Customs launch puttered out to us. Friendly officers looking very smart, their brilliant white short-sleeved shirts contrasting handsomely against their dark arms, their polished shoes shining like their grins, "Happy Christmas man," they greeted us. "Sorry you missed it. Permission to come aboard?"

"Happy Christmas. Welcome aboard." They came and sat in the cockpit, opened their briefcases and took out a pile of forms to be filled in. They left chewing happily on toffees.

A splash of oars and "Happy Christmas". It was Trish from RALPH ROVER. We had met in the Cruising Association Library. It seemed fantastic to be greeted by name within minutes of arriving on the other side of the ocean. With their small daughters aged four and two, Ray had taken a sabbatical year and they were circling the Atlantic. Other sailors rowed up asking how we had fared, giving information and inviting us on board their boats for drinks. How good it was just to talk. Everyone seems to get verbal diarrhoea when they first arrive, babbling non stop, sharing experiences. We wanted to phone home but had no local money and were told everything ashore was closed.

The New Zealand delivery crew of PRINCESS IRENE invited us for drinks. They were enjoying sailing the British built, brand new super-yacht, to Auckland for the owner, who was too busy to make the voyage himself. They took us down to the master cabin, flung back the dressing table triple mirrors and there was an 800 watt Sailor Radio Telephone. "Would you like to phone home?" asked Gillaine. She turned it on and spoke into the microphone.

"Portishead Radio, Portishead Radio, this is PRINCESS IRENE."

"Yes PRINCESS IRENE what can I do for you?" Gillaine handed me the phone. I gave the number.

"Hello, hello." Noel's voice, clear as a bell. I couldn't speak for happiness and choked with tears. Peter took over. Yes, all three children were there enjoying Christmas together. Paul had flown from the States to be with them. I sobbed my greetings. How wonderful to know they were all safe and well and together. After putting the phone down we enjoyed socialising and didn't get back to CLYPEUS until well after midnight.

When the holiday was over, our first priority was to get mail and money. We borrowed coins from RALPH ROVER for the bus into St. Johns. WOW! It was an experience. We squeezed into a mini-bus already crowded with people. It pulsated with loud throbbing Reggae music. The relaxed passengers were clapping, crooning, swaying with the roll of the bus and saying "Yea man!" Driven fast over pot-holed roads we bounced and rattled along. The happy-go-lucky atmosphere was exhilarating. The centre aisle had let-down seats, so that if someone at the back wanted to get out, everyone down the centre aisle had to get out before them, then climb back in. The driver was paid through his window when passengers reached their destinations. It was very difficult to hear how much, as the steel band on his radio blasted your ears.

Mounds of green bananas and plantain lay in the market place alongside the wharf. We lined up in the Bank. Yes, our money for the next three months had arrived and yes, there were over 70 letters and cards for us but we would have to pay 20 cents each for them. I burst into tears and asked for the Manager.

"There was no mention of payment when you confirmed you would hold our mail," Peter said. We were then charged a mere $5 and excitedly picked up the pile of assorted packages, letters and cards; sat in the corner and had our real Christmas feast of love and greetings.

That evening, now we had local money we went out for a meal to celebrate our safe arrival. Feeling very fortunate and mellow we rowed home. Peter unlocked the door and held it open for me. As I stepped into the cabin it was obvious that somebody had been inside. Things had been moved. "Did you leave our passports out on the navigation desk?" I asked.

He pushed past me. "No, I didn't. They were in an elastic band with the travellers' cheques and all the money and I put it at the back of the drawer. Oh! No! All the notes have gone, the American dollars as well as the Eastern Caribbean dollars."

All the money we had brought from the bank that morning had been stolen. All we now had was the change from the $100 we had taken for our celebration evening ashore. We had locked the door but had left a hatch slightly ajar to keep the boat cool. As it was after midnight there was little point in rowing back to the police post to report the theft.

First thing in the morning we dressed smartly and went to report the burglary. The Duty Officer listened politely but didn't bother to write anything down. Peter looked incredulous "You are going to make a report aren't you?"

"No Skip," said the policemen. "There isn't any point. It happens all the time."

"You mean you aren't even going to make a note of how much money was stolen, or my name or boat name?"

"No Skip, you would be so far down the list of people hoping to get some of their stolen goods or money back, there'd be none left by the time they got to you."

I butted in, "Don't you even try to find the thieves?"

"Well Ma'am, we try, but you've got it and they haven't. The people here are poor and you're rich or you wouldn't have a boat." With that, he smiled politely and turned away.

"But; we're not rich," spluttered Peter. "We've got a boat because we have saved all our lives and sold our home."

The Policeman wasn't interested and there was nothing to be done. As we rowed disconsolately home we acknowledged the truth of his statement. Although we consider our income modest, we have more than the Islanders dream of owning. We passed a Western Australian boat SHOESTRING from Fremantle Sailing Club, where my sister has an S&S 34. The man on deck looked down at us and said, "You look as though you need a cup of coffee. Come up and have one."

We gratefully climbed aboard and exchanged names. Don and Ann listened to our tale of woe while the kettle boiled. We would have no money for New Year celebrations as the banks had already closed for the holiday. Our planned flight to see

Paul in New Orleans for Mardi Gras in February would have to abandoned.

They gave us coffee and comfort and insisted on taking us out to dinner on New Year's Eve. The evening finished off in a courtyard beside the lagoon. We danced under the palm trees to the mellow throb of a steel band. Cream frangipani and red hibiscus blossoms decorated our green-coconut-shelled rum punches. The moon shimmered across the water and brilliant stars sparkled. Glasses clinked amid chuckles of laughter. Cicadas chirped and tree frogs chimed.

Thanks to our new friends, the world looked good again.

Lat 17° 00'N. Long 61°45'W

Three weeks in Antigua passed quickly. It seemed a fertile and verdant island but the vegetables are poor and so are the people. Nobody appeared to till the soil or fish the reefs. In the shops we noticed that eggs and frozen chicken necks were imported from the USA The children look well cared for and clean but nobody was in a hurry to provide a service.

The adults appeared to think, if they sat around long enough, dollars would drop into their laps and were disappointed and aggressive when they didn't. Their philosophy seemed to be 'we had to work hard as slaves, now we're not slaves and therefore, don't have to work.'

Nelson's Dockyard in English Harbour was historic, well kept and an all-weather safe anchorage. The old naval workshops have been tastefully converted into fashionable holiday accommodation.

We explored beaches, towns and islands, carefully threading our way through our first coral reefs. It became easier to distinguish the deep dark blue water, changing to aquamarine between twenty and ten feet and then taking on a brown hue as the coral neared the surface. I was in heaven, snorkelling over the coral in the clear warm water. I had never really believed that I would be actually swimming with such colourful fish. Long-spined sea urchins seemed the worst obvious hazard. Although you didn't mean to touch them, sometimes the current pushed you onto the end of their black spines.

Tiny coral cuts or blisters are an insidious problem. A mere scratch turned into a painful septic staphylococcal ulcer which, if not attended to, could eat right through to the bone. My swim fins rubbed a small blister on my ankle which became a tropical ulcer and the first bitter taste of a staphylococcal infection. It laid me low and in bed for three days. A daily scrub-out followed by a dusting of anti-biotic powder and no swimming was the recommended cure. Painful, but it worked.

A shore hazard, apart from voracious mosquitoes, was scorpions. While sunbathing on the beach one day there was a scream, much scuffling and urgent shouting for a taxi behind us. A tourist had slipped on her shoes without looking in them first, and had been stung by a scorpion. We learned later that, thanks to quick medical assistance, she recovered with no lasting damage.

Black frigate birds wheeled around the sky zooming down to steal food from the beaks of other seabirds in flight. Pelicans dived in formation one after the other. Tree frogs chimed at night and cicadas screeched. At 6.30 p.m. darkness descended quickly and thoroughly as there were no street lights.

A colourful paper poster advertised the *Ambakaila Folk Dancers*. At the specified time we rowed ashore and stood for an hour waiting, watching the chatting crowd of patient local young people. Bright-eyed coconut crabs scuffled in and of their holes which dotted the black earth. Mosquitoes buzzed around our ears. Ambakaila means 'under the house', the dances were those of the servants and slaves in the olden days. After a shaky start the calypso music became so loud we had to lean back to try and get out of its way. The dancers had marvellous rhythm and for their colourful market place calypso story, even the local audience was quiet and interested. The intense Rastafarian bongo-drummer held us spellbound.

Some of the young men watching were very smart; white socks were all the rage, but their slim grey shoes, sharp trousers and pastel bomber jackets looked expensive. Perhaps that was where our money had gone?

I talked with a friendly teenage girl. She told me the usual story of young people; that there was little to do on their island. "You can either dance or play cricket," she said.

"What about swimming and snorkelling?"I asked.

"It's not right for girls to swim. We don't having bathing costumes so have to go in the water in our dresses and they cling. We don't have any masks either, so we can't see under the water like the tourists."

We left English Harbour on 23rd January 1984. Sailing south between the islands was exhilarating and boisterous at times. Careering along in winds of 20-35 knots didn't seem as worrying as it would have done in the grey Solent. A warm sun shining steadily from a bright blue sky certainly took the sting out of rough weather. Our days were full of sunshine, sea, and happy chatty interludes with a rum punch or cool beer in our hands.

A few Pirogues sailed between the islands

We sailed towards South America anchoring at many islands. I had no idea they were all so different: Verdant, French Guadeloupe, then Isle des Saintes: a small group of islands set in clean, clear, water with very little visiting traffic, just the odd pirogue. There is much inter-family marriage. The French Navy helps solve the problem, in their own inimitable way, by calling every five years for a little rest and recuperation and perhaps to add a few more genes.

Dominica was mountainous, with hot sulphur springs and lakes near the summits. Tropical rain forest covered the slopes, with hardly any level ground. It supported a poor agricultural community. Here the currency reverted to East Caribbean dollars and food was measured in pounds and ounces. One night just before dawn, anchored 200 metres from the beach, Peter who was sleeping on the saloon settee, was woken by the boat pitching and the sound of bare feet padding down the deck. In a panic he grabbed the only thing handy, a large plastic torch. As the big native, who must have climbed up the anchor chain, lowered himself into the cabin, Peter shone the torch at the doorway to reveal a naked, black male torso climbing down. The intruder hesitated, but continued to descend. Peter threatened him in his gruffest voice, "Get off my boat or I'll call the police."

A pretty insubstantial threat under the circumstances and the man was in no hurry to move until Peter called to me "Shirley. Quick. Get the gun." I reached for the revolver above our bed, but didn't know where to start looking for the ammunition in the dark. Fortunately, the threat of a gun was enough to change the intruder's mind. He retreated, jumped overboard and swam ashore. Standing trembling with shock in the cockpit with our arms around each other, we watched him calmly walk along the beach to a house. A few seconds later a light went on and, through the window, we watched him towel himself down. Dawn was breaking so we dressed, clean and smart, to go and report to the police. Speculating about how Peter would identify the man gave us some grim smiles.

In the Police Station the result was much the same as before, no interest, the policeman on duty didn't want to know. However, I could see some gold braid behind a half open door, so pretended some minor hysterics about strong young men climbing onto our boat and murdering defenseless tourists in their beds. The gold braid appeared, apologised to us and waved to the Duty Officer to make a note. He then returned to his room and firmly closed the door.

We adjusted to the situation. They were not going to change. It was up to us to do something. From them on Peter slept with the revolver under his pillow and a machete by his side. Fortunately we didn't have to use either, because the next pirates in Union Island boarded during the night, removed my purse from my handbag and left us sleeping without hearing a thing. Life goes on!

Michael, a young English friend doing voluntary service overseas took us on an eight hour mountain hike up through dripping rain forest to Boiling Lake, a volcanic sulphurous bubbling lake. Peter and I dropped out in Desolation Valley where steam spurts up through the valley floor. I ate my picnic lunch submerged up to my neck in a hot sulphur stream. It eased my aches and pains so well I positively galloped home. Michael pointed out the pens where the original cannibal Kanaks fattened prisoners-of-war, like cattle, for their tables.

At Trafalgar Falls, the water tumbled into cascading pools. We swam in the calmer pools revelling in the glory of pristine warm water surrounded by luxuriant undergrowth. It was wonderfully fresh and unspoiled. The day ended in a nearby hotel soaking in a hot mineral pool in our bathing costumes, supping rum punches. -I've never been so relaxed and couldn't keep my feet on the bottom.

We left Dominica with Michael and his friend joining us for ten days to Martinique. 25 year old William was on holiday for three months; an expensively educated young man who had decided that there was an acute shortage of plumbers in London's SW3 district. He had taken a trade qualification, lived in Eaton Square and worked hard locally tending to burst pipes and minor repairs between November and March, then pushed off somewhere warm for an extended holiday. It was good to have energetic young men on board, eager to hoist sails and pull up the anchor.

Arriving in Martinique was a pleasant surprise with chic women, large modern super-markets and good restaurants. Michael was amazed that two islands, only forty miles apart, could have such different life-styles and economies. Instead of the cars being ten year old Fords, here there were many Porsches.

In St. Lucia, our friends left us. It had been great to have young people around but it was good to be on our own again too. St. Lucia was the most cultivated of the non-French islands and had a bustling market, good hotels and three safe harbours. When we booked in at Rodney Bay we made two big mistakes - we filled the diesel tank with fresh water because we hadn't noticed a fender resting on top of the water filler. Secondly, the Immigration Officer offered us a two week visa but we were so sure we wanted to get on to Panama we asked for just a four day visa. However it was such a social time - joining the 'Jumps Ups' at waterside hotels and meeting up with old and new friends, we ended up paying $50 for a visa extension. The boat boys were a nuisance demanding a fee to "Look after your dinghy Skip?" We didn't realise that by not paying for their services they would extract money other ways – by stealing or damaging the dinghy.

Happy boat boys serenaded us with 'Yellow Bird' and calypsos

Bequia was a small and relatively prosperous island. Their seamen and fishermen are internationally respected and in 1984 there was still a small whaling station on an adjoining island. They still used open boats and harpoons, but a whale hadn't been caught for three years. Large white sun-bleached bones were lying around and huge cauldrons stood waiting to be filled with blubber. Bright young boat boys serenaded us with *"Yellow Bird"* and calypsos and we were happy to give them money.

CLYPEUS almost sank here. Safely anchored, on two anchors, amongst other yachts, we went exploring for the day. On returning in the evening our home was tied up behind a large yacht LISTER LIGHT. Evidently the engine of a visiting fishing trawler had failed. Wind and tide swept her onto our anchor chains. The weight of the trawler's keel was gradually pushing CLYPEUS down. Fortunately a Swedish yacht-owner nearby saw what was happening, grabbed his metal shears, rowed over, and cut our anchor chains. CLYPEUS bobbed back up, free, and was caught and towed to LISTER LIGHT. Later the fishermen dived to recover the anchors and chains and replaced them on deck. We never saw any of the drama nor did we manage to trace our quick-thinking Swedish saviour.

Friends on FRIARS GOOSE, Amanda and Mark, had guests Sarah and Jonathon on board who happened to know young Royals whom they met ashore in Basil's Beach

Bar. Interest was expressed in FRIARS GOOSE so Jonathon invited them on board to have a look around. Their friends replied "Sorry, we would love to come but must get back as Mummy is lonely on her own. Why don't you come for lunch and showers?" Sarah declined as Mark had given instructions that they were to leave that afternoon. When Amanda heard the story she lectured her guests that forthwith they were never to refuse a shower - especially a royal shower!

Tobago Cays was beyond my wildest dreams: a long coral reef surrounding small uninhabited islands in a turquoise sea. Snorkelling was so rewarding, the colourful fish and coral so easy to see in only six to seven feet of water over white sand. Anchored in the flat shallow water behind the reef the full force of the Trades blew over us, so there were NO MOSQUITOES.

Only a few miles away at Union Island, my purse was taken from the cabin whilst we slept. However, during the following six years across the Pacific and in Asia no money was ever taken.

Mopion Island was a perfect cartoon miniature desert isle of about thirty square metres of white sand, one palm tree and a little thatched shelter.

Author John Caldwell and his staff ran a well-kept private hotel on Palm Island. His book 'Desperate Voyage' tells how, in 1946, he sailed from Panama to Australia to claim his wife after WWII. An excellent raconteur, he indulged us as we would be following his route and captivated us with his adventures.

At the hotel on Petite St. Vincent guests hoist a flag outside their cottage for room service and a waiter drives to them in a sand-buggy. Two gentle golden labradors greeted us and we enjoyed a companionable walk in the shade with them right around the island.

Poor, sparsely vegetated Cannoun Island had no road; about 250 people with one shop. Dirt tracks criss-crossed between houses to the Church. The surrounding white sand and blue sea didn't have the romantic ambiance of the more prosperous tourist islands. Here, you could see that life was still hard.

Carricou seemed dry but well-cultivated. The cosmopolitan people were happy, charming and friendly. It was market day. Bullocks were being loaded onto a small inter-island sailing trading vessel, for sale in Granada. The young bulls were hoisted

by a sling under their stomach but were not happy about it, bellowing, as they disappeared down through a hatch. One escaped to be chased halfway around the town. He tossed aside market stalls in his path, to the amusement of most people. Once re-captured he was lowered snorting and kicking into the hold, past the goats and sheep tethered on deck.

I needed more exercise, perhaps I could generate electricity by cycling on deck? Peter said my efforts would be worthless but did support the bicycle against the

Bullocks were slung into the hold snorting and kicking

Perhaps I could generate electricity by cycling on deck?

mast, lifting the back wheel off the deck so that I could pedal away – I wondered if I'd be the first person to cycle across the Atlantic!

St. George's is an old Georgian town on Granada's magnificent harbour. Behind the town, green hills enlivened with dashes of orange flame trees, looked cool and colourful in the brilliant sunshine. Fragrant spice and nutmeg cooperatives were open for visitors. The much-publicised waterfall was a disappointment after Dominica's magnificent falls, but we had the thrill of walking behind the cascading water and swimming in the pool.

On the way to Prickly Bay pear we passed the new airport which still received only American military planes and no commercial flights. The perimeter and a couple of burnt-out buildings were patrolled by jeeps full of soldiers carrying automatic rifles. The locals said they were happy with the occupation but anticipated having to re-elect corrupt officials when the Americans left.

On Monday 19th March, exactly one year since leaving London we sat in the shallows of the warm Caribbean and pondered. Had we made the right decision to seize the day and disrupt our comfortable Wokingham life? For us, yes it was. We both agreed we loved being close to nature and living such a simple uncomplicated life. There were problems: missing family and friends; the limited water supply. General 'living in the tropics health problems' of which we had been unaware. No refrigerator meant that all food spoiled within a day or two; fresh fruit and vegetables were squashy and flyblown within hours. Our own skins and bodies were susceptible to infection from the tiniest cut or blister. And of course, we are the "constant grockles". Looked upon as tourists who should be cunningly fleeced or just plain robbed.

That evening we set sail for Islas Testigos wondering what Venezuela would have in store for us?

Had we made the right decision to 'Seize the Day'?

CHAPTER FIVE

VENEZUELA
Lat 11°24'N Long 63° 10'W
March - May 84

A whale, as big as a single-decker bus rose close to the boat, blew, dipped its head, lifted its tail and disappeared. Where would it surface next? Under us? No, we saw no further sign of it.

It was on this stretch that two Frenchmen in their yacht saw a life raft with two survivors in it. They lowered their sails, started the engine and went to help. As soon as the supposedly exhausted men were brought on board they pulled a gun, took over the yacht and forced the crew into the life raft with nothing, not even water, and set them adrift. Fortunately they were picked up by fishermen within 24 hours, unharmed. Their boat was found months later drifting and towed into Willemstaad harbour where it lay abandoned, unclaimed and deteriorating for many months. We were blissfully unaware of this tragedy and nothing spoilt our sail south.

At first light, Islas Testigos rose brown and dry from the sea. We anchored, swam and had breakfast while flocks of large black frigate birds wheeled high overhead and squadrons of pelicans crash-dived in 'V' formation into the sea.

The sun was very strong now at 11° from the Equator, the glare on the sea and white sand hurt our eyes. A fishing boat chuffed up and asked for oil. Peter was able to give them a can and they gave us fish.

On land while waiting for the Customs officer some small boys came to talk. One cheeky eight year old, whose name was Jesu, gave me a baby parrot and was disappointed when I tried to make him put it back in its nest. I wished later that I had accepted his generous gift, but I didn't know the faintest thing about raising parrots. If we had managed to feed it, it would have been great company.

The Customs Officer gave us a glass of cool orange squash when we checked into his green moondome home. Wow! This was the first time a Customs Officer had been generous.

A large yacht anchored in the bay and the German skipper invited us to join a beach BBQ. Twenty-one people gathered: German, Scots and Dutch all from the chartered yacht, the Customs Officer with his wife, baby and six year old daughter, plus the energetic local school teacher. (The school had 32 children from kindergarten to 13 year olds.) plus the five Venezuelan fishermen, whom Peter had helped during the morning. They provided countless lobsters and fish.

The yachties provided the salads and rum punches, the Customs Officer produced a bottle of champagne and three bottles of French white wine - not sure about the schoolteacher - I guess he provided bon homie and most of the entertainment by singing operatic arias. The language problems were prodigious.

Oh! and one handsome, blonde, dark eyed fisherman played the guitar, but much too delicately and softly for the mood of the company. We chatted, sang, danced and ate from seven until midnight. The only song everyone knew was *'Happy Birthday'* so, although it wasn't anybody's birthday, we sang it many times.

In Testigos we decided to change from our original itinerary and sail to New Orleans to see Paul, (the robbery had deprived us of our air fares), and spend the hurricane season somewhere in the Mississippi Basin. Our new plan would be to continue along the Venezuelan coast to Curacao then turn north to Jamaica, the Cayman Islands, Mexico and USA and pick up our original itinerary at Panama one year later.

A fast daylight passage took us to Carupano on the north coast of Venezuela. The sun was bright and the blue sea lumpy, it kept dumping white water into the cockpit. Peter's hat, a gift from Andrea, blew off and foolishly we started the engine, to circle around to pick it up. As usual we were trailing three lines - a generating propeller which gives us four amps of electricity when sailing at 5-6 knots; the log impeller which shows us speed and distance and feeds the information into the Satnav; and a fishing line with a spinning lure. All three caught each other and wound themselves around the propeller shaft. We had no choice but to enter a port with no engine.

CLYPEUS sped into the small harbour in a brisk wind under full sail. Fortunately there was room to round up into wind and pull the sails down before we hit anything.

On anchoring, I donned thick gloves, mask and flippers and dived to cut the impacted line and free the propeller. Having sawed through the lines, I surfaced for the umpteenth time clutching the bread knife, and noticed a large red American yacht had anchored behind us and guess what? There was a little blonde lady climbing down their swimming ladder in snorkel and fins, also wielding a bread knife. Her husband was standing on deck making encouraging noises, just like mine! I decided she was my sort of person and we have since kept in touch with Americans Barbara and Morty on HUNTRESS.

A young Peruvian/French sailing couple changed $5 into bolivars for us and showed us the dry and dusty town, and the bus stop for the out-of-town Barclays Bank. An old Dutch colonial house set in manicured gardens. On saying our names at the reception desk a sudden hush descended, typewriters silenced, telephones were held away from ears. The receptionist made a phone call and announced "The Manager would like to see you immediately." What had we done? What was wrong?

A Secretary came to lead us into his office. He stood up, hand outstretched and welcomed us with "We are so pleased to see you. You are three weeks later than your money order implied, we thought you had drowned. Would you like coffee?

Overwhelmed with kindness we sat back and enjoyed morning coffee, biscuits and a chat. The Manager gave us airmail copies of The Times and eventually said. "I suppose you would like your money. Miss Jones?" She returned a few moments later with a large roll of U.S. dollars. .

"Here you are." He handed Peter the roll of notes, which he accepted and thrust into his pocket. He couldn't possibly check them under the circumstances. No receipt was asked for. So we left the Bank with $2,000 or was it $3,000 we had arranged?

A fleet of eight large rusty Korean fishing vessels were based in the harbour, similar to the ones in Santa Cruz. Huge hauls of big tuna, or perhaps they were dolphins, we didn't see their heads. It made our hearts sink as heavy open trucks thundered by on their way to the fish meal factory loaded with the stiff frozen bodies of large leaden-grey fish, their ice-encrusted tails pointing to the sky.

The Peruvian couple showed us the vast market where, apart from luscious fruit and vegetables, plastic goods had the price moulded into them. Prices have remained unchanged for many years thanks to the rich oil deposits in Lake Maracaibo and places. We were also taken to a house barbecue where the owner employed teams of small boys to pick up aluminium beer and soft drinks cans and then exported them back to the USA. I invited them on board for tea, but his wife couldn't climb down to the dinghy. He came on his own and enjoyed a Devonshire cream tea. We could hear him boisterously telling her all about it as he rejoined her on the jetty.

On March 27th we sailed from Carupano to Pampatar on duty free Isla Margarita where our mail was waiting in the Harbour Master's office. At a large hotel in a tourist resort we were able to telephone Andrea, now a fully qualified State Registered Nurse. We were very proud of her but so sorry not to attend her award ceremony. She confirmed she had sent more letters and photographs to the care of the Pampatar Harbour Master.

The palm fringed golden sand beaches were spectacular although the interior hills were barren stone mounds. The shops and stalls were fascinating with a terrific variety of unusual and cheap goods from Brazil and Mexico.

While Peter worked on the engine, I went by bus to Pampatar, to collect the mail

Isla Blanquilla firing practice

and hopefully buy needed Venezuelan charts from the Harbour Office. The officious Port Captain greeted me effusively. He was a dark, plump little man, squeezed into a white gold-braided uniform. In a charming manner he invited me to share a glass of white port in his dusty office. Then he insisted on giving me the charts, refusing any payment. He was so like the image of every corrupt South American government officer in every movie you have ever seen, I just couldn't take him seriously... until he buttoned up the top of my blouse in a most familiar way and I began to worry. I stuttered fictitious excuses as to how I was already late meeting Peter. Hastily I picked up my bag, our mail and the charts and managed to back out of his office thanking him for his generosity and briskly walked out of the building and round the corner. As I sat at the back of a dark local cafe and sipped my fruit juice while waiting for the bus, I wondered; did he really want his evil way with me? Or are we just so brain-washed we automatically think the worst? I don't know, but you certainly can't afford to offend, as even petty officials have absolute power in such remote islands.

Thanks to his charts we sailed on to Isla Blanquilla for a blissful solitary week of sailing, swimming, snorkelling and exploring. The island of white cliffs and dry grass had just one empty house and a deserted air strip shimmering under the hard bright sun. We practised firing our revolver at driftwood targets on the beach.

The next group of islands to the west, Los Roques, consisted of dozens of small islands and reefs surrounded by an enveloping outer reef making the waters inside calm and clear. We had been told that this was where lobsters actually jump into your cooking pot! We swam and snorkelled and came face to face with groupers, angel fish, damsels and trumpet fish, in only two or three feet of water. The colours were incredibly bright, both of corals and fish.

A yacht lay high and dry on the outer reef. We anchored and rowed across to see if we could help. A young German couple with their two daughters aged four and eight had hit the reef and holed their 40' yacht DEMI. On leaving the Venezuelan mainland they had travelled so fast during the night they had reached the reef long before expected and hit it. Alvert and Berndt had spent two months clearing a path over the coral. Now, with a block and tackle borrowed from local fisherman, over the four hours of high tide each day, knee-deep, they dragged DEMI a few more inches. On reaching the calm deep water of the lagoon they hoped to mend and re-launch her. Already their wetsuits were tattered and torn and sea sores looked painful on their ankles and knuckles.

Fishermen had helped them build a shelter of driftwood and palm leaves on a nearby islet, and the girls played happily in the sand and their makeshift house while Alvart and Berndt worked. DEMI wasn't insured and was all they had. Their hope was to patch her enough to sail back to La Guira and live there until repairs were made and then continue their voyage to the Pacific. They were showing such courage and determination to get DEMI afloat again. Not a moan or groan from any of them. I hoped I could be as positive in similar circumstances. We gave them coffee, sugar and fruit and they insisted on having us for a meal - fresh bread baked in their pressure cooker on a driftwood fire, grilled lobsters and fish. Berndt took Peter spear fishing and from then on Peter often caught our lunch or dinner in the waist deep water. We took their water carriers and messages to The Guardia National on Grande Roque where there was a small fishing village but no telephone.

Then came one of the happiest and contented weeks of our lives. We approached a deserted, sheltered, white sand, coral-reefed bay and anchored. In the morning we found thirteen dazzling white Venezuelan yachts surrounding us. It was Easter holiday week and the anchorage was full of happy families: slim, tanned girls in brief bikinis and bronzed young men darted around on windsurfers. Happy children swam like fish between the yachts or revved up the dinghy outboard to pick up their friends. Parents enjoyed the social round of sunset cockpit cocktails and often included us. SUPERCILIOUS invited us to lunch and we noted the generous Venezuelans ate their meals the French way, vegetables served first and the meat eaten separately.

Local fishermen came round to sell lobsters but, just as we were buying a pair, a Fishing Authority boat whizzed by. They immediately dropped the full sack and faded into the scenery. However a young man later dived for the sack and shared them out. He gave us a huge lobster which we barbecued on the beach in the evening in a romantic spot on our own. Tasty morsels were dipped in garlic butter and washed down with a cool bottle of Rose. Food of the gods!

Our new friends had invited us to moor in their Country Club Marina at Puerto Azul on the mainland. A fantastic complex with three swimming pools (one with a glass end fronting onto a restaurant) cinema, restaurants, and bowling alley. On arrival we were greeted on all sides by the friends we had made in Los Roques who introduced us to the efficient Harbour Master. He refused to let us pay for our berth as he said the owners, who were voyaging, had already paid the annual fee.

Up up and away in the Andes in the swaying funicular cars

CLYPEUS rested there safely while we visited the capital, Caracas, and went up into the Andes. The overnight bus took fourteen hours to trundle up to the old University town of Merida. The journey only cost US$ 3.50 for each 200 mile journey, but the mountain road was terrifying. Chasms dropped away on either side as the bus coughed and lurched its way round the S bends. Ventilation was good - there were rust holes around our feet for the wind to blow through, and taking my shoes off I felt the cockroaches crawling over my toes.

Snow capped peak in the Andes

The longest funicular railway in the world reached the top of snow-capped Pico Bolivar. At 12,000 feet it was giddy-making, brilliant, and worth the terror of the bus. Descending in the swinging funicular cab we talked to a Dutch couple. On learning Willemstaad was our next port of call, Lony and Levien gave us their address and asked us to call them. We agreed.

Friends of our hosts in Teneriffe invited us to their Caracas home for a night. It felt wonderful to be within a loving family and be looked after again. Juan and Carmen had an Amel ketch in Puerto Azul which he had sailed from La Rochelle, so we had much in common and we enjoyed every moment with them.

An assortment of pleasant American yachtsmen befriended us. Their boats were unbelievable. Even in 1984 some had water makers, full size washing machines, dryers, micro-wave ovens, freezers, fridges, garbage disposal units and garbage compactors, galley bench tops with concealed built-in-motor-bases for coffee-grinders, food processors etc, as well as electric anchor winches, roller furling headsails and mainsails. HUNTRESS had an automatic vacuum cleaner (little holes in the wainscoting of the cabins sucked any dust out.) Windseeker boasted a walk-in workshop complete with work-benches, drills and lathes and a similar Perkins engine to ours, just to generate their electricity. The silly thing is, that they can't go to remote places in the Pacific like us because they can't carry enough fuel for their engines and generators. So although we don't have ice, we can go wherever we want.

Barbara and Morty, on HUNTRESS, and in their mid 60's, have lived on board with their dog PITA (which Morty says stands for 'Pain In The Ass') for nine years and see no reason for stopping to live ashore yet. They fly home to see their family twice a year in New York or Florida. Barbara, a gentle lady, Morty was a fast talking, former marina owner from New York who initially quite intimidated me with his sharp wit and brusqueness. When they came for drinks on CLYPEUS they always brought ice with them. To most Americans life without ice is hell, where as we Brits enjoy most of our drinks at room temperature. Peter was dispensing drinks. Morty looked at his well-filled glass as Peter handed it to him, and said in disgust:

"You Brits are so mean! I bring my own bloody ice and you still only give me one lump!"

A basic Anglo/American misunderstanding: we think we are being generous filling the glass with alcohol, they think we are mean not filling it with ice!

Stocking up with stores in La Guira was easy as the supermarkets had a wide selection of foods and with the exchange rate of 13 bolivars to the pound, it was economical. The port officials wanted a fee for booking out, but we had spent every bolivar at the supermarket. In the end they just said "OK, OK," and stamped our passports and papers.

In strong winds CLYPEUS bounded towards the Netherlands Antilles.

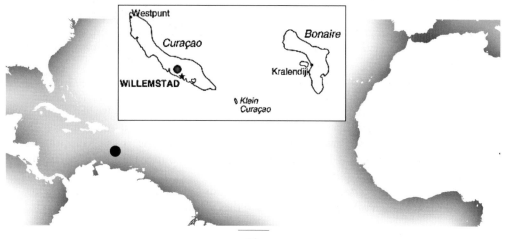

CHAPTER SIX

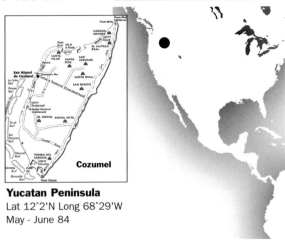

Yucatan Peninsula
Lat 12°2'N Long 68°29'W
May - June 84

May was spent in Curacao and Bonaire which were flat, arid, islands, but the seas, coral and fish around them are outstanding diving areas. The cost of living was high, about five times that of Venezuela. Postage and phone calls were reliable but expensive. The Dutch influence was still strong as they poured money into the Antilles economy to keep the population stable, although the strategic necessity of the oil tanks and ship bunkering facilities seemed over.

Dutch architecture in Willemstaad, Curacao

Two hours after tying up at Willemstaad Quay, a sudden knocking on the cabin roof startled us. "The Officials." Peter said in dismay. "We should have gone ashore immediately, not cleared up first." We apprehensively went out into the cockpit. "What kept you? We have had the air conditioning on in your room for five days already." It was Lony and Levine, the couple with whom we had exchanged addresses in the swaying funicular cabin. Their casual invitation had been sincere and they had been coming to the harbour to look for us every day. After escorting us through Customs and Immigration, they whisked us to their modern home and we luxuriated for five days with our own bathroom and air conditioned bedroom. It was wonderful.

I was pleased to still have little gifts on board I could take with me: a little Wedgewood dish and a colourful teatowel of Welsh Castles.

After reading so many sailing books before starting this journey, we had assumed that only 'real' voyagers like the Hiscocks and Smeetons were spoilt and pampered by strangers when they went ashore. But now, we began to realise, it was happening to us. Lony cooked delicious Dutch meals - meat balls in butter with small beetroots. Indonesian spicy meat dishes with rice.

One sunny day we took them and their friends sailing to Spaanisch Water. After anchoring for lunch off a white sandy beach they all jumped overboard and scrubbed the Willemstaad oil from CLYPEUS's hull. We were delighted.

We spent a lazy Monday morning watching the lady skippers from the Assiento Sailing Club enjoy their weekly race around the buoys. It was very relaxed and amiable as they called the course directions to each other.

Goodbyes were hard. Would we ever meet our generous friends again? This is one of the sad aspects of cruising; the wonderful people you meet for just a few days, probably never to see again. We try and keep in touch, hence the letters this book is based on, but nobody's life stays still, and gradually communications fade. We still keep a warm place in our hearts for all those kind friends we have made and will never forget. It is a joy to remember them again as I write now.

Short friendships can be so deep and lasting. Language communication may be poor but understanding and empathy cut right across language and culture barriers. Our voyage has cemented our belief that most people are kind to others - in all countries. In this respect women are more fortunate than men being less competitive and sharing common problems and tasks. We can talk cooking, laundry, babies, children, mothers, on varying levels. Most women are so generous with their love and sympathy and pathetically receptive to praise - they seem to get so little.

Six days of fast, rough sailing to the North, with the wind on our beam, brought us to Jamaica. We by-passed Kingston having been warned of its rough reputation and unhurriedly rounded the eastern corner, sailing with ease in the lee of the island, admiring the luscious countryside, parklands, elegant mansions, fine estates and hotels.

Montego Bay had always sounded so romantic and sophisticated but the native town down by the Harbour was dirty and unkempt, with cockroaches and rats visible even in daylight.

Jamaican Customs Officers made a farcical visit on board. They were very officious and insisted on coming see where our guns were stored but our Avon rubber dinghy wasn't quite what they expected and sat on the wobbly sides cringing in horror in case sea water touched their well-polished shoes.

Dawdling, anchoring in small bays and swimming in the clear green water. Towards Negril on the western shore, we gazed with awe at the mountains, rivers, and mansions with parklands sloping down to the sea. Ruminating, in green meadows in the shade of splendid trees, were the first cows we had seen since Guernsey.

Fishing by indiscriminate dynamiting had destroyed much of the coral. A couple of times we were offered 'guanja', the local name for marijuana. The guys remained friendly although we always refused. Local villagers paddled out in their dugout canoes to chat and told us not to be afraid. Nevertheless Peter slept in the main cabin with our weapons by his side - quite unnecessary as it turned out, but we were getting more worldly-wise.

Having a rest day, anchored in a small bay, a big tourist catamaran anchored near-by. We both had good books and took little notice. Snorkellers suddenly caught our attention: black heads with a snorkel sticking up, followed by a shiny pink bottom being propelled along by black flippers. They were nudists with no distinguishing costumes. It made a bizarre scene!

122 miles of sloppy sailing brought us to Cayman Brac, the smallest of the three Cayman Islands. We didn't mean to visit this particular island but CLYPEUS was rolling so atrociously with the wind dead astern, that we turned onto a broad reach for an

easier ride. Peter called on the VHF for procedural help and spoke to the Lloyds Agent who informed Officials of our arrival. It was Sunday evening and the efficient British Customs Officer and Agricultural Officer visited within an hour and charged US$17.50 for the privilege of acknowledging our arrival on a Sunday. The hum of the mosquitoes ashore made spraying the inside of our cabins seem a little ridiculous.

My first encounter with a five foot barracuda occurred here: a long slim fish with a big mouth and many sharp teeth. (I should point out that Peter doesn't swim happily. He hates the water and getting his feet wet. He says that's why he has a boat.) I was snorkelling on my own a long way from CLYPEUS and noticed the large, sabre-toothed fish watching me closely. I swam away and he followed. Swallowing my panic I tried to remember all I had been told about barracudas - they are curious, cowardly and shy. Shy? with a smile like that?

CLYPEUS was too far away for a sprint so I turned and faced him, looked into his eyes through my mask and deliberately swam towards him appearing as aggressive as I could. He backed off, turned tail and swam away. My courage then deserted me. Perhaps he had gone for re-enforcement's? I raced for home and found myself sitting in our cockpit having incredibly scaled the narrow ladder in flippers!

Several encounters later it does seem that barracudas are just curious and interested. Under-water photographers have told us that by the time they have set up their cameras and tripods, there are usually two or three barracudas looking over their shoulder to see what they are doing. I still don't point my finger at them or let my arms wander far from my sides. A hand would be just a tasty mouthful.

Peter caught a small barracuda about two feet long off Little Cayman and I swam over to a blonde diving couple, sitting disconsolately on the rocks, to ask if it was safe to eat - many fish cause ciguatera poisoning that can affect our nervous systems permanently.

"Hi!" I said. "I'm from that sail boat. We've just caught a barracuda about a foot long. Will it be OK to eat?"

"Sure. Young barracudas are OK. It's the build up of poison in the larger ones you have to watch."

We continued chatting and I learnt that they were American dive masters managing a hotel/diving school. They had only been there a couple of months and it was a disaster. Neither the generator nor air compressor was working, so they had no lights or air-conditioning in the cabins; no full dive tanks and more guests arriving every day. Nobody could come and repair the equipment for a couple of weeks.

"I expect my husband could mend them." I offered. After all the problems he had cured on ours, and other people's boats, I now had absolute faith that he could mend anything. "I'll go and ask him if he will come and have a look."

Peter agreed, so they drove us to the hotel. They fell about his neck when, after a quick inspection, he said he would try and repair their equipment. They made us very welcome. He did mend both generator and compressor whilst I swam with the divers over amazing coral walls where the depth went from 50 to 2,000 feet in one precipitous cliff. It was sad I couldn't dive because I have high blood pressure. However, I could still see the sandy seabed at 50 feet. I watched big rays, their skirts fillibrating across the white sand with cleaning fish nibbling their backs; sea cucumbers, crabs, crays and all the tropical aquarium fish you have ever seen; only much bigger, and of course barracudas.

The divers saw sharks but I didn't. In shallow water we gathered conch. The

Cleaning the conch we had just picked up in the shaloow lagoon

insides, once cleaned and chopped, were marinated in lime juice making a delicious hors d'oeuvre. For four days we swam and ate with these young, happy American guests, exchanging addresses and hoping to meet in Houston or London.

At Grand Cayman when Peter booked in and took our guns to Customs, he had to BUY the forms before filling them in. We only stayed two days as it was so expensive and Mexico was calling.

A white passenger liner flying a Russian flag was aground in the bay with Schmidt tugs buzzing around it. The cost of such an avoidable accident must be astronomic. What do they do with the hundreds of passengers and crew?

The colours fade on the mahimahi's death

On the way to Mexico we sailed through great clumps of pale brown fronds of Japanese seaweed floating on the surface resembling, what I have always imagined the Sargasso Sea would look like. The weed fouled the fishing lines so we pulled them in. When the surface was clear we let them out again and just as we rounded the southern end of Cozumel off the Yucatan Peninsula we caught a six foot dorade (mahi-mahi). Blue, green, gold and silver whilst in the water but, as it died on deck, so its colours dramatically faded and we imagined its pathetic little soul released and winging upward.

The anchorage between Cozumel and the mainland looked calm and inviting. We shared our six kilos of fish with the crew on BLACK JACK, a large American yacht anchored close by. The Skipper was a Sociology Lecturer from California with a crew of students, all on their way to Nicaragua to try and find out what was really happening.

A grand local dance in the large Market Hall was advertised and Bob, one of BLACK JACK's crew, came with us. Being the only gringos amongst 1,000 locals. the Manager of the Hall came and sat with us and scrutinised each young man who, bowed and offered me his hand to dance. My men were involved in a political discussion so I had a wonderful time. My partners were all great dancers but Peter dragged me back to the boat at 3.30 - the dance went on until 5 a.m. Green Cozumel was full of happy, dark skinned, high-cheeked Mexicans and American tourists. The tourist trivia and gift shop trinkets were really unusual, well-made and attractive. Mexican weaving, embroidery, blankets, pottery and jewellery were good and inexpensive. Squelching the impulse to spend, spend, spend, I only bought a hand woven blanket for Paul, whom we hoped to see in a few days, and charming ochre-pink pottery pigeons moulded in a simple pleasing shape. Later I found it very hard to later give them away.

The pictures and stories of the Mayan civilisation and pyramids had fascinated us in National Geographic Magazines and we planned to visit Chitchen Itza. BLACK JACK agreed to look after CLYPEUS whilst we took the ferry to the mainland and local bus. The ancient bus took us for miles through dense forest on the flat limestone Yucatan plateau, it seemed just trees, trees and more trees. Suddenly, in a violent downpour of rain, the bus squealed to a halt in the middle of the dripping jungle. There were no signs of habitation and nobody else dismounted. The driver indicated this was where we should get out and gestured vaguely towards an adjoining road. Wonderingly we descended into the rain.

The driver immediately engaged gear and the bus splashed away on its scheduled route. Within seconds we were soaked through and with our hair and clothes plastered against our bodies, we paddled towards the hoped-for site of the Mayan Pyramids and Temple ruins.

Chitchen Itza pyramid

Chitchen Itza did not disappoint us. The Mayan Pyramid with 365 steps, The Temple of A Thousand Pillars, Pyramid ruins, Observatory, Ball Court, Nunnery, Sacrificial Cenote Well, were all fascinating. The ruins of the twelve hundred year old civilization, were even more exciting than anticipated. We were able to wander where we wished, up and down the pyramids, in and out of the temples, tunnels and chambers. If only we had had the foresight to bring a torch. Passages and steps led to inky blackness and we were too frightened to venture too far. The blood-curdling tales of the various human sacrifices and altar rites, where the still beating hearts of the sacrificial victims were laid on the chest of their greedy god Chacmool. The Ball Game Court was still in good condition and it was easy to imagine the players passing the ball from hip to knee to elbow and up through the stone goal circles. It was difficult to imagine how the game ever ended though, as the Captain of the WINNING team was beheaded by sword on the spot. Evidently this was the supreme moment of his life never to be equalled. (I guess he was never given the chance to find out)

A young American honeymoon couple gave us a lift to the nearest town to find a hotel, but unfortunately we 'lost' a $100 note during the early evening, so couldn't afford another night in the hotel or see the 'Sound and Light Show.' We had planned another day and night, but in those days, before credit cards were universally acceptable, unless you had cash, it was 'no pay, no stay'.

We spent the following morning at the site studying the Observatory. The Mayans accurately calculated star movements and a calendar for centuries ahead. They calculated the world would end on May 5th 2000. We have looked on our computer star charts and indeed all the planets are clustered together on that date, which together with the moon's gravitational pull, could topple the earth. However, we now know they were wrong!

Returning through the miles of jungle our eyes were more accustomed to the scenery and we noticed thatched mud huts with families living in them. Each appeared to have a new small concrete water tower with a cement, one room house built alongside. The doors were usually open. The only furniture appeared to be woven hammocks slung across the room with perhaps a chair on the earth floor. Dogs, chickens, piglets and naked children ran in and out. Cozumel seemed very sophisticated.

The social round of cocktail hour in cockpits resumed. American guests brought a friend along to our evening: a tall, quiet, epitome of an English explorer in long khaki shorts, socks and sandals. John was an archaeologist who contributed to Mexican Tourist and Archaeological Books. He was returning to the UK the following day for a health check up, because whilst in a Mexican hospital with malaria; he had been accidentally injected with hepatitis. His liver consultant happened to be our brother-in-law, so John took a 'hot' message home.

Snorkelling around Cozumel was superb, so were the margaritas! Sad stories of poorly supervised diving expeditions were told. The bar on board would be open for divers to buy alcohol on the way to dive sites and swimmers were not counted back on board at the end of a dive. One poor tourist had been caught in the propellers as they started for home; others simply never arrived back in their hotels.

On the 15th June we tore ourselves away from Cozumel to make for New Orleans as the hurricane season was almost upon us and we longed to see our son, Paul.

New Orleans

USA
Gulfport 30°20S 89°26'W
June 84 - Feb 85

New Orleans

CHAPTER SEVEN

It took seven days to cover the 700 miles across the Gulf of Mexico from Cozumel to the USA. Three of those days were spent motoring over a glassy calm sea with dolphins and dorades as escorts. Five dolphins played while I lay on the bowsprit with my hand dangling. I could have touched them. I wanted to touch them, but at the last minute couldn't help involuntarily drawing my hand away. They swam on their sides squeaking and really looked into my eyes in a friendly way. Scars and scratches on their backs were caused by what? Do they fight or had they just played too close to boat hulls? Twice a trio of dorades, a male with two females, swam alongside all day in the shade of our hull.

Thunderstorms brought rain and filled the water tanks. Sleek black triangular fins of sharks cut through the water as we entered the "forest"; the nickname for the oil rigs in the Mississippi Sound. As night fell, many lit up and it seemed wondrous sailing quietly on calm sea between the twinkling Christmas trees; until we realised there were some broken-down unlit rigs. We counted 40 oil platforms around us at one stage, mostly unmanned.

As we approached Louisiana Peter tried, on the VHF radio, to contact Paul in New Orleans where he was Port Superintendent for one of the large oil companies. All the channels were busy, the lady operators ignored him. He handed me the microphone. I called once, "Venice Radio, Venice Radio this is British sail boat CLYPEUS"

"Yes, Sail Boat CLYPEUS what can I do for you?" was the immediate interested reply. I guess a woman's voice on the male dominated marine frequencies made a pleasant change. She put us through to Paul who told us to make for Gulfport where Customs and Immigration Officers would be waiting.

Peter worried about Customs and made me write a list of all our medications with strong drugs in them, and every bottle of alcohol.

Our first sight of America was a lone Inter-Coastal-Waterway navigation mark on a pole in the middle of nowhere. On July 21, we anchored off Ship Island, a nature reserve. It was good to find clean walkways, smart, friendly wardens and clean public

Our first sight of America

toilets with SEATS and PAPER! Oh America! We knew we had arrived. Archaeological sites and undeveloped countries are fascinating, but civilisation has attractions too.

Peter wouldn't come ashore as we hadn't booked in but I explored a fort defended in the Civil War by the largest cannon ever made, but never fired. A few trees dotted the island, mostly scrubby bushes on the sandy soil and noticed several small black birds with red feathers on their wings, chirping and hopping around. I met the Warden and asked: "Please can you tell me the name of those black birds with red wings?"

He regarded me warily. "Would you believe 'red-winged blackbirds?" he kindly replied with a grin.

The night was hot. We slept on deck covered with sheets from the top of our heads to under our feet and awoke with red, itchy, mosquito bites across our foreheads and toes. We seemed to be floating on watery green soup. Thin sea -snakes squiggled swimming with their heads high and sea spiders scuttled across the surface, while mosquitoes zoomed onto any uncovered body-part.

Arriving in Gulfport at midday we passed a hundred or more yachts, flying colourful spinnakers, gathering for the start of the Gulfport to Pensacola Race. It was a magnificent sight.

Paul was waiting for us at the quayside. I was dying to jump up and hug him but we dare not make contact until the Officials came on board. They couldn't have been more kind - it is much easier to bring a yacht into Mississippi than get off a 747 at Chicago.

A colleague of Paul's, 'J.B.', drove us along the coast to lunch at a Plantation Home. It looked so romantic, straight out of *"Gone with the Wind"*, with tall white columns from roof to the ground. Pink and white magnolias bloomed in the garden. Our plates were heaped with sea food, all fried in batter, including the oysters and soft-shelled crabs.

In his motor boat JB guided us to Diamond Head Marina through a tortuous narrow water-way. CLYPEUS slid through shallow alligator-infested swampland following a wayward sluggish channel, grounding four or five times. As dusk fell so the mosquitoes homed in - not quite as big as pigeons, but the people of Louisiana have named these mosquitoes their 'State Bird'. At last we tied up at a safe marina berth at 10 p.m. and Paul drove us to his home near Baton Rouge.

Now we were to be land-lubbers for six months during the hurricane season. We planned to be ready to set sail in February and via the Panama Canal, be in Tahiti by July and in New Zealand for Christmas.

Paul's 56' steel yacht built single handed from his own design moored in Cajun country

An amusing aspect of life in America was, that nobody was really interested in our voyage across the Atlantic until we mentioned that we had no refrigerator.

"How long did it take y'all?"

"Thirty days."

"What, you lived for thirty days without ice? Wow! How did y'all manage?" From then on there would be great interest.

It was lovely to be with Paul and for a month we enjoyed his home. He proudly showed us the 56' steel yacht he was building all by himself on the banks of the Mississippi. We had hoped to tour the U.S.

together, but he couldn't get time off. He loaned us the money to buy a car, a Chevrolet Citation with 'four on the floor' - a manual gear box. We rented a tent and circled the States inland - we had seen enough sea for a while.

In five weeks we drove 8,000 miles around USA. I sang our destinations as we drove towards song titles. From the *'Mississippi Mud'* to *'Way down upon the Swannee River'*, past *'My Old Kentucky Home'*, through *'Georgia, Georgia'*, up onto *'Old Smoky'* and along the *'Trail of the Lonesome Pine'* taking the *'Country Road to West Virginia'*. Over the *'Banks of the Warbash'* and the *'O-hio'* to *'Chicago, Chicago'*. West to the *'Black Hills of Dakota'* down through the Rockies until we were *'24 hours from Tulsa'*, on to *'El Paso'* then east *'Deep into the heart of Texas"* where the stars really did shine bright, and back to *'Bourbon Street Rag'* and Cajun Country. Peter is a very patient man!

Southern hospitality is 'sumthin else'. After only two hours driving we stopped for breakfast (sausages, eggs and syrup) with new friends from the Marina, at their Pensacola beach-front vacation home. The little bottle of pretty white shells and clean silver sand picked up that morning, still grace my shell collection.

Paul attended a meeting in Gainsville, Florida, and we continued south to stay with Sally (whom we had met in Venezuela) at her waterside home in Homosasa Springs. In her motorboat she skidded around mangrove channels to see and play with the wild, mild, manatees in the clean warm river where the temperature of 72 degrees is just right for rearing their young. Nobody seemed to worry about alligators.

Swimming with the wild, mild manatees

Alligators

Disney's Epcot Centre and Kennedy Space Centre were both mind-boggling. Epcot's humanoids were uncannily realistic and I left scrutinizing people to see if they were real. Americans should be justifiably proud of their achievements.

In a Kentucky State Park, when we came to set up camp, our rent-a-tent had no pegs. Peter surreptitiously crept round in the dark with his pocket-knife trying to find suitable twigs, for replacements, without rousing the Park Ranger.

Kennedy Space centre

They flew us in their Beechcraft Debonair

In Huntington in W. Virginia, we stayed with friends from England. A typical Midlands 'high tea' awaited us, thin bread and butter, ham salad, fruit cake and pots and pots of tea with milk and sugar. There was so much to talk about. Next day they flew us in their Beechcraft Debonair to Greenbriars Country Club, 150 miles away across the Appalachian Mountains. (The magnificent Club House resembled Buckingham Palace surrounded by three world class golf courses.)

We arrived in Chicago in time for the *'Sail Boat Venetian Night'* on Lake Michigan. Joining the families sitting picnicking by the lakeside, we watched in wonder as dusk fell and brilliantly lit yachts and cruisers slowly motored past, their lights depicting different themes. The firework display was the longest, brightest, most thrilling display we had ever seen. The noise of the explosions reverberating from the sky-scrapers behind us was deafening.

In Milwaukee, Peter's former business colleagues and friends welcomed us and invited us to stay in their ultra modern condominiums.

Then, we were on our own, right across Wisconsin, Iowa, S. Dakota's Badlands, (where you are asked not to pick up dinosaur bones or fossils). To Mount Rushmoor where the four Presidents' heads are carved high and huge in the solid chalk cliffs. On through Wyoming to Cody and the Buffalo Museum where I felt an affinity with the pioneering women.

We camped in Yellowstone Park and were warned very forcibly about the bears, which look tame but are still wild and dangerous animals. Notices read:

'All food to be stored in the trunk of the car,

Do not indulge in sexual activity,

Ladies should not camp during their monthly cycle,

All litter to be carefully disposed of in the bear-proof bins.'

Madonna of the Prarie. I felt an affinity with the pioneering women

Yellowstone Park. First snow on 6th September

It was bitterly cold as we tried to sleep in the tent, and awoke to the first snow of the year on the 6th of September.

I particularly enjoyed the wide skies of Wyoming and the lean, jeaned, cowboys and girls who still work hard on their horses. Speeding south through the Tetons, to Dinosaur Quarry where a museum has been built over the cliff face to cover the dinosaur excavations. We watched archaeologists painstakingly brushing between the bones - (only Americans would think of, and construct, this 'mammoth' project).

I asked a friendly attendant if she knew where we could go square dancing, or any dancing for that matter. After discussion with her workmates, they decided "Kay's Bar" would suit us. We booked into a motel, showered and I carefully dressed in a skirt and blouse and Peter smartened up with a tie and clean shirt. We drove on and on out of town and eventually saw a flashing red light above a one-storey wooden shed. This was Kay's Bar. Timidly we entered.

A slim, blonde, red-trousered, sixty-year-old sat at a card table, took our money, and asked,

"Where y'all from?"

"England"

"My! Is that so? I don't get many customers from there. Well, have a nice evenin'!"

We did! We were in real cowboy country. The blue-jeaned, range-riding couples one-stepped their way around the darkened floor. The twinkling coloured lights behind the bar showed me that I was the only lady wearing a skirt. Everybody wore a stetson. If the man was taller, his stetson brim overshadowed hers, but if both were the same height they had to keep dodging brims. After a 'Millers Light' we rose to join them and were welcomed with many "Howdy's" and broad grins. It was a friendly and, not sober, companionable evening.

At Salt Lake City Citadel a smooth-talking guide conducted us around an elaborate series of showcases depicting the Mormon story. Beautiful bronze statues graced the gardens. The tour finished in the Tabernacle where we sat and counted our blessings while listening to a recording of their magnificent choir singing the Battle Hymn of the Republic.

Bryce Canyon was amazing, the wind-eroded red sandstone columns outlined eerie shapes, one resembled Queen Victoria. We camped beside mind-boggling Grand Canyon and took a morning guided walk down the trail. Our Ranger carefully picked up any litter: perhaps just a cigarette butt, or piece of chewing gum and put it into a small plastic bag in her pocket. She also checked the water bottles of any backpackers who passed. At one of the evening lectures in the Visitors' Centre a Warden told of some of the problems the Park Management faced. One was the proliferation of donkeys down in the Canyon. They were destroying the natural vegetation. Many had been air-lifted out in a net slung beneath a helicopter.

In Arizona's Walnut Canyon we walked among the exposed Pueblo Indian cave dwellings, the entrances only four feet from the cliff face. Every mother must wonder how they kept their toddlers from falling off the edge.

As we drove across the Arizona desert towards the Petrified Forest it was a surprise to hear the "News in Navajo" on the car radio. Roadside native stalls sold attractive silver and turquoise jewellery. I couldn't resist some earrings.

At El Paso we expected to see horses hitched to rails outside log cabins but we approached the city via a six lane spaghetti junction overpass! In New Mexico the Carlsbad Caverns were an hour's walk down, down, underground, to reach the enormous galleries, stalagmites and stalactites. The vast caverns were big enough to hold a full size football pitch. However it was only a three second elevator ride back up to the surface.

At the campsite we chatted to a young couple who were cycling around the USA She had a little cart on the back of her bike for her poodle. They shared with us an Indian verse:

> "Walk tall as the trees
> Live strong as the mountains
> Be gentle as the spring winds
> Keep the warmth of the summer sun in your heart
> And the great spirit will always be with you."

In Houston Kathy and Bill whom we had met at the dive school on Cayman Brac welcomed us. As well as taking us to museums and 'Theatre under the Stars', Bill showed us his workplace. He was an Emergency Room Doctor in one of Houston's busiest hospitals. We saw what he meant when he had said it was "pretty stressful."

Another day's driving across Texas: 850 miles at 55 miles an hour - the other definition of eternity. On past lonely nodding donkeys patiently pumping oil. Eventually driving over the swamplands and bridges across the Louisiana bayou, to Paul's home near Baton Rouge.

What a land of contrasts! America has virtually every natural scenic delight the earth has to offer. We camped on sites where it was too hot to sleep, and we camped in the snow with frozen noses. We watched out for bears in the mountains and rattle snakes in the desert. We stayed in lovely modern homes with every conceivable convenience yet passed shacks where people still had no piped water, electricity or telephone. We crossed raging torrents and dried-up river beds. America really does have the most fantastic, breath taking, scenery too.

'Breath taking!' What an over-exaggeration I've often thought when reading travel descriptions. But, one late afternoon, driving east over an escarpment in Arizona, we crested the brow of the hill and suddenly, there was a dramatically green valley beneath a deep crimson cliff, the colours exaggerated by the soft golden glow of sunset. The scene really did take my breath away, so much so, that I couldn't ask Peter to stop for a photograph, but tried to imprint it forever on my memory.

There were some lessons to be learned too, relative to our cruising life. In the islands, people have little use for money so we trade for vegetables and fruit with good second-hand children's clothes. At Lees Ferry, crossing the Colorado River up-river of the Grand Canyon, there were five pathetic little gravestones alongside a small homestead where the ferryman and family used to live. A plaque told the story of how a wagon train, when passing through, had given the ferry family their unwanted children's' clothes. They didn't mention that their young ones had died of smallpox. Consequently all five of the ferryman's children perished from smallpox and the homestead was abandoned forever. Since then I have made sure that any clothing I buy for trading, is given a good wash in disinfectant and laid out in the sun, before being given away.

All through America we met nothing but friendly, helpful, happy people. Yet, tuning into the local radio stations as we passed through towns, we heard about murder, rape, kidnapping, shoot-outs, and drug raids. It was difficult to understand.

I marvelled at the Pioneers, particularly the women and what they must have endured. One of the monuments in Salt Lake City brought tears to my eyes: just a small bronze statue of a little family pulling a handcart, all they possessed and lived with, as they walked from Missouri to Utah. To us, the Mormons have some peculiar ideas, but what faith they must have had to survive that journey as families, build such a beautiful city and make the appalling dry, salty, stony land, into fertile fields. We were impressed. Camping ourselves really brought home to me how awful it must have been having babies, caring for children with little water and no bathrooms. Cooking; and just surviving in the dust, dirt, heat, snow, rain, flies, ants, mosquitoes, Indians on the warpath, unscrupulous cowboys and religious persecution. I shall try never to complain again when the boat is rolling constantly.

We did stay in motels for three nights. The cheapest one gave us a laugh. Situated at the eastern edge of Flagstaff, Arizona. It looked perfectly OK when we inspected the room. However, on getting into bed, we realised there was a large shunting yard near-by and the 'Atchison, Topeka and Santa Fe Railroad' pounded alongside the bedroom window in mile-long goods trains all night. The mighty diesel engines sounded as though they were ploughing between our pillows. However, the room had a clean BATHTUB and HOT water - who cared!

Southern living in Louisiana and Mississippi coastal area was hot and humid. Swamps and lakes oozed around mangrove trees between towns and hamlets on the Gulf Coast where the Cajuns live. Further inland, the cotton fields, sugar cane and Old Plantation Homes are set in the dark fertile farmland. New Orleans and the French Quarter were full of contrasts from the old cathedral to a chic new shopping mall, where, on a balcony, a gentleman in black tie and tails played Chopin Etudes on a white grand piano beneath a crystal chandelier. It was World's Fair time and in mission halls and on street corners, small groups of Dixie-land musicians played jazz or

Cajun Festival music makers

blues. Many of the older men looking so distinguished with their white hair topping their smiling brown faces.

In Baton Rouge, Louisiana's State capital, we attended Paul's Church of Christ. We found a congregation of loving, dedicated, friendly people who welcomed us into their homes. Paul had great faith so we did our best to understand and took instruction. Before leaving, Paul baptised me and the Pastor, baptised Peter.

CLYPEUS then received our undivided attention as we prepared for the Pacific. A stranger stood watching us rubbing down wood for varnishing. "Have you any air conditioning?" he asked.

"No, unfortunately," Peter replied.

A few hours later the man returned carrying a window-air-conditioning unit. "Could you use this for a while?"

"Wow. Yes, please. When would you like it back?"

"When you're ready." He left his address. "Bring it back when you've finished with it." Peter fitted it into the forward hatch. We were so grateful. Now it was possible to retire from the enervating heat and sleep at night.

In October a wonderful unexpected surprise arrived. My parents in West Australia sent us the air-fares to fly to see them for Christmas. By shopping around, and having plenty of time, we managed to fly via England and be in Wokingham for the birth of our first grandchild Laura Billing on the 18th of November 1984. All was well with our family so on December 1st, we continued on to Perth by Garuda Air.

For the first time in 26 years my 78 year old parents had all three daughters with them for Christmas. The sun blazed overhead, but 'the Fremantle Doctor' wind that blew in from the sea each afternoon dissipated the heat. My father organised video-filming a family potted pantomime of ALADDIN and we finished up with an edited 33 minute epic for posterity. (Who's posterity?) Is a sample of the level of comedy). It has proved a happy but poignant reminder of our family fun and my mother's unstinting support for his unusual projects. What a difference from last year's lonely Christmas Day at sea!

On our Garuda flight back to England it was mandatory to spend two days in Bali. The people were gracious and beautiful. The terrain was of lush paddy fields, jungle and high mountains, yellow sand beaches and warm sparkling sea. Hindu statues and shrines dotted roadsides and gardens, parks, beside trees and on the beach. Each morning there would be a fresh offering before the shrine. Perhaps only a hibiscus blossom; or a little woven banana leaf basket containing a piece of apple, an orange segment, a few grains of rice and a frangipani flower.

A Balinese Ballet was performed in the hotel - not quite our idea of graceful dance: gestures with curled fingers, sticking out knees, neck craning from side to side, and grotesque make-up; but beautiful movement, splendidly dressed with an exciting story line including horror and humour.

Our waiter mentioned that a cremation was being held the following day in a nearby village. He arranged a taxi for us. I had read that cremations in Bali were quite a social event. The embalmed body is stored for months or years while the family save to prepare all the clothes, food and jewelry the relative will need in Nirvana. For rich folk a huge pagoda shrine is constructed of bamboo and paper and carried on the shoulder of 50-80 men. We saw a family looking out of the upper windows as it slowly processed. Lesser mortals are put in large paper-mache dragons, bulls or horses, elaborately painted and decorated and carried by 20 or 30 men.

One immense procession accommodates all the village deceased so that they can travel to heaven together. Cacophonous bands in traditional dress walk between the wobbling edifices, blowing bugles, beating gongs, cymbals and drums and swinging bells. Interspersed are women carrying colourful towers of fruit, eggs and rice cakes on their heads, as well as rolls of batik.

They process to a field where cremation pyres are prepared and after prayers and sprinkling essences, a torch is put to each separate shrine and offerings. Later the ashes are gathered and families sit round in a tight circle to perform other private rites. There were many tourists as well as locals. Everyone behaved with suitable discretion.

We returned to New Orleans on 14th January after flying 35,000 odd miles and 32 take offs and landing without a hitch. Our economy tickets taught us - less money, more landings.

In February, Misco Marine in Gulfport had a pre-season bargain offer where CLYPEUS could economically be hauled out. The boatyard was a mere thirty miles along the coast so we pushed off from Diamond Head Marina and launched ourselves onto the sea once more.

We pushed off from Diamond Head Marina, Mississippi

What a chapter of crises! Our water tanks were frozen solid and the SatNav failed. We were severely reminded how pitiless is the sea as we jiggled our way out to Bay St. Louis and tied up for the night to a partly completed jetty. The wind rose, the swell increased, we were banging against the jetty. In the dark at 1.30 we moved a hundred yards out and anchored. At 4.30 Peter ratcheted the anchor up again so that we could motor out with the tide to clear the shallow pass under the railway bridge. Once through, he let go the anchor and we snatched a couple of hours sleep. As soon as it was light at 6.30 in a cold northerly wind we set off again only to go aground on the shifting sandbanks. At 9.30. Peter had managed to kedge us off by 10 am. Then the engine failed at 10.10 before we were out of the narrrows. In a panic we hoisted the sails. The engine had sucked one fuel tank dry so he had to bleed the fuel system. As he hung upside down to suck the diesel through the pipes I steered us through the winding channels under sail. We arrived at Misco Marine at 1 p.m. Ah! The joys of sailing! It certainly cut us back down to size after six months of land-lubbing and just talk.

Louisiana was freezing, unprecedentedly cold, and to lighten the boat, we had carefully taken all our cold weather clothes back to England. CLYPEUS was chocked up in the yard fully exposed to the freezing rain, sleet and bitter north wind - not good painting weather.

An example occurred here of how difficult it is to balance income and expenses. At the bank, I changed a £100 travellers' cheque and only received US$99.40. On the steps outside I had a little weep - losing $50 on each £100 wasn't going to help our finances.

It was hard leaving our son and friends but it would be good to head south and be warm again.

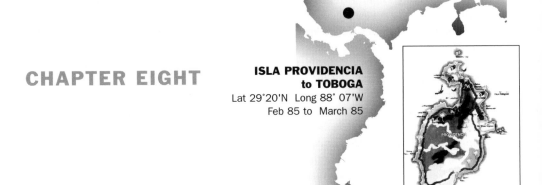

CHAPTER EIGHT

**ISLA PROVIDENCIA
to TOBOGA**
Lat 29°20'N Long 88° 07'W
Feb 85 to March 85

The first eight days of the voyage from Louisiana to Panama caused us to question our sanity. CLYPEUS was tossed around in huge seas like a cork in a cold wash cycle. The oil rigs I had romantically called 'sparkling Christmas trees' on the way north last July, were now, in February, a terrifying hazard, especially the abandoned, unlit, structures.

A friendly Mississippi tug boat gave us a call on the VHF. The captain's slow southern drawl was welcome, even if his news was not. "Hi y'all. This here rough weather's goin a get a durn sight worse. Jus keep on headin south and you'll get to the sunshine," he paused, "sometime, I guess."

Once through the Yucatan Channel, in the lee of Cuba, the sun peeked out and the seas grew calmer. At last we were able to eat and sleep again while heading for Swan Island, a dot a hundred miles off Honduras. Although we had a new mainsail on board Peter was loathe to use it, so all spare time was spent with a leather sailmaker's palm on my right hand, stitching.

From my journal I see:

'FEBRUARY 20th 83°W. 16S (between Cuba and Panama)

Sitting in the sunny cockpit in the Western Caribbean off the Honduras coast plough-ing through a pale blue sea only 7-8 fathoms deep (40-50 feet). 1062 miles and 14 days out of Gulfport. There is a fresh wind and dollops of spray keep hitting me. Reefed main, working jib and staysail up, doing 6 knots on course for Isla Providencia, before getting to Colon hopefully on 27th to meet Sheila James who is going to join us for a couple of weeks. Pooped twice, once with door open: bucket job to clear bilges.

Feb 22nd Arrived at Swan Island which is the same size as Alderney, (about 4 x 1 mile). It looked idyllic with coconut palms, white sand beaches, coral reefs. On shore the metre long iguanas, land crabs, frigate birds and boobies nesting were quite unafraid when we walked close to them.

The eleven inhabitants comprised:- eight Honduran soldiers on two weeks rest and recuperation. They seemed incredibly young (they screech around in jeeps at night, shoot-ing up the iguanas with their AK 47's.) two Americans who were manning a radio station for NOAA whilst the area is being surveyed by the U.S. Navy; and Jerry a tall, handsome young Honduran farmer. He cares for 250 Brahmin cattle: beautiful, clean, healthy looking animals; pigs, chickens and a vegetable garden. He proudly showed me his hound-dog with her eleven lovely pups and offered me one. I sadly refused as some countries enforce strict anti-rabies laws. Jerry was trying to interest the soldiers in helping him as they had no other duties. Old Quonset Huts, relics of U.S. Military and United Fruit's former dominance dot the island.

Jerry came and invited us to supper the first evening - lobster tails, baked in butter, delicious! The Americans cooked supper for us the following evening and I cooked supper for them all at the house on our final night. For some reason they didn't wish to eat on CLYPEUS *as she rolled and gyrated in the bay.*

They encouraged us to use the shower, bath, washing machine and their home. We explored, swam, gathered coconuts and took photos of the tame wild life. I won't mind so much if we are not allowed long in the Galapagos Islands now as I feel we have been to a relatively unspoiled island."

The soldiers turn the lighthouse out when they go to bed at 10 p.m. so we left by 7p m. to make sure we were well away from the island before they did. We calculated two and a half days sailing to Isla Providencia but on arrival couldn't find the pass between the coral reefs. Eventually, at 4 p.m. a dugout canoe with an outboard powered out. A native pilot, Captain Blood, climbed aboard and offered to guide us in through a shallow pass to pirate Henry Morgan's Island.

Isla Providencia had been British but was given to the Colombians by Queen Victoria. The Islanders (all colours from coffee to black) speak a Victorian Caribbean English, mixed with Spanish and Creole.

As we anchored, the dugout came to pick up Captain Blood.
"How much do we owe you for piloting us in?" Peter enquired.
"Foh de big yachts $15 but foh yoh, only $10". He replied.

We only had a US $20 note, so gave it to him and asked if he would be kind enough to bring us the change in pesos so that we could buy some bread and fresh food.

"Sure Skip, tomorrow" he replied clutching our $20 note (now with the rate of exchange it was £20 sterling, as well) and disappeared over the side into the canoe.

"Oh dear" we thought, "we've done it again, parted with our money too easily. We will never see him or our money again."

A few hours later the port captain and immigration officer arrived together with a smartly dressed gentleman who spoke no English but carried a clipboard with many forms. We assumed he was the customs officer but found out later that he was an officious shipping agent. Our harbour fees for entering were US$12 and the agent's fee another US$12 for a sheaf of forms in triplicate suitable for a cruise liner.

Ashore we looked longingly into the window of the village store at appetizing fresh buns glazed with white icing. Fifteen-year-old Audrey introduced herself and suggested we try them. On our admitting we couldn't, because we had no pesos, she insisted on buying us one each. They were probably only about ten cents, but such generosity from a stranger who wore no shoes is thought provoking.

Our assessment of Captain Blood's avarice was wrong. Next morning, first thing, he arrived in his dugout with 1,150 pesos, a big toothless grin and an invitation to come to his house for lunch on Sunday. "Jus aroun de corner of de bay in yoh dinghy, you see mah house. You come 12 o'clock and mah wife she make you good fish stew".

In our Sunday best, at 11.30, Peter started rowing the few hundred yards to lunch but, against the wind and tide. An hour later, absolutely exhausted, we tied up at their jetty and were led proudly into a wooden unpainted shack with glassless windows. The living room, bedroom and kitchen were spotlessly clean and tidy with two chairs, no table but a defunct white enamel chest freezer on which stood a fan and two black and white T.Vs, none of which worked because there was no electricity.

The kitchen had a tap, a plastic bowl, and a shelf on which stood a draining rack with crockery and cutlery. The cooker was a wood fire resting on a sheet of tin at waist level in a little bay window. On the burning sticks balanced a big iron pot containing a simmering stew of trigger fish with yucca, plantain and sweet potato. Captain and Mrs Blood made us welcome, and after a delicious lunch, proudly showed us their six chickens, two pigs, two dogs and a puppy, and made us good coffee.

Mrs Blood shows me seeds she has planted

Mrs Blood, who didn't speak English, took me into the bedroom - two tidy, clean single beds, no cupboards but two string lines hanging across the room with all their clothes neatly folded on them. There was one small shelf with an array of nail polish bottles. She insisted on giving me one, her nails and hands were in much better condition than mine and she was obviously trying to encourage me. When we ran out of gestured conversation she just looked out of the window at the aquamarine coral-studded sea. Capt. Blood couldn't read but was able to show Peter the way out through the reefs on a wall chart.

Audrey took us to her home, another shack, and to her grandparents'. Grandma was a big black mammy and Grandfather, a wiry, white, Englishman whose father had come out on a sailing ship. He himself had sailed square-riggers between Providencia, Colombia, Panama and Honduras.

Just before we left for Panama, Audrey hailed us from the beach and handed us a plastic bag with a huge lobster and two fish in it. I'd given them biscuits, sweets, magazines and clothes, with no thought of having anything back. The lobster was so big we couldn't cram it into the pressure cooker, even after taking off the claws. Peter had to bash its nose in with a hammer and squeeze it into the pot. It was good, but I almost ruined it by adding a tiny quarter of a small red pepper Mrs. Blood had given me - it was a chilli, a very hot chilli.

Capt. Blood shows peter the way through the reef

*Ploughing down to Panama -
the plughole of the Caribbean*

Three more days of exhilarating sailing and at 1 a.m. on the 28th February, we entered Colon Harbour, the entrance to the Panama Canal. With train-high seas roaring down behind us, we surfed in between brilliantly lit cargo vessels towering above. Peter said it felt like entering the plughole of the Caribbean. It was thrilling to be amongst so many lights and to hear the throb of the ships' powerful generators. At 2 a.m. we dropped anchor in 90' of water on the flats off the Panama Yacht Club, had a wee celebratory dram, and slept. Our friend from Portugal arrived and joined us for two happy, but frustrating weeks trying to sail east to the San Blas Islands. The strong wind was continually against us. We visited Porto Bello, the terminus of the Gold Road where the Spaniards loaded the Aztec gold into their galleons. In the 16th Century it was a city, but now is just a poor village with roofless ruined customs warehouses and stone forts.

Porto Bello - Ruined Spanish gold warehouses

Warily hiking on paths through the jungle monkeys shrieked down at us, but we saw no snakes or other wildlife. A week passed as we enjoyed swimming in the warm clear water and the beaches revealed many unusual shells. Sitting on the path outside the Panama Yacht Club were Cuna Indian women from the San Blas Islands decked in heavy gold armlets and anklets, selling their exquisite molas (embroidered collages of traditional designs. The bright material is folded back and stitched to expose the different coloured layers). We bartered half-heartedly not wanting to beat them down too far and then found out they commuted to Panama by chartered helicopter to sell their wares. A matriarchal society where the women hold the money, make and sell molas, and the men farm and keep house.

Beside a pontoon lay DEMI. They had spent seven months in Port Azul repairing their yacht and were now on their way again. Well, they would be, when their passports were replaced, as they had been stolen in Colon the previous week.

We volunteered to be line-handlers for INTERLUDE's transit of the Canal. It gave us a good idea of what to expect and we enjoyed the train ride back from Balboa to Colon.

There was a good market and supermarket in Colon. However the crime and mugging rates were so bad we were warned to remove any jewelry, not to carry hand-bags, or wallets, and to take as little money as possible when shopping. On average three yachties a week were mugged in broad daylight. I armed myself with a can of baked beans in a plastic bag and swung it aggressively as we walked along. At the supermarket, the manager refused to let us leave until he had called a taxi and made the driver back up to the door for our purchases to be packed in.

Working out stores for eight weeks or so was difficult. I had no idea what type of food would be available in the Galapagos, if any; then there would still be another 3,000 miles before we arrived in Tahiti. We had plenty of cans, rice and pasta on board, and baking bread was exciting, as I could never anticipate how it would turn out. I regularly sowed and tended mung bean seeds with varying success: either a few mouldy little shoots fought for life on the lint at the base of a jam jar, or a veritable forest sprouted which we could never eat before the roots exceeded the shoots. We wouldn't be bored with our diet during the month-long crossing.

Wilma our pilot, sees us into the first lock

On Tuesday 19th March, coincidentally the exact two year anniversary of leaving St. Katherine's Dock, we made our transit through the Panama Canal. A hot, busy, day that started at 04.30 for us and our three line-handlers who were sleeping on board, ready for the 04.45 arrival of our pilot. It was a surprise when she arrived on time. Wilma, our Panamanian Adviser was a pretty 25 year old who did a good job, although Peter found it very difficult to take instructions from her on his boat.

Underway by 05.00 in the pitch dark, amidst a maze of lights from buoys, ships and street lamps, the waning sliver of moon was just rising as I steered across the main channel and then from red buoy light to red buoy light up towards the first lock. Peter was busy with ropes and instructing our line handlers.

The first lock was the most traumatic, because the water fell the greatest height from Lake Gatun. We followed a towering merchant ship into the lock. High above us on the quay, the dockers flung down ropes with hard monkey knots on the end. We tied our 100' ropes to them and the nooses were pulled up and slipped over bollards. Then it was up to us to keep the yacht in the middle as water whooshed, bursting up in the centre and raced away to the sides. The strains on the four corner ropes were immense as we tried to keep the boat central. The water bubbled and boiled ferociously against our hull with a chuckling, sucking noise, reminiscent of riding the overfalls in the Alderney Swinge. (Really, normal British summer holiday sail-ing to the Channel Islands prepares you for most sea states you are likely to meet on a

Panama cut

circumnavigation - excluding warm water).

CLYPEUS motor-sailed at the mandatory six knots through the canal and 26 miles of Gatun Lakes - it is necessary to keep up a good speed if you are going to get through in one day. We lunched on deck, in spite of the glaring sunlight, anxious not to miss glimpses into the Panamanian jungle. It was hot and humid. The air felt thick and moist to breathe. Monkeys chattered in the overhanging trees and vines as we passed close to islands.

Going down the Pacific side of the Canal at Miraflores, yachts enter the lock first. A large cargo vessel followed us in, with the power of the wind and water behind it. We prayed it would stop before it smashed us up against the lock gates. It towered above us blotting out the daylight, but did slow and stop in time. At Balboa at 4 pm., we dropped off the crew, picked up the last of our mail and headed to Taboga - a hilly tropic isle with golden sand, Spanish houses, palm trees, one shop, two hotels and pretty pink and purple clam shells on the beach.

Taboga Island was such a lovely, unexpected surprise, our first Pacific Island with the skyscrapers of Panama City, fifteen miles away still visible. When swimming we found that the water was about 10° cooler than the other side of the isthmus, only 70° as distinct from 80°. It felt fresh and invigorating but looked a dull green, not as clear and blue as the Caribbean.

Peter thinks I ought to mention the big psychological traumas we work up to before ocean crossings. Leaving Taboga to sail across the Pacific, the tension was the same as when we first left England, then Gibraltar, then Teneriffe and lastly the USA. Each time we leave we try and be at peace with our family in case we never see them, or land, again. All debts must be paid and our affairs put in order. Plus, of course, planning future landfalls, money transfers, mail drops, food, fuel, spares and water.

We enjoyed one more rest day ashore and planned to leave the following afternoon on the tide when the wind freshened (as it did about 3 p.m. most days) take a quick look at the Perlas Islands and sail on to the Galapagos Archipelago, crossing the Equator at 88° 30'W. However another unexpected sojourn delayed the start of our Pacific adventure.

During the night our anchor dragged and wrapped itself around LIBERTY's chain and we waltzed around each other until the morning. It is a situation when you make either good friends or lifelong enemies. It was our fault, but, in the morning rafted together, Robert and Linda (doctor and nurse wife from San Diego and Nebraska) forgave us for disturbing their sleep, and breakfasted with us. They were such good company we partied with them and a Chilean yacht for a couple of days. Robert is one of those clever young men with the irritating habit of being able to speak with authority on any subject. It was difficult sometimes to accept his views, but on investigation, we always found him to be correct. Fortunately he had great charm, an incisive wit, an impish sense of humour and we thoroughly enjoyed his company. Linda was a slim, quiet, efficient and supportive wife.

Our new friends told us of the splendours of Cocos Island, a pirate island with buried treasure deep in the Doldrums. Even if we didn't find silver, the fishing would be fantastic and the abundant lobsters could be caught by hand. Wild boar roamed the island and the friendly wardens not only helped you shoot them, but showed you how to smoke the hams. It was decided to rendezvous on this unspoilt, Costa Rican isle. "Only a diversion of 150 miles," Robert said. LIBERTY was a Bruce Farr 36' racing machine which enabled them to make fast crossings; our sedate CLYPEUS couldn't keep up with them, so we left first, promising to do our best to meet them at Cocos island.

CHAPTER NINE

Galapagos

TOBOGA to GALAPAGOS
Lat 29°20'N Long 88° 07'W
March to April 1985

Quietly unravelling our anchor chain, we headed south for the Perlas Islands. Panama City's skyscrapers gleamed pink in the morning sun against the backdrop of dark green mist-shrouded mountains. Cormorants, in flights of ten to twelve, swooped low over the water in V formation. Flights of pelicans skimmed motionless, low across the glassy surface, with only an occasional wing-flap. Terns and pelicans dived for their breakfast, others spiralled up on air currents. The Gulf of Panama teemed with life.

At Saboga Island I rowed ashore to beach-comb, but found only a few shells and no seaweed. Piles of sand above the tideline might be where turtles nested? Digging produced no evidence.

We had enjoyed the minimal tides of the Caribbean and now must re-adjust our thinking to an 18' rise and fall. We anchored for the night near a rocky plateau. At mid-tide our depth sounder showed only 7'. We decided to move. In the starlit but moonless night, as we slept on deck, I lay watching the dark ocean slurping around the emerging sleek black rocks. It looked as though El Pacifico was licking her lips, just waiting for us to make a mistake.

Next day on Isla Contadora we bought bread (sliced, wrapped in plastic) and remarked on the smart hotels, Rent-a-scooter and Duty Free shops. We left before lunch and hoisted the genoa which hadn't been up for many months. Fishing was good. A short log extract reads:

> *11.30 Caught Blue Runner Jack*
> *11.55 Lost Blue Runner Jack, (it slipped off chopping board on aft deck)*
> *12.10 Caught Blue Runner Jack*
> *12.30 Ate Blue Runner Jack - delicious!*

Shoals of sardines poppled the sea surface and swerved as one - how do they do it? We caught another fish for our dinner and had it stuffed with breadcrumbs and herbs and baked in the oven.

The night of March 24th was moist and dark. Phosphorescence lit the sea as our wake tumbled and sparkled like the Milky Way. Dolphins swam through shining tubes of light exploding in a fountain of stars as they broke the surface. Many ships passed on their way to the Canal. Now our clocks were six hours after GMT.

Sailing west along the north coast of the Gulf of Panama, the mist and smoke from evening fires dotted the brown mountains as they disappeared and a night of stygian blackness descended. The fresh northerly wind was steady but next day it faded and we started motoring across an absolutely calm and smooth sea. We were almost on the Equator:

For eight days we hoisted and lowered the sails like yo-yos for any puff of wind. The engine was on more than it was off. We poured buckets of sea water over our heads to cool off. After dark, small squid propelled themselves up onto the deck. Thunderstorms developed each evening but at last, in the glow of an orange dawn, we sighted Cocos. The waterfalls sparkled as the sun rose. At 14.00 as we joined LIBERTY and five other yachts anchored in the North Eastern Bay, Veronica (now eight) and Yvonne (four) from DEMI, rowed to greet us with "Welcome to Paradise."

The 450 mile voyage from Isla Contadora had used much of our precious diesel. In a frustration of calms, contrary winds and adverse currents, it had taken nine days and we had covered 690 miles. It was worth it.

Cocos is a high island, covered in virgin rain forest. Two wardens had been installed by Costa Rica in 1978 to protect the wildlife. They live in a hut on the beach, stamp passports and generally make sure nobody destroys the environment. Water flowed down from a mountain stream through a plastic pipe into a pierced beer can, providing a continuous cool and refreshing shower for all. Within a hundred yards of their shack was a river swimming hole and laundry pool.

The wardens, delighted to have company, led us miles up the pristine boulder-strewn river bed with impenetrable jungle on either side. Another glistening waterfall greeted us which had a ledge behind the falling water where we could walk and survey the jungle through a rushing, silver curtain.

I actually did catch a lobster in my hands (wearing kitchen gloves), and speared some fish. At low tide we filled a bucket with enormous oysters for fresh meat on the next leg. Whilst snorkelling we saw many sharks both white tips and hammerhead (who do have a taste for human flesh). The hammerheads skulking along the bottom took no notice of us, but we took the precaution of climbing back into the dinghy and hung over the side watching them through our masks until they meandered on.

Cocos island's enormous lobsters

The other yachts were American, German, Swiss and Australian, no other Brits. Guitar from Florida invited us all on board for a 'bring-a-dish" Easter Saturday party on their spacious foredeck. We sat, contented, on a balmy starry evening, sipping iced drinks, listening to our host playing his guitar and softly singing cowboy songs and '40s' melodies. The moon came up over the mountain to shimmer across the water towards us.

Cocos was so perfect we stayed seven days and spent our time enjoying the company of other happy, satisfied, sailors. It seemed a great achievement to be in, and enjoying, such a remote place. Everybody was self-sufficient, in their own space-capsule, and while anchored we could allow ourselves to relax and enjoy the moment.

However, it had to be paid for, and as we steered a little west of south for The Galapagos Islands:

> *'The sun came up upon the left.*
> *Out of the sea came he!*
> *And he shone bright, and on the right,*
> *Went down into the sea.'*
>> Rhyme of the Ancient Mariner

On Sunday, April 14th we sailed across the Equator at 89°52'. Our bottle of wine, clad like Neptune with crown and trident, a gift from friends in Mississippi, was undressed. Neptune received a splash and we downed the rest with fresh oysters chopped small and marinated in lime juice.

Our bucket of large live oysters was proving a good source of protein. Oyster chowder made with potatoes and longlife milk was delicious. The shells of our 'fresh meat' were as big as dinner plates lined with oyster-pink mother of pearl. When the outside deposits were scrubbed off they made attractive, though heavy, ash trays. It seemed criminal to toss them away. However Peter didn't share my attachment to them, and insisted they were too heavy to keep. So over the side they went.

It took six days to cover the 350 miles to Tower Island in the north of the Galapagos group. We just hoped we would be able to buy diesel fuel somewhere in the islands.

Blue footed Boobies were completely unafraid

At dawn on April 15th, stark rocky islands rose out of the sea ahead and we made for Tower Island, the nearest of the famed 'disappearing' or 'enchanted' Galapagos Islands. In the olden days the galleons often couldn't find them, the currents are wild and treacherous and with mist and the sun immediately overhead navigation is difficult. We anchored in Darwin Bay, the caldera of an extinct volcano. The shoreline was a circle of sharp black rocks with grey scrub vegetation. Thousands of sea birds: masked boobies, blue and red footed, and brown boobies noisily roosted, wobbling on slender branches, their webbed feet, inefficient for perching. They constantly twitched as they struggled to keep upright.

Liberty arrived

Menacing black frigate birds circled high, the inflated red balloons in their necks brilliant against the sky. Sea lions raised their whiskery snouts out of the water and eyed us questioningly. Red and orange Sally Lightfoot crabs skittered around the black rocks. We didn't go ashore, just gazed in wonder at the busy, riotous, bird-life. A few hours later LIBERTY arrived and anchored close by and we were able to welcome them with drinks and a meal.

It was a spellbinding landscape and Herman Melville describes it well:

"In many places the coast is rock-bound, or more properly, clinker-bound; tumbled masses of blackish or greenish stuff like the dross of an iron-furnace, forming dark clefts and caves here and there, into which a ceaseless sea pours a fury of foam; overhanging them with a swirl of grey, haggard mist, amidst which screaming flights of unearthly birds heightening the dismal din."

The Encantadas (1841)

The brown boobies were funny. They wheeled around over the boats and twanged into the rigging. They settled on the pulpit and wouldn't be shooed away. They were making such a mess on deck Peter tried to frighten them by blowing our fog horn close to their heads. They just poked their beaks up the horn inquiringly to see where the sound was coming from. He eventually assisted their take-off by gently lifting their tails with a piece of wood. Sometimes they turned their heads to give him a reproachful look as they fell into the water but didn't seem to mind and were completely unagressive.

The stony, grey scrub-covered hills of Santa Cruz were shrouded in mist as we sailed down the eastern side and round to the anchorage in Academy Bay where the Darwin Research Institute is located. One shop had a little fresh food available and diesel was poured from big oil drums into our five gallon plastic containers. The bottom 6" settled into a layer of water, rust and dirt. Nylon tights stretched over the filler provided an extra filter as Peter funneled it into the fuel tanks.

Black marine iguanas roasted on the black rocks like statues, holding their heads

*Tortoise 500 years old at the
Darwin Institute*

Pelicans were friendly and greedy

high, only yards from CLYPEUS. They were impossible to photograph - black on black.

There was plenty to see on Santa Cruz Island. The tortoises at Darwin Research Station were aged from 5 days to 500 years old - alive when Shakespeare was around. The Institute gave us fascinating leaflets on their studies and conclusions. 1982-83's El Nino warm currents had disastrous effects on the iguanas, penguins, cormorants and flamingoes. The marine iguanas had been affected by an unusual Giffordia algae which they ate as they cropped their usual diet of seaweed. Many died and it was found that extraordinary amounts of fat had accumulated in their livers. As the sea returned to its normal temperature so what was left of the iguana population stabilised. How little we understand the complex effects of global warming.

Our 'permisso' had arrived, but in 1985 yachts were not allowed to visit the other islands without a National Park Guide who cost US$30 a day plus his bed and board. For a large yacht or tourist vessel this is reasonable, but not for a small yacht with only two people on board. We do understand the difficulties the Equadorean Government must face to preserve the environment, yet allow the isolated agricultural community to enjoy some of the prosperity that tourism brings.

A group of us walked two miles over painfully sharp black cinders, to the white sand of Tortuga Bay. We surfed in the cold Humboldt current and shampooed our hair in the breakers (family shampoos work well in sea water). A local boatman, Rommy, guided us to the other side of the narrow isthmus to the warm shallow lagoon where huge manta rays were mating and big sharks slid along the bottom. Rommy jumped into the waist deep water and exulted "Look! Even the sharks are friendly in the Galapagos!"

"Foolish man," I thought, but indeed none of the marine creatures did seem in the least aggressive towards humans.

Vernon of GUITAR gave a well-attended, free, concert in the local hall of easy melodious jazz music. Boatman Rommy led us to The Booby Trap night club to dance. Rowing home across the moonlit water to sleep on deck ended a perfect day.

Every day was spent as thought it may be our last. LIBERTY invited us for a celebration breakfast of strawberries and pink champagne, followed by savoury and sweet crepes. An expedition to swim with the sealion was abandoned in heavy seas.

Examining weather charts ashore, the time was approaching to launch ourselves out into the Pacific. A final farewell dinner was organised. As I fished for our first course, the tribe of hungry puffer fish took every piece of bait before it reached the edible fish below. The first three were thrown back before I realised they were not going to allow me to catch anything else. American cookery book *'Living off the Sea'* gave a recipe for puffer fish scampi with the assurance that it wasn't poisonous as long as you didn't puncture the stomach. When twelve puffer fish were lying dying and grunting on deck, I stopped. The fillets cut from beside the backbone did look like firm white scampi. Deep friend in batter they were delicious - I took the first bite.

Before leaving we tried to send letters, but the post office had run out of stamps. They took our money and promised they would be posted when the stamps arrived. They were.

Apprehensively we left the Galapagos Islands for our longest ocean crossing of about 3,000 miles to Hiva Oa in the Marquesa Islands.

Peter posting letters in Post Office Bay -
They did reach our family

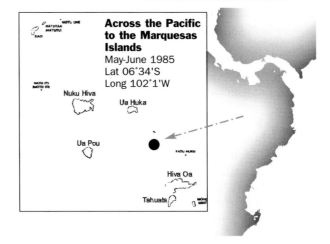

Across the Pacific to the Marquesas Islands
May-June 1985
Lat 06°34'S
Long 102°1'W

CHAPTER TEN

Our voyage across the Pacific was the realisation of our dream; as an extract from my journal shows:

30th April 1985,

I swam ashore on Floreana and saw pink flamingoes wading in the lake just behind the beach; a fur seal hiding in the shade beneath a rock; penguins swimming flat like platypus. Turtle tracks led to deep wide holes in the white sand above the high tide mark. Hundreds of little red crabs skittered to their holes in the sand, then poised half in and half out, watching which way I walked before deciding whether to carry on with their game or disappear.

Underwater there were thick-spined sea urchins, the spines as thick as pencils. I saw one giant clam - the type that could snap shut on Tarzan's foot and hold him under; also green, red and yellow parrot fish, a shoal of blue and yellow striped margate and large conch and helmet shells.

On the short run to Post Office Bay we caught a big grouper (8 lbs). After a tasty lunch the rest of the fillets were bottled using the pressure cooker.

7th May 1985.

Seven days out of Floreana - 780 miles travelled, 2,300 to go to Hiva Oa. Fantastic sailing now, after the first three days when we motored SW looking for the Trade Winds. We found them and are tearing along at 6 knots (7mph) over an untidy pushy sea that keeps intruding into the cockpit. It is too rough to do much but sleep, read and eat bananas - they are ripening fast.

On Saturday we sailed 145 miles - our best ever 24 hour distance. The colour of the Pacific here is a weak dark blue with white caps sparkling in the sunshine. A big swell, like low hills slowly roll up behind us from the SE, with undisciplined waves with white horses from the north racing over it. The main and genoa are up and we are trying to make 250° (WSW). On our fastest day Peter had two working jibs boomed out wing and wing as well as the staysail and main. He is taking sun sights every day.

Little storm petrels are still flying and dipping between the waves, so far from land. Flying fish skim the surface during the day and squid at night.

Using the pressure cooker instead of the oven to bake our bread has improved it 100%. It now no longer resembles a small Elizabethan brick. A covering of mould *develops after the second day in this heat and humidity so I'm getting plenty of practice. Our diet is still varied with Galapagos fresh fruit and vegetables. Nina Cotton in Mississippi gave me a box with hand written "Southern Cooking" instructions. So this morning we have had hominy grits with our eggs and bacon (tinned) and we'll have corn bread with our paprika beef goulash and stir-fry cabbage tonight..."*

During the thirty day crossing of 3,060 miles we experienced no bad weather, no problems, averaging just over 100 miles each 24 hours. Happy days of lounging around, thinking, reading, embroidering, writing, eating and occasionally attending to the sails; taking sights and comparing them with the SatNav. We lay on deck observing the white puffs of Trade Wind clouds floating in the blue sky, listening to the rasp of ropes on winches as they took the strain. Standing on the bowsprit, rainbows glistened in the sparkling white spray as our bow sliced through the water. The ephemeral creamy bubbles curled back along the hull disturbing floating logs which rolled away and little crabs scuttled up to the dry side. Hoppy insects jumped from frond to frond on clumps of seaweed as it undulated on our bow wave. Flying fish careered in straight lines smacking into whatever got in their way. Some areas had grey pumice floating on the surface, which was worrying. Was an underwater volcanic eruption about to take place? During night watches I worked on a sonnet.

We spent time in separate cabins listening to different programmes or tapes. During calms Peter inflated the Avon to scrub off weed growing on the hull. In the

SONNET

by Shirley BIlling

NIGHT WATCH

In the lingering midnight watch I make
Plans, while scanning billowing sails on high.,
Phosphorescent tresses that trail our wake
Flash incandescent transits to the sky.
Cascading foam slips down the curling wave,
Tumbling from our bow to leave no trace,
The Ocean's mine, I do not fear its grave,
Its deep will keep our souls in watery grace.
Swooping dolphins, glist'ning bodies dancing
Through tubes of light to burst in bright boquet
Turn their heads, their bright eyes glancing
With mine, to meet the tranquil dawning day.
  Our young ones prospered being left alone,
  We found adventure, and heireith for home.

Peter inflated the Avon to scrub off the weed and Goose barnacles

Ocean bath

evenings we often sat at the saloon table playing Scrabble; the soft light of the oil lamp glowing on the red velvet upholstery, aware of the creak of straining sails and the swish of water along the hull. The alarm punctuating the game every fifteen minutes for a look around outside. No ships, no major upsets, no intrusions, no whales or dolphins and still no albatrosses.

We caught and ate two dorades, made bread, pancakes, cakes, yoghurt, sprouted beans. The rice purchased in Academy Bay was infested with weevils, more black little insects appeared in the big plastic jar each day. We didn't dare just throw it away as we didn't know when we would next be able to buy stores, so did some experiments on de-weeviling rice. Eventually, the most efficient way appeared to pour the rice into a bowl of water and spoon the weevils off when they floated to the surface, then spread the rice out on baking tins to dry in the sun. However, not all the weevils wanted to swim! Further close inspection as the rice dried, allowed us to extract drowned bodies and any eggs.

We had plenty of water thanks to Peter's ingenuity. He had fitted two wooden strips along the sides of the cabin top to direct rain down a copper tube each side. When it rained, we would wait for a few minutes for the salt to be washed away, then push on plastic piping to feed the run-off into the water tanks. We cooled off by pouring buckets of water over our heads then mist-sprayed with fresh water before drying off.

During the voyage I read about twenty books. Determined to improve myself I started with Sir Thomas More's *Utopia;* an easy read with astonishingly modern views for the Sixteenth century. Virgil's *Aeneaid;* but it was too gory; I tired of the bloody battles and gave up serious reading and enjoyed Melville's *Typee*, four Michener's; two Dick Francis'; and many others. I mulled over known and unfamiliar poetry on audio tapes and books. Peter read even more. He enjoys spy thrillers so sat reading about emotionless killers in freezing slush in Berlin while on watch, living many people's dream in the blue Pacific.

Our baptism and renewal of faith in the USA had many positive side effects.

Half way celebration 1485 miles sailed from Florena 1488miles to Hiva OA

One was that we began to use God to avoid confrontation with each other. We used him as our mediator and needed him on a practical level. He is the other person we spoke to: our Counsellor. While staying with Paul, who wants to be a missionary, we became accustomed to holding hands around the table and saying grace (just like The Waltons). I found I could now say, "Thank you Father for this food and please bring us safely to harbour. Please help me understand why Peter won't wash the dishes immediately after our meals. Amen."

Now Peter knew that I really cared about this silly problem. The division of labour is - I cook, he washes the dishes. It is a constant bicker that I want it done NOW, while he wants to read his book.

He, in turn, had the opportunity to say "Dear Lord, we are grateful for all your blessings, but please help Shirley to remember to put the pencils back in the rack on the navigation table." I agree, it's infuriating to dash to write down a radio message or gale warning and not be able to find a pencil, and I do try hard to comply.

We both navigate, we both steer, change, clean and mend sails. Peter maintains engine and gear, I maintain cabins and stores. We have learned to meld our accomplishments and acknowledge our weaknesses. We have had time together which we will never regret.

On May 20th, twenty-eight days out of Floreana we still had sixty miles to our landfall. After eating the last grapefruit for breakfast, we nonchalantly busied ourselves on deck pretending not to look for

Mid-Pacific sextant sight. Bearded skipper land. Gradually Hiva Oa and Mohotani rose out of the mist.

The Satnav said we had travelled 2958 miles from Floreana, the Stowe trailing log only recorded 2848, so CLYPEUS had received a boost of 90 miles of current. We approached Hiva Oa, happy with our life at sea, but still pleased to smell the sweet aroma of land as it wafted across the water.

Rounding Hiva Oa's stone breakwater we were surprised to see seventeen other yachts already at anchor. Every boat had sailed at least 3,500 miles and there was a great feeling of camaraderie. New Dutch friends on ROSA invited us on board for an Indonesian 'reis staffeal'.

The camaraderie didn't extend to all the French Officials. The Bank Manageress was so officious she reduced me to tears. We'd walked the mile or so to her office and arrived near to lunch time which didn't suit her, so an appointment was made for 2 p.m. However, the gendarme took longer with his immigration form-filling than expected and we didn't arrive back at the Bank until 2.15 when she severely scolded us for our tardiness. Peter made a point of saying (in halting French) that he thought the Bank was there to provide a service for us. (The expected bond, for the cost of air fares back to the country of origin, was banked and then refunded on departure from Tahiti with no problems).

Two charming teenage Polynesian girls befriended us on our exploration of the village. It was impossible to buy fruit and vegetables, but once you made a Polynesian friend they would give you all you needed. They insisted on taking us home and picking pamplemousse from a tree in their garden. The fruit was luscious, like large grapefruit but juicier and sweeter, each segment exploding deliciously in our mouths. The French baguettes, butter and wine were all the standard French, government-regulated price, but anything else was very expensive.

All six Marquesa Islands were green and fertile with dramatic mountains, cliffs and stone outcrops. When first visited by Captain Cook the population was 70,000, but now, fewer than 10,000 people are left; due mainly to contracting white man's diseases. In the valleys, on river banks and beaches were black volcanic stone foundations of large, abandoned villages. Our Polynesian friends led us up the valley to see, in the distance, tikis carved into the mountainside, similar to those on Easter Island but without the topknots. The people seem so friendly and gentle it is amazing to think they were still practising cannibalism in 1910 - during our parents' lifetime. Our Western education had taught us to think of them as 'backward'. It came as a surprise to realise they were actually navigating and making voyages of thousands of miles, before the Norman Conquest of England and were able to preserve food and vegetables to last journeys of several months.

A week later we motored south to Vaiahu village on Tahuatu. (In Polynesian pronunciation, every vowel is pronounced. It makes for a soft and musical language). Handsome young men paddled out with bananas, limes and pamplemousse and were happy to trade them for the small screwdrivers, and packs of playing cards, we had brought with us for the purpose. Wild horses galloped along the cliff top, their flying silhouettes dark against the blue sky. Pigs and chickens seemed to be the only livestock.

The copra trading boat that comes once a month was their only source of outside goods and, as it was due, we were asked to move CLYPEUS. We motored across the bay and re-anchored. The pretty, red-steepled, Catholic church beckoned and we were anxious to say 'thank you' for our safe ocean crossing. Because of the voracious 'no nos' (tiny biting insects) Peter put on his long trousers and I wore a sleeved blouse and long skirt.

The Copra tarding boat which visits once a month

Rowing ashore in the inflatable dinghy, we misjudged the swell and 'Ooops' a rogue wave turned us upside down. From a jumble of arms, legs, water and sand under the dinghy, we eventually struggled ashore pulling it behind us. An elderly Polynesian had just finished watering the church garden and offered us the hose. We sprayed each other down, fully clothed, squeezed out what surplus water we could and stood in the back of the church for the service, dripping puddles on the stone floor. Another pre-ordained baptism to humble us?

The hymn singing in Polynesian and French was harmonious and soothing. At the end of the service feeling emotionally refreshed and happy, we slipped out into the dark night and carried the dinghy to launch it from the jetty beyond the breakers. Peter rowed towards where we had left CLYPEUS. I peered into the darkness.

"She isn't there. I'm sure CLYPEUS was just about here." We rowed around in the dark anxiously searching for our home, trying to judge the distance from other anchored yachts.

"Perhaps we haven't come far enough," Peter panted, rowing hard with his back towards the empty space.

"She's gone. I know this was where we were anchored. I took a bearing on that cliff-top tree and the church spire when we anchored and again before we left." Peter stopped rowing and turned around, puzzled, but still not sure if I knew what I was talking about. Slowly he scanned the dark sea surface.

"She could be hidden by the dark cliff shadow." In an awed whisper he said, "I did turn on the galley fluorescent light in case it was dark before we returned," and pointed to a faint bluish light way out at sea. "That must be CLYPEUS right out there," he gasped in horror and, without thinking of the consequences, rowed as hard as he could towards the faint light.

Eventually we caught up with the light and the dim outline of our drifting home. She was happily bobbing away to the west. Clambering aboard, he started the engine and we motored back to our original anchorage now that the copra boat had departed. Nightmares worried us for weeks as we realised we would never have been able to row back against the wind and current if it hadn't been CLYPEUS. We would have been at the mercy of two thousand miles of ocean and the few small islands between here and Australia.

In an uninhabited sandy bay I dived to clean the propeller and snorkelled for shells. A magnificent white murex sat in the bottom of a rocky cleft through which a fast current ran. I swam down, grabbed the shell and pulled. He was strong and held on tight. I reached the stage of thinking 'it's either him or me' when he suddenly let go and I shot to the surface, red-faced, but clutching my first real shell. It took a long and smelly time to get him cleaned out. I've never collected another large live shell again, except to eat. Fortunately I didn't notice any cone shells as I had no idea that many have a lethal sting.

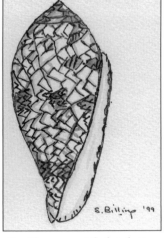

Textile cone with fatal sting

After a moonlight sail on a gossamer sea to Taiaha Bay on Nuku Hiva we anchored and made for the Post office and our first mail drop since Panama. It was wonderful to hear from all our family. We spent most of the day in the Post Office trying to phone home but only managed to get through to Hilary in Australia to confirm my parents' flights and arrival in Tahiti. They were already on their way to meet us via New Zealand.

The Post Office closed at 3 p.m. so we sat on the beach with ice creams and gloated over our letters. We managed to buy a chicken, the first fresh meat for five weeks, and a bottle of wine. Next day we confirmed all was well with our family.

I was eager to see how much of Melville's book *'Typee'* rang true. We anchored and rowed up the river as far as a small village, bearing gifts of scented soap, cigarettes and balloons for the children, but there was nobody to give them to. Two miles up the valley we could see, a long way off on the mountainside, waterfalls and impressive black stone tikis. It started raining, hard, so I held a large young banana leaf over our

Banana leaf umbrella

heads in place of an umbrella. When the rain stopped, we sat high on the red earth river bank and watched sleek, brown children fling themselves off the rocks below and swim, squealing and shouting with delight. They looked natural, uninhibited and happy and were not the least interested in us. In the village of a few woven, thatched houses, we stood outside the white painted wooden Church listening to harmonious choral singing, but not a soul appeared. The humid fertile valley was full of food - trees bearing mangoes, breadfruit, guavas, pamplemousse, limes, lemons, bananas, and not enough people to eat them. Rotting fruit lay beneath the trees. We didn't manage to make contact with anybody. Perhaps they were hiding in the Church in case we brought disease?

Ua Pou's granite monoliths pierced the clouds and gave the island a fairy castle look. The island's fifty strong dance team was practising their 'tamourraa' for the South Pacific Arts Festival to be held in Papeete during the two weeks prior to the Bastille Day celebrations. The young men whacked their knees together and apart and the girls rotated their hips so fast our eyes could barely follow their movement. The whole village was helping make costumes from natural fibres and shells.

In Hakahau Bay, anchored off the village, we took a long walk up the valley beside the river, but it was muddy and bug-ridden, damp and infinitely depressing. Stone sculpted tikis stood alongside moss-covered stone steps which showed where ancient houses and villages had been. The humid valley was deserted; abundant fruit rotted on the trees. It seemed an unhappy place. We wondered what evil thing had happened here. Not to be discouraged we climbed to the water-shed but came down again bitten and itchy and retired to bed by 7.30.

The following day, June 3rd, we left for Takaroa in the Tuamotos, the 'Dangerous Archipelago'. So named because the low islands are difficult to see until you are close and ocean currents run strongly between, and onto, them. A Taiwanese fishing vessel almost ran us down. It took no notice of our VHF radio call. Peter shone the '1,000,000 candle power' search light at their bridge and they changed course, just in time. Our boat couldn't move fast enough to get out of their way. We both felt frightened as well as seasick.

The wind disappeared, sails were slatting: time to start the engine. Unfortunately the generator rope caught in the propeller and jammed the shaft completely. We poked and prodded with the boathook from the stern, launched the dinghy and tried to free it but it was immovable.

"I'm sorry, you will have to go over the side and cut it loose," Peter said, "we must have the engine in case of emergencies."

I looked at the three mile deep ocean. What was down there? Sharks? Barracudas? Sea monsters? But this is part of our teamwork . He doesn't like the water, I love it. He has to do rotten jobs like dismantling the toilet when it gets blocked, changing foresails on the bucking deck, sucking diesel pipes to encourage fuel through. Now it was my turn.

While he took down the sails I donned a padded woolly hat, tying it under my chin in case the boat slapped down on my head in the swell. I pulled on fins, mask, snorkel and thick rubber gloves to prevent my hands being cut on the barnacle-coated propeller and hull. After tying a rope around my waist in case CLYPEUS sailed away without me, I lowered myself fearfully into the ocean.

The water was very clear down to purple depths. Clutching the bread knife I took a few deep breaths and dived. I could see the line compacted round the propeller shaft. Sawing hard with the knife, gradually a few strands broke away. I had to breathe. Popping to the surface I gasped for air and took a quick look around to make sure there were no triangular fins circling. Would something strike, and bite off the lower half of my body? Down again, grasping the propeller to hold myself down I sawed furiously. Bobbing up for air I was thankful for encouraging noises from Peter on deck. Down again, and again, until the propeller moved. Not all the rope was clear, but I'd had enough for one session. Back on deck, even with Peter's kind congratulations, I threw up.

By mid-day a breeze blew which was sufficient to raise the cruising chute and we puffed along behind our huge, light, green and yellow, billowing sail. CLYPEUS danced, like a staid matron after too much sherry.

On Thursday morning as it was calm, I dressed up and went over the side again and managed to completely clear the rope from the prop..

We whispered along in light winds then started the motor to mutter on until the wind freshened, then

'The fair breeze blew, the white foam flew;
The furrow followed free...'

and we worked hard trimming the sails to increase our speed as we were close to Takaroa, our first Pacific atoll.

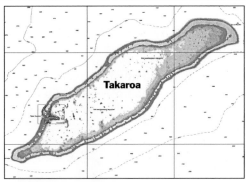

TUAMOTO ISLANDS
TAKAROA to TAHITI
May 85 - July 85
14°28'S Lat. 146°00'W Long

CHAPTER ELEVEN

Waving palms beckoned us to the tiny island of Takaroa. Motor-sailing as quickly as we could we tried to arrive before sunset, but adverse currents held us back and we had to stand off all night. CLYPEUS glided on a silver sea as we quietly sailed to and fro beneath the moon, taking turns to keep a bearing on a flickering lamp ashore. A pink and orange sun eventually rose through the slim palm trunks just a mile away.

As soon as it was high enough to see the underwater dangers, I stood on the bow rail clutching the forestay and shouted directions. We'd timed our entrance for slack water and gently nudged in against the last outflowing from the lagoon. On a July Sunday morning, we tied up to the jetty outside Canadian yacht PAMINO.

The Tuamoto Islands are low sandy islets under threat of drowning if global warming raises the sea level just a few more inches. We managed to stop at only Takaroa and Ahe on our way west to Tahiti and met gentle, hospitable Polynesians. Every morning, brown laughing children swarmed all over the boat watching our every action. From breakfast-time, little brown noses were pressed against the windows. Big dark eyes watched our every move. In the evening, their more discreet parents would wander along the quay nonchalantly carrying a guitar. If invited on board for a drink they sat in the cockpit and entertained us with their soft voices and melodious music.

The children, plump with life and laughter, happily sang into my tape recorder in French, Polynesian and even a few songs in English: *Happy Birthday* and *The Grand Old Duke of York.*

We were welcomed to wander freely down sandy paths between the coconut palms, frangipani and oleanders. The islanders encouraged us to pick hibiscus blossom to put behind our ears. Every lady had a flower tucked into her hair, so did some of the men.

The Islanders live a meagre existence on fish and coconuts, but now black pearl oyster farming is making headway and the economy is looking up. However, there is little soil on the islands, only sand, so fresh meat and vegetables are rare. A few palm leafed plaited homes remain, but most have been replaced at the expense of the French Government with smart little concrete houses with sliding glass doors and

A bonny grandmother taking oysters to have a hole drilled, to be suspended in a lagoon

solar panels to supply electric batteries. France was still pouring money into the economy to keep the inhabitants happy while they continued testing atomic bombs in the southern Tuamotos.

The Polynesians attitude to children gave me food for thought. One day I sat on a log chatting to a bonnie grandmother, while she picked tiny seed oysters from a twiggy branch which had been lying in a sheltered corner of the lagoon. She carefully laid them in a plastic bowl of sea water. In halting French, we exchanged names, ages, the weather, the last island from which we sailed. She told me a new life is about to start for her island. A Black Pearl Farm is being set up. This was the first year.

Honore showed me the tiny oysters of about one centimeter diameter. "They will 'ave a 'ole drilled so that they can be strung on a line to 'ang in ze water and grow. When they are two centimeters diameter, a Japanese expert will come and insert a little plastique ball. It will annoy the oyster so much it will cover ze ball in black pearl. C'est bon," she said. "Soon we will not need French money or French atomic explosions. Now we will have somesing more than coconuts to sell."

A beautiful young woman with long black tresses and a flower behind her ear walked by. She was obviously very pregnant. She waved and shouted "Bonjour Honore"." My companion waved back, returned the greeting and proudly said to me

"That's my baby."

"What do you mean, your baby?"

"That girl wishes to go to college in Tahiti. We like our young people to have many lovers before they marry. We like to make sure they are fertile and can have children. So, I will have her baby and bring it up as my own. She will still be its first mother and I will be second mother. I'm lucky to have been promised the baby. Zer is great competition for it. We all love children. There is always room in every house for one more child.

"What about the father? Who is he? Doesn't he want the baby?"

"Who knows which of her lovers is the father? Does it matter? We are one big family on this island."

"But what about inheritance? What if he has money or property?"

"No problem. We all own everything and share. He, or she, who needs something uses it, then passes it on. Young people sometimes get accused of stealing when they go to Tahiti. But they aren't stealing, they don't know what stealing is. If they need something they use it, then give it back."

"What a pity the rest of the world doesn't live by your rules. You make us seem so selfish."

We sat companionably in the sunshine. Honore serenely continued her task while I contemplated her people's generous and uncomplicated lifestyle.

She confirmed our experiences that the poorer people were, the more eagerly they shared their few belongings.

Suddenly there was great activity in the village; palm fronds were being tied to decorate the verandah of the village hall; children with plastic bowls were rushing around beneath the frangipani trees picking up the sweet smelling fallen blossoms. The quay and sand walkways were swept because Monsieur Fosse, the President of French Polynesia, was coming to visit the island.

In the morning, the little girls we had befriended woke us up. When I emerged in my sarong they told me to bend my head and put a lei of freshly strung frangipani and tiare flowers around my neck.

Another put a flower crown on my head and told us to be ready to welcome the President. I was delighted to have a lei and coron made for me.

At ten o'clock a smart open motor boat arrived. After a few 'heavies' landed and made sure the launch was secure, a dapper, silver-haired, gentlemen in a white short-sleeved shirt, grey trousers, brown socks, carrying his polished brown shoes, stepped ashore. Local

Little girls made me a Coron and Lei. I was delighted

dignitaries welcomed him with kisses on both cheeks and when his feet were back in his shoes, he was escorted to the village hall. With the children we watched through the windows.

After a feast and many speeches and a tour to the lagoon, M. Fosse departed and the island prepared for the evening's entertainment - a dance in the village hall. The yachts' people were invited.

We enjoyed a convivial evening dancing with, and talking to, our hosts and the children. All were included, mothers with babies in arms and little boys running and playing tag between the dancers as we waltzed, quickstepped and tried to hula.

Copra rats had to find new homes when the copra collecting boat made its six monthly visit and anchored offshore. All the sacks of copra stacked on the quayside were transferred by whaleboats to the ship. Our first intimation that we had unwanted guests aboard was finding grains of 'black rice' on the floor.

We borrowed a trap and set it with cheese - no response. Perhaps Polynesian rats didn't know about cheese? A piece of coconut proved better bait, and bang! Peter picked up a poor brown and white, fluffy, furry creature by its tail, threw it overboard and gave back the trap. Next morning; shock horror! More black rice. The trap was re-borrowed and the wife was caught - were there babies? We searched and worried for a few days but no nasty smells developed.

The other five yachts had more trouble. Rats ate the cording around their upholstery and nibbled through plastic plumbing pipes. Eventually they were all cleared but it took a while as the rat-trap passed from boat to boat. Poison isn't practical, for the rat may crawl into an inaccessible corner of the bilge to die.

The copra sacks on the quayside were transferred leaving the rats nowhere but the yacht

Children launched themselves into the 12ft deep pass

Each afternoon, after school, exuberant children came running and launched themselves into the 12' deep water of the pass from anything that would give them extra height: boats, bowsprits, oil drums. They had no bathing costumes but wore shorts and 'T' shirts. Sometimes they dived or jumped, but often just threw themselves at the water and came up grinning, shouting and waving to us for approval. They were unsupervised and seemed to be unaware of the 7-8 knot current flowing out of the pass between the coral reefs. Their white teeth shone with glee as they told us there was a big moray eel just below our boat. "Come see. Come see?" when they identified it from our tropical fish book.

"No, thank you, perhaps another day." I had already severely frightened myself on the other side of the pass. Peter had rowed me across to the aquamarine shallows on the far bank and while snorkeling in the bright sunshine and delighting in the variegated corals and brilliant fish, a large shadow passed over the sand nearby. I looked up and saw a twelve foot steely-grey shark gliding along near the surface. Immediately

I swam low and tried to hide behind a coral outcrop. Surfacing to take a breath of air and not being able to see Peter or climb out of the water, I sank again to see what was happening. Yes, the shark was still there, just moseying around, but when a remora sucker fish detached itself and started swimming towards me I nearly died of a heart attack. Somehow the thought of a remora trying to suck onto me seemed just as frightening as the shark. Fortunately by this time Peter was nearby and rescued his gibbering wife.

I asked the children if they were afraid of sharks? Apparently, not particularly. Yes, sometimes children were taken, 'mais pas souvent' - but not often! Later I dived with them to visit their large pet moray eel which I had understood were fierce, voracious, and slimy. The smooth, brightly coloured head shyly smiled out at me from his hole under the quay. The children stroked his head - I didn't!

It was sad to leave these friendly people, but I was excited at the thought of seeing my parents who were flying in to meet us in Tahiti in two week's time. Ahe had an excellent reputation for hospitality and friendliness to yachts.

However, 'The Dangerous Archipelago' lived up to its name. The stories of unpredictable currents between the palm tree covered low islands are not a figment of the imagination of poor navigators.

On the blackest of black nights, with a faint breeze, we rolled along uncomfortably with just the big Genoa up. Off watch, I lay clutching the side of my bunk to stay in bed, feeling sea-sick when I decided the imagined thunder of surf echoing in my ears was actually real. Peter was on watch but only concerned with warding off seasickness.

I called out "I'm sure I can hear breakers!"

"Shouldn't be."

"Well, I'll go and look while you check our position on the SatNav and chart." On deck the air seemed to be vibrating with thunder and, from the bow I could see we were heading straight towards a line of phosphorescence that showed breakers crashing on the reef only a couple of hundred yards away.

As I screamed "Go about."

Peter shouted simultaneously "Yes, we are almost on Manihi."

He turned on the engine, spun the wheel and turned into the mounting swell; which at first carried us towards the breaking reef. Gradually we beat away from the crashing foam, our hearts in our mouths.

What if the engine failed? The south-westerly going current had unobtrusively carried us close to the north shore of Manihi, which we had programmed to avoid on the SatNav, but obviously by too close a margin. We motored towards the eastern end of the island and safely rounded it. Seasickness and weeks of safe sailing across the ocean had dulled our watch keeping.

Morning showed us Ahe atoll in the distance and I finished reading 'The Hurricane' by Nordhoff and Hall, an exciting story about the people of these very islands. Ahe is only a few metres high and there is always the fear of a hurricane washing the sandy soil away for ever. Global warming, and the consequent rising sea level is a positive threat creeping closer every day. The surf pounded against battered lumps of coral balancing on the edge of the pass as we entered the blue lagoon and followed the five miles of marked channel to Ahe village to join four other anchored yachts: Tucumcari, Maira, Escoffier and Amarua.

The Ahe villagers and Mamma Fanna, who are famed for their generous welcomes, were tired. Until the advent of self-steering and satellite navigators, visitors to these lonely atolls were few. Now, in 1985, they had already hosted over thirty yachts.

On the VHF Heinrich of MAIRA called us, "It's Maggie's birthday. We're having a bring-a-dish-supper with Ronny and Anne in their house on the island. Would you like to come?"

"Happy birthday Maggie. Yes, please. We'll bring something."

Scots Ronny and French Anne, of ESCOFFIER with their new baby, had taken up residence for a few months and had rented a native thatched 'A' frame home on a small sandy peninsula surrounded by ironbark trees. Bernard Moitessier had lived in this house after dropping out of the Round the World Race after circumnavigating one and a half times in June 1969.

Mamma Fanna in her muumuu, (a full cotton dress with short puffed sleeves) and shell necklaces, and Harry, the island chief, in his loose shirt and waist-to-ground sarong, joined us for a happy evening. Their English was better than our French, and we were able to chat and sing along with Heinrich and Ronny as they strummed their guitars. We had our first hesitant taste of raw fish. The thinly sliced red tuna, marinated in lime juice and coconut cream was delicious. Suddenly thunder rolled and roared, gentle rain turned into an appalling downpour. The wind screamed through the ironbarks. The party came to an abrupt halt.

Fearful for the safety of our boats, we gathered our belongings; bundled little Maira and baby Lieff into wheelbarrows and ran, the men pushing the barrows before them, through the wall of torrential rain to the jetty. Jumping into our dinghies we each made for our own tiny anchor lights. All the anchors had held, and after careful inspections we checked on the VHF that everybody was OK.

A quiet day followed, swimming and baking bread. In the evening we rowed ashore to dance and sing with the locals who strummed their guitars beneath the palm trees under a canopy of stars. The lack of teenagers was obvious and we learned that they were all away at school in Tahiti. A village with no young people is a subdued and gentle one.

In the lazy days that followed Peter helped repair Heinrich's radio, AQUA VIVA's log and AMARUA"s SatNav. I chatted with the ladies ashore, looked for shells and snorkelled in the blue lagoon. Giant clams glowed with iridescent bright bluey-green lips, snapping shut as my shadow passed over them. Little bottle-brush anemones looking like brilliant red, blue and orange Christmas trees, tucked themselves into the coral as I came near. Small white-tipped sharks slunk over the white sand beneath aquamarine water. I cautiously swam out over the edge of the reef. It was scary; were there big sharks out there? The edge of the coral looked pink, then purple as it disappeared down into the dark blue abyss.

On Sunday evening we joined the villagers in the Sanito Church for a happy service with guitars, singing and talking. Afterwards socializing in French and English, we munched cakes, doughnuts, coffee and Koolade until 10.30 p.m. From what we could gather, not many islanders spoke English and many had no French, just Polynesian. Life on the islands was simple and unhurried. Fishing and extracting the copra from coconuts, with a curved metal tool, were the main occupations. No great effort was needed to live comfortably; another mouth to feed meant just a few more hours fishing.

On Monday I rowed ashore to say goodbye to Anne and Ronny and thank our hosts with cakes and home-made fudge for the small children. My Cannon 'Sureshot' camera hung around my neck as I paddled knee-deep to pull the dinghy to the beach. Noticing a pretty cowry shell underwater I bent to pick it up. Of course my camera reached the water first and dunked under. Spoilt forever! I was absolutely furious with myself for being so stupid and unthinking. Peter took it apart and tried to dry the pieces but it never worked again.

Beneath the palm trees, my lady friends Tego and Juliette generously gave me pretty shell necklaces that they had made themselves and said it was a traditional gesture in the hope that we return to their island one day. The thought of the number of hours of work involved in finding and cleaning the shells, then sorting and drilling holes in them to thread on the nylon fishing line, made me feel very humble as I offered my purchased gifts of scented soap, perfume and embroidered handkerchiefs. However Tego and Juliette were delighted, as they had no way of obtaining such luxuries.

Unwinding the anchor chain from around a coral head so that we could depart was easy in the shallow, clear, water as I shouted directions to Peter at the wheel. However, the five or six remora sucker fish now attached to our hull gave me the creeps.

We motored out of the lagoon into a dead calm and for four days, occasionally using the engine, but mostly drifting, eventually saw the smudge on the horizon rise from the sea to become Tahiti's dramatic mountains. Swirling clouds obscured dark craggy peaks. The mountain tops of nearby Moorea Island pierced the white clouds to the north west. They looked exciting islands in which to greet my parents.

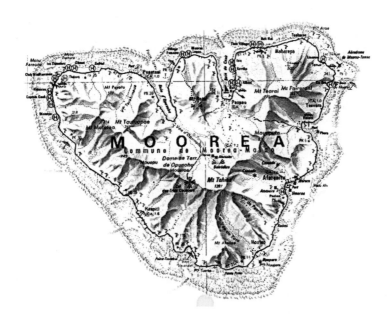

CHAPTER TWELVE

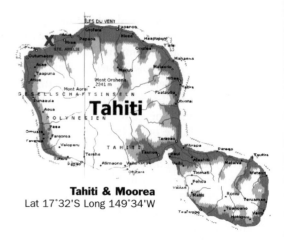

Tahiti & Moorea
Lat 17°32'S Long 149°34'W

Within Tahiti's smooth, safe, lagoon, French warships lined the harbour and busy ferries bustled out through the pass to other islands. Linda and Robert were waiting to catch our lines as we tied up in the 'low-rent' district alongside LIBERTY.

We hurried along to Papeete's sea front, to the first street of shops since Panama. What I wanted most was a glass of fresh cold milk. Peter's dream was a bottle of cold beer. After the first delicious sips we sat at the outdoor cafe table and watched with renewed fascination, the condensation running down the outside of the glasses. Nearby we bought a long loaf of French bread, hot, crispy and full of holes, which we took to a park bench and ate before it cooled.

The sophisticated shops had smart dresses, chocolates, vacuum cleaners, gold jewellery, black pearls. We ogled through the windows. The noise and smell of traffic assaulted our ears and noses. Life seemed so fast, noisy and polluted.

In the afternoon we slept and adjusted to civilisation. After a glass of wine on LIBERTY we walked to the 'vans' for supper - mobile kitchens parked along the waterfront offering international food. I chose chicken chow mien and ice cream. Tahiti seemed to offer everything anybody could ever want. We took time to sit and watch the smooth, bronzed, smiling, passers by; flowers decorating every person and building.

At 5.30 next morning, in the dark, I went to the market. Fish of many colours were hanging above the stalls on lines that disappeared into their mouths and came out through their gills. The bare electric light bulbs overhead made them sparkle and shine in serried ranks according to size and colour. Beneath lay glistening bright-eyed assorted fish on stone slabs.

Fresh vegetables and bananas were piled in small family-sized heaps. Juicy red halves and quarters of water melon dotted pyramids of fat, green, globes. Comfortable smiling lady stall vendors wore flower wreaths on their dark hair and most men had a flower behind their ear.

Back on board we spent a busy day tidying ship, taking on water, and I did the laundry in the municipal granite trough. Communal wash day is so much more fun than our lonely western way. The ladies talked and sang as they scrubbed, helped each other wring and fold. It was a very social occasion. Peter climbed the mast to twist the navigation light back into position. It had embarrassingly turned itself around he then started repairing the cockpit floor which appeared to be sinking.

I cleared out lockers, laying clothes and linen in the sun to air. Food cupboards were washed out and boric acid laid in the corners to discourage cockroaches.

On Monday, as soon as the offices opened, we booked into immigration, paid our cruising fee and bond, which was settled at US$1,300 (the cost of two single economy air fares to England). At customs - no problems. Peter took our guns in during the afternoon. The Bank of Tahiti gave us a stack of mail they had kept for us for no charge and happily we returned to CLYPEUS to wallow in news from home.

At hotels lovely girls danced, we enjoyed watching on lagoon-side lawns

We spent the next week socialising and looking for a suitable hotel for my parents' visit. Each evening we would hear 'the drums, the drums' with their insistent erotic rhythms echoing across the water. As soon as dinner was over I would follow the sound to watch the fantastic hotel cabarets of Tahitian hula. Beautiful girls swayed and undulated wearing a coron of flowers or high head dresses, and coconut shell bras, above long grass skirts slung on a flower or shell band around their hips. Flowers around their ankles and bare feet made it easy to appreciate the whole body movements of the strong athletic girls beneath their romantic exterior. The performances usually took place on the lagoon-side lawns. I sat on the grass with the warm breeze sighing through the palm tree fronds which fluttered and filtered the moonbeams as they shone down on the dark water lapping the shore. It was better than my wildest dreams.

At Maeva Beach Hotel a powerful mature woman peeled the hard green outer fibrous husk off a coconut with her strong white teeth, then with the side of her hand chopped the brown coir covered nut three times. She raised the overflowing broken nut above her head and poured the spilling milk into her mouth. We were impressed - it still takes us ages to get into a green coconut even with a machete.

Snorkelling in Maeva lagoon, wearing rubber gloves, I saw a beautiful blue/green spiney star fish and tried to pick it up to show Peter, but before I actually touched it, received a very painful sting. It was a Crown of Thorns. Even with my arm in a sling the pain stayed in my hand for over two weeks and the flesh of my thumb is permanently damaged.

The 'le truk" busses gave a noisy boisterous ride with amplifiers and 10" speakers vibrating the whole vehicle with Polynesian and French music. They are open-sided vans with a bench down either side for passengers. Smiling faces studied us from the opposite side with interest. Most had a flower behind their ear or a flower crown on their heads and were carrying children, shopping baskets crammed with fish, taro roots, melons or flowers.

An arena had been erected on the wide harbour front to accommodate The South Pacific Arts Festival. The international festival introduced us to dances, songs and plays from all the Pacific Islands from Hawaii across to The Philippines and from Easter Island to New Zealand and Australia. The different ethnic dancing, costumes, and colours were mind boggling. It was an anthropologist's dream to have so many different island communities showing their traditional skills. How some small isolated islands could produce a team of fifty attractive good dancers was amazing.

The first night of dancing took my breath away and from then on I was a slave to the progamme. That first performance was a pageant by the Tahitians depicting a tradition-al wedding - seemingly hundreds of beautiful bronze young people in white grass skirts and high head-dresses danced their hearts out. The tamouraa was so exciting it made one's blood race. From then on, it just got better. The Cook Islands brought 200 lovely young dancers plus two pigs to enact their pageant.

Australian Aboriginal young men, delicate and fearful, jumped like kangaroos, stalked like emus and brolgas, held feathers behind their backs to imitate lyre bird tails as they mimicked the birds' courting dance. One dance portrayed hunted kangaroos; their eyes darting, their nerves a-twitch, ears and neck muscles tense, with the thrum of didgeridoos evoking fear.

Papua New Guinea men with head feathers and bones through their noses

Guam's grand display showed how their traditional island dances had been influ-enced by the Spaniards and Americans with fast waltzes and changes in historic costume, right through to rock and roll. The Papua New Guinea men with head feathers, and bones through their noses, danced an amus-ing penis dance with make-believe long and flaccid replicas strapped around their tum-mies that they swung and twirled with non-chalance. Their girls, their nipples like pol-ished copper, sang in high shrill voices (not surprising)!

The plays and storytellings were fascinat-ing. The audience was often warned that 'Christians may find this play upsetting,' and by our moral standards the stories were cer-tainly different. They told of: multiple wives, incest, cannibalism, elderly gentlemen's prostrate problems which were all enacted and were usually a source of great amuse-ment.

We watched traditional tattooing into a young man's back with black ash being jabbed into the skin with a thorn tied onto the end of a stick. No antiseptic, just what looked like a dirty rag, dipped in ash, to wipe the droplets of blood away.

Choirs of fern-wreath-crowned large ladies and thinner older gentleman sat in clusters on the floor of the sand arena, swaying back and forth as they sang hyminees - long harmonic rounds of Polynesian song.

In the temporary village, typical houses of the different islands showed crafts and local food. Men from the Solomon Islands chipped away at elaborate wooden carvings following the form of knotted tree roots. Strong men waving chainsaws, fashioned dugout canoes in a matter of hours. New Zealand Maoris danced and sang, the girls twirled balls of straw called pois on strings, and warriors, with tattooed faces, stamped the war chant and stuck out their tongues down to the bottoms of their tattooed chins.

The normal Christian Sunday service in the church opposite our mooring was inspiring. A dignified congregation of ladies, all in white long dresses and white straw hats, and gentlemen in dark suits, highly polished shoes and white shirts, sang with fervour. Some hymns were unaccompanied and some sung with the organ. The 23rd Psalm sung in Polynesian by a full church of gentle melodious people was unforgettable. Four babies were christened after communion, their heads touched with water and their names read out beneath the beautiful stained glass window. No altar, no cross, no statues, just a simple white interior inside a white wooden, red steepled church.

We sailed my parents to Moorea

July 10th was boat cleaning, shopping and anticipation day, before my seventy-nine year old mother and father, Ivy and Henry arrived. We borrowed a wide-stepped boarding ladder so that they could climb on and off our boat with ease.

At 5.30 next morning we took le truk to the airport loaded with flowers and champagne. I bought flower and shell leis to drape around their necks as they came through the arrival lounge. We waited and waited. Where were they? Their flight wasn't listed. Frantic enquiries. It transpired that the New Zealand Air plane had come in yesterday - none of us had realised that flying across the dateline they would lose a day. How disappointed they must have been, not to be met at the airport. We could imagine that Ivy thought CLYPEUS had sunk and we had perished.

We rushed to the Bel Air Hotel, where Air New Zealand accommodates stop-over passengers, and at 6.30 woke them with flowers and champagne. Their relief that we were well and safe helped mitigate the terrible guilt I felt, and we breakfasted beside the pool looking out over the lagoon. They had enjoyed their three week tour and reunion with

Henry's brother Andrew and his wife Rose in New Zealand and were planning on continuing their round the world flight to London in one month's time, although my mother caught my eye with a worried look.

We took a taxi to CLYPEUS and from the cockpit watched the canoe races on the lagoon. In the Festival village we saw fruit carrying races and elegant Samoan dancing. On many evenings Ivy joined me on the free Arena bleachers and didn't mind seeing more of the dancers' backs and bottoms, than their fronts and faces. Ivy and Henry moved into town so that we could easily walk to see each other and attend the concerts. However the air pollution from the heavy traffic combined with fumes from the nearby power station caused allergies and a chest infection in Ivy and she became very ill. She didn't want to continue their journey around the world. She felt she wasn't well enough. A French doctor came and saw her and prescribed some drugs. Robert visited and told us her heart was weakening and it probably would be best if she went straight home.

In private she confessed to me that Henry's increasing memory loss (nobody actually said the word Altzheimers and in those days, it still wasn't a well-known condition) was a great worry and keeping track of him in airports was becoming difficult. She was never sure he would get back to her, and their hand luggage, before their flight took off. He seemed blissfully unaware of his problems and was very disappointed. He found it hard to accept her wishes.

As soon as she was well enough, the four of us sailed across to pristine Moorea, rented a small chalet under the mountains, and anchored CLYPEUS just a few yards off-shore. It was idyllic. For the first few days we all rested but later hired a car and explored right around the verdant coastal plain of this mountainous island. We had a wonderful time together, time for our fun-loving parents to be our friends not just our mother and father.

Back in Tahiti we sailed them back to the Bel Air and anchored just offshore in the lagoon. Ivy sat in the dinghy while I snorkelled; I was longing to find a beautiful shell for her. I slid over the side of the rubber dinghy and gently flipped down to the reef. There, resting on the first shelf, was a large tiger cowry, empty but pristine. Proudly, I was able to give her a perfect specimen. We returned to CLYPEUS and, as she reached from the dinghy for the ladder to climb onto the deck, so the dinghy slid inexorably away from the hull and I couldn't hold it. To my horror, my aged mother slowly slipped inevitably under the water. Horrified, I grabbed her arm and dragged her up. She was laughing and stayed laughing. God bless her!

Unfortunately Ivy really wasn't well and after their month in Tahiti they organised to return directly to Western Australia. Our last dinner up in the mountains on the terrace of the Belvedere was a fitting climax. The sun sank in a blaze of glory beneath the sea as we sipped our cocktails. By the time dinner was served the moon and stars blinked down from a velvet sky.

Sadly, we took them to the Airport the following day. Ivy looked tired but happy and loving, and my undemonstrative father actually held my hand all the way in the bus to the airport. We had a tearful farewell at the end of a wonderful time together. I stood on the runway until their plane taxied off and roared away to the west. As I counted my blessings I realised what a lucky woman I was to have such bold and indefatigable parents. How long before we would see them again?

CHAPTER THIRTEEN

Society Islands Bora Bora
August 85
Lat 16°29' S Long 107°42'W

On Friday August 16th 1985, after eight glorious weeks, we left Tahiti, our dreams of 1968 more than satisfied. Beneath low cloud and drenching rain, Moorea island, only half a mile off, was invisible through the deluge. Landing at Kia Ora, we made for the disco on the old wooden schooner in the lagoon hoping to dance the night away. Unfortunately it was sinking, the ballroom floor was submerged.

In Cook's Bay we succumbed to soporific lotus fever, whiling the days away relaxing, snorkelling, and painting Christmas cards. The bow anchor in 50' of water and the stern tied to a palm tree, it was perfect. Robert greeted us each morning with a grin, sighing "another shitty day in paradise."

I painted Christmas cards

Poor weather forecasts gave an excuse to linger. Walks up into the hills revealed avocado trees dropping their soft dark green fruit, coconuts crashed to the ground, breadfruit, bananas, pineapples, pamplemouse, paw paws were all ready to pick or buy. Red ginger flowers, like canna lilies, brightened the hedgerows; tiare flowers alongside the lagoon perfumed our evenings.

Living in French territory inspired us to cook each other elaborate farewell dinners as someone expected to leave, but then the weather would deteriorate again.

Avocado with French garlic dressing, Prawn Provencale cooked with cream and wine on green noodles, Chocolate Mousse, with duty free French wines, brandy and cold beers, we were surviving!

Days passed, ladies varnished bright work, painted, wrote letters, read, cooked, washed and baked farewell cakes; the men tinkered with engines, varnished, painted and read. Laughing, carefree days.

On the 28th August, with our huge Blue Peter flag flying at the masthead (the international signal of departure), playing *Rule Britannia* on the cockpit loud-speakers, we lowered the flag, and tore ourselves away from this particular paradise and headed west

Cook's Bay. Canadian Vera varnishes their bowsprit

for Huahine.

The passing depression left the sea unsettled. It was still too rough to enter Araara Pass to Pareu. The sun reflected rainbows through the blue-and-white spume as the swell crashed onto the reef. We turned out again and carried on until we could enter the difficult to distinguish Farerea Pass, in what seemed an unbroken line of pounding surf. A narrow passage of deep blue water opened up and, with our hearts in our mouths, the tide swooshed us into beautiful Maroe Bay.

Two young wahines paddled out astride an old windsurfer bringing us gifts of melons and papaya. They shouted "Bonjour" as they paddled towards us. We waved back "Bonjour". Their return greeting was too vigorous and their unstable craft capsized. They splashed around laughing and catching the fruit and a plastic bag full of audio tapes, replaced them all on the board, and pushing it before them, swam to Clypeus. We gratefully accepted the fruit they handed up and helped them on board.

"Je m'appelle Lisette." the taller girl smiled and dripped.

"Je m'appelle Marrietta." the younger one offered. "Parlez vous Francais?"

"Un peu." I went below and got them clean towels. They dried themselves looking sorrowfully at their bag of audio tapes. They

Huahine

had hoped to listen to them on our tape recorder as they had no batteries for 'le transistor', and now the tapes were ruined.

Peter gently took them. "Pas de problem" he said and spent the next few hours carefully unwinding the cassettes, by twiddling the reels on pencils, and drying every inch while the girls took me home to meet their mother. I took gifts with me in the dinghy and after being introduced, we collected little sister Lydia and went for a walk along the beach to gather pretty, tiny, yellow winkle-type shells. When I returned Peter had dried the tapes and we took them ashore. The girls were delighted.

In the morning their big brothers offered to take us underwater fishing. Through my mask I watched them jab a metal rod into the brilliantly coloured blue and green, purple and brown, delicate flesh of the giant clams which sheltered in coral clefts. When the clam closed tight around the rod they waggled and wiggled until the whole shell came free. Both young men hid behind coral mounds under water for many minutes holding their breath and waiting until they were sure of spearing a fish. The brothers made us a delicious clam and coconut curry. While we ate at their scrubbed table, the whole family sat around and watched. They were Seventh Day Adventists so couldn't eat shell fish - crustaceans are forbidden food for them.

The well-favoured family had 15 children, one of whom was adopted: nine boys and six girls. Two were away at College and the rest all at home from 23 years down. Mother was mid-40's petite, with, long black hair and a soft smile. Father Noel was a smooth skinned, big, brown teddy bear of a man, handsome and gentle.

They farmed three areas on the motu of coral. Four cabbages, or four melon plants, grew in each two foot diameter circle dug out of the coral, spaced about two metres apart. Fresh earth was brought from the main island by canoe every other year. The melons were draped out over the sun-baked surface. Before and after school the young children, with buckets, watered each plant individually, taking turns to pump up the brackish water from the well. The warm, showery weather allows them three or four crops a year which are taken by the weekly supply boat to Papeete Market.

Mother took an outrigger canoe with an outboard motor across to the main island to fill their canisters of drinking water every day. Seventeen year old Marie Louise, the eldest daughter at home, seemed to spend every day on her knees beside the tap on the mainland doing the laundry.

Their house had no electricity or water. Cooking was by propane gas and lighting was one Coleman pressure lamp in the kitchen. A flashlight shone their way to bed or to the outside privy or shower, which was just a plaited screen around a bucket and dipper.

The younger children went to school at 6.30 each morning in the community power boat. Noel worked on the Inter-island Ferry, as well as trading their crops. In their garage

Father Noel was a smooth-skinned brown teaddy-bear of a man, handsome and gentle with 4 of his 15 children

beside the tap on the main island were two Land Rovers and three boats, each with a powerful outboard motor, one of which Peter mended for them.

We had three meals in their home with the family as spectators. Mirielle, Lydia, Augustine and Marcel would come on board, sing or play cards and giggle. When they left, Lisette, Marietta, Jimmy and Christopher would come. They were obviously disciplined to visit in groups of four or less. Their French was marginally better than ours but each child had a quiet dignity and assurance, until they dissolved into giggles.

They were a happy, loving family and a marvellous advertisement for their way of life. Noel drove us around the verdant main island and introduced us to brothers and aunts. Only one hotel and few tourists, who appeared to make little difference to the economy and traditional occupations of farming and fishing. Noel and four of the younger children came for a sail in CLYPEUS. He took the helm with confidence and care.

Scraping the hull clean was no problem for me in the clear water. Anchored in ten feet, every grain of sand could be seen from the deck. From underwater when looking up, I could see a clear reflection of the sandy bottom on the underneath silvery surface of the lagoon. Wearing a mask, with eyes at surface level, I could see above and below the water equally clearly at the same time. Within the pale blues and greens, fish were visible twenty metres away among coral heads

Eventually we had to leave. Lisette and Marietta gave me shell necklaces they had strung together themselves from the tiny yellow shells. A tearful farewell followed with flower and shell leis draped around our necks together with cabbages, melons, tomatoes, beans and jam placed quietly on deck. We gave perfume and eye-shadow to the girls and pencils, with erasers on the end, to the boys along with home-made fudge.

As we sailed around the north of the island we passed a Polynesian couple walking

A Polynesian couple walked along the shore

along the shore. The man wore a short flowered pareu and carried a spear, a raven-haired wahine carried a bucket full of silver fish. They made a perfect picture to keep in our memories as we left one of earth's most beautiful places.

On entering Fare, the main town of Huahine, we were back in a modern world with three supermarkets. We walked to see the ancient Marae (place of worship) at Anini Point, passing M. Fosse's home. The cabbages and melons were shared with Americans Susan and Ted on TYCHE. They lent us Seven Seas Cruising Association bulletins giving information on cyclone procedures.

One day on the beach we chatted with Vicky from DOROTHY ANN and discovered that they had lived in Wokingham. Accepting her invitation for a cup of tea with Josh and their three teenage daughters, we found so much to talk about, we stayed for supper. They were circumnavigating east-about and had sailed through the Med and down Red Sea to Australia.

The following evening over spaghetti bolognaise on CLYPEUS we swopped yarns, warnings, addresses and advice. DOROTHY ANN was not in very good condition and appeared overloaded. (However she did many more miles before sinking the following year in the Atlantic when almost home. The fortunate family was picked up by the P & O Liner CANBERRA and carried in great style to Southampton.)

To arrive in New Zealand before the cyclone season, it was essential to keep moving. We could see the high islands of Raiatea and Tahaa over the sparkling sea - an easy day's run. The chart showed it was possible to stay inside the calm blue waters of the lagoon and encircle both islands in a figure of eight .

A joyous sail downwind to Noa Noa Pass was brought to a sudden halt. The gentle swell gathered speed and strength as it rose up in a surge of pale green water to break and crash onto the reef in a mountain of thundering foam. Big waves were breaking right across the Pass making it unsafe to enter at this state of the tide. We anchored and rowed to tiny offshore Noa Noa island and walked right around collecting shells, and pen oysters. We tried to shoot fish with the spear gun but they were too quick. Swarms of hungry mosquitoes harried us.

Scrubbing shells having made chowder with the insides

The view was glorious; rainbows sparkled through the pounding surf; waving palms bordered the yellow sand and dark green verdant jungle climbed the mountains to grey cliffs atop. It inspired me to get out my oils again and I painted until the Pass quietened. We cautiously entered the lagoon and anchored in Baie Faaroa.

Raiatea was heaven. Contented islanders, few yachts, virtually no tourists and a landscape of cloud-topped mountains sloping down to a lush flower-filled coastal plain. I noticed four seven-fingered lambis truncata from the dinghy so swam down and picked two up; they weighed about a kilo each. A narrow black slit indicated a large pen oyster, which live buried verti-cally. The ones found yesterday had made a delicious chowder with onions, white sauce and pepper. Peter passed down a rope lassoo which I placed around it. He pulled from the deck and voila! some good fresh food. We are hopeless fishermen - our hunting only extends to animals that don't move.

On a glorious sunny day we anchored for lunch amidst a selection of blues. Water about 24' deep over clear white sand gives my favourite aquamarine blue. Happy dolphins swam past, leaping and turning three times in the air, then standing on their tails and flipping backwards. The depth of our keel is about six feet so we risked motoring through the channel marked on the chart 'for small boats only', to reach Apooti without retracing our wake. I stood on the bow and shouted directions to Peter at the wheel.

"Left a bit...Straight on...Quick, quick, left again". It was exciting. With our hearts in our mouths we went very slowly especially when the channel shallowed. Gently scraping the sand we made it to Apooiti Marina, and there were Susan and Ted on TYCHE. They took our lines and called out "Ready for a cold beer?"

Removing the flesh from large shell fish without destroying the shell is a problem. I asked Susan if I may put my plastic wrapped Lambis Truncata in her freezer overnight. She agreed and when it defrosted next day the flesh slithered out easily, ready to cook.

Walking home from shopping, some well-scrubbed young Americans offered a lift. They turned out to be Mormon missionaries and were interested to come on board for a fruit juice. They invited us to their church arranging to pick us up. Mormons are very active in the South Pacific: on every island we saw at least one standard Mormon cream brick church, easily distinguishable by the adjoining high fenced basket-ball court with floodlights on tall poles. It's good psychology for enlarging their congregations as there is little else for the young people to do after dark. The Mormon school or youth club is the only place the young can acquire free paper and pencils.

Susan and Ted came on board for dinner. A happy evening, but it was here that I discovered my true Royalist feelings. We were discussing currency and illustrations on notes. I fetched an English five pound note. We examined the Queen, and then Abraham Lincoln on the U.S. dollar. Suddenly I noticed Ted was drawing a mustache on the face of the Queen.

"What do you think you're doing?" I declared angrily.

"Don't you think it's an improvement?" he chuckled as he regarded his handiwork.

"No I don't. How dare you deface our Queen. It's as though you drew a mustache on a picture of my mother." I was incensed. Patriotism boiled in my veins. He looked sheepish and apologised; but they all thought my anger hilarious and I soon laughed with them, but remained surprised at my depth of feeling over something I had never even considered. I knew I didn't want a politician as Head of State and considered our Royal family above corruption, but that was all.

When it came to being picked up to go to the Mormon Church everyone else ducked out. However, I was interested and enjoyed my morning. The Preacher greeted me and handed me over to a Polynesian lady who translated the service and then took me to the women's meeting where they discussed various domestic issues in a positive and helpful way. The Preacher gave me two shell and seed necklaces as I left, one for me and one for my husband whom he hoped would accompany me next week.

On Monday we meant to leave for Tahaa but it was raining so we busied ourselves with little chores: Peter fitted an extension from the toilet pump to pump the bilges. I re-covered my sleeping bag with the hibiscus-printed cotton bought yesterday. We left Apooiti in low cloud as we continued our figure of eight around. During breakfast we listened to yachts chatting on the Ham Radio net and heard that LIBERTY was still in Papeete.

Gently we sailed around the island exploring secluded bays. School children were fishing with rods during their break-time outside a school; a lady, wading up to her waist in water outside her house, was fishing with a spear for lunch.

Bora Bora, how romantic it sounded, was the next Island to the west. We could see its mountain wreathed in clouds. Playful dolphins joined us again in the lagoon, spinning and turning in the air, flipping their tails on the surface. Leaving through the Pass was rough despite there being no wind and we had to motor all the 25 miles to Bora Bora.

Taking our guns ashore to book in, we collected our mail. A letter from Rosemary told us that Laura now had two teeth and is nearly walking. I had never considered that we might miss our grandchildren's first years.

A well-stocked supermarket greeted us and we talked to an American lady who owned a boutique. Thirty thousand American troops were stationed on this island in World War II - some postings weren't so bad, were they? Climbing the mountain we found huge bronze, naval guns cemented into the rock and pointing out to the Pass. The whole American Navy could have anchored in this magnificent lagoon - Perhaps they did?

My mother had sent me $20 for my birthday and I tucked it into my pocket hoping to buy a hand printed sarong. However, walking along the beach a fisherman approached. He held out a little wooden box. In it was a selection of misshapen black pearls.

"$25 pour une," he said.

"J'ai $20 seulement," and flashed my $20 bill.

"Choisez," he replied magnificently; so I did, a baroque grey pearl drop, the size of my little finger nail. I had it set in gold later and it is a lovely reminder of a perfect time in our lives.

As we sailed away huge manta rays with a span of about five metres were slowly flapping around us so I eased myself into the water, to join them. They slowly continued on their way taking no notice of me. What magnificent creatures they are as their wings undulate through the clear water.

Moored off Oa Oa Hotel I talked to a sailor on a nearby yacht who said they were on their way back to Australia having been away for ten years.

"Ten years," I repeated in shocked amazement. "How could you stay away that long? Don't your family mind?"

"It hasn't seemed long," he said. "We took jobs in England so that we could tour Europe, and our families have got on with their lives without us. It's no big deal," he said as he saw the consternation on my face. I never dreamed for a moment we would be staying away even longer.

145 miles further west, in the narrow pass into Mopihaa lagoon the tide was flowing out so strongly that CLYPEUS couldn't make any headway against it even at full throttle. We anchored, dragged then re-anchored again. In the sunset glow turtles played around us and mated in the calm lee of the low atoll. The wind blew hard in the rigging all night but CLYPEUS didn't drag although there was only 30' or water at the bow and over 100' at the stern. Peter wrote in the log:

> "At 11.00 a.m. waited for Wild Spirit to exit pass then motored in. Ran at about 2000 rpm against estimated 6 knot outflow and 20/25 knot headwind. Just prayed and it all went OK. Beautiful lagoon."

Mopihaa was our last French Polynesian Island. One small, earth and sand covered, isle in a necklace of coral reefs. No permanent inhabitants, but some friendly itinerant fishermen from Tahaa. The jeep they used for carrying fish and gear wasn't working.

Peter mended the alternator, brought one of CLYPEUS's batteries ashore and started it with jump leads so that they could re-charge their battery. The re-vitalised fishermen gave me cowrie shells and bosun bird tail feathers. I am very lucky to have such a practical engineer for a husband. They also took us to the windward reef to show us 'chapeau dur' - hard hats. On a boulder being battered by the surf they prised the armour-plated domes from the rock.

"Cette place seulement dans la monde." One fisherman murmured.

"Really! This is the only place on earth they are to be found?" I exclaimed as I turned the grey golf ball sized crustacean in my hand. It was a type of sea urchin.

"Qui, nous avons du formaldehyde."

Peter was astonished. Why should itinerant fishermen on a lonely atoll have formaldehyde at hand? We didn't find out, but they put the hard hats in a bottle of formaldehyde for me.

With Bob of TUCUMCARI we went on a coconut-crab hunt Creeping beneath the palms was eerie as the moonlight flickered through the gently waving fronds. We hoped we didn't actually catch anything. After criss-crossing the island a few times without seeing any signs of life we sat on the soft golden sand beach and had a quiet singsong and tried to identify some new stars in the sparkling southern firmament.

I know you are thinking; come on, come on, where's the action? Where's the disaster? This is a sailing adventure, right? Yes, we thought so too, as our idyllic life continued we waited for the wrath of God to strike us and took great care not to give Him an opportunity. Eventually He did in Chapter 21, so if you want more than just descriptions of beautiful places and fascinating cultures, go for it. Otherwise live this dream with me as we sailed on towards the Cook Islands.

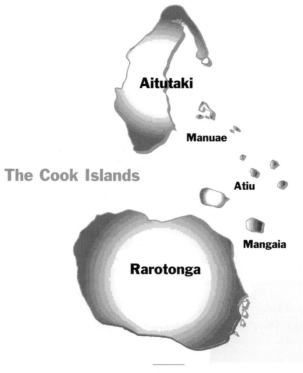

Aitutaki

Manuae

The Cook Islands

Atiu

Mangaia

Rarotonga

**Cook Islands,
Rarotonga - Palmerston**
Lat 18°52'S Long 163°12'W
Sept - October 85

CHAPTER FOURTEEN

Whales played and blew in the sparkling, deep-violet-blue sea as we bounced towards Rarotonga where our mail would be waiting. As the night rolled on so did we, purposely gybing a couple of times to try and lessen the sickening rolling. Serious navigating was necessary to pass through the unlit northern Cook Islands during the night with no room for error. Peter took sextant sights to check the SatNav. As he called out the sun's height every second, I wrote it down. The calculations were done using the Hewlett Packard navigational calculator, then re-checked with the SatNav. We were right on course for the gap between tiny Manuka and Mitiero Islands. The black night slipped past and we never saw the unlit motus.

When within range of Rarotonga the local radio announced "Avarua's cinema will be open Friday AND Saturday evening." Wow!

Eventually we motored into the tiny harbour and tied up alongside New Zealand yacht WOODWIND.

"Cup of tea?" offered a carpet-slippered man on deck. "I'm John, that's my son Ken. Ken put the kettle on."

We stood on deck and talked about how John was trying to refloat the classic yacht YANKEE which had been aground on the reef for twenty years. Ken emerged from the cabin with mugs of tea and great slabs of delicious fresh bread, butter and strawberry jam.

The Harbour Master did not make us welcome. Blasting was going on within the small commercial harbour and there wasn't room for yachts. I explained that I had written to him months ago asking if we could pick up mail here and having had no response assumed it would be OK. He grudgingly gave us a four day pass to attend to our business.

Walking to the Post Office we met tourists from New Zealand. The lanky, short-shorted, freckled girls with auburn hair, mingled with the well-rounded dark skinned, and sarong-clad, local girls. I hadn't realised that New Zealanders were such an easily distinguishable race before. A crowd surging around a street stall opened up to reveal ICE CREAM imported from New Zealand at 40 cents a cone (about 15p). It was fresh, creamy and delicious, a highlight after expensive Tahiti.

We danced the night away on two evenings at Banana Court, the local night spot. The cover charge was NZ $1, (about 40p or 50c US) It was great, full of locals, a good band with an Ella Fitzgerald type singer, who was there because of her rhythm and voice, not her face or figure. The Cook Islanders are natural uninhibited dancers and between every half-hour of western dance was half an hour of tamoure dancing. I loved watching these beautiful young people dancing their traditional dances as the natural way of spending their evenings. Although they had to wear shoes and western clothes to be admitted to the hall, their body movement wasn't restricted, hips rotated, knees whacked together, eyes and shoulders with arms outstretched, co-ordinated and challenged each other.

We sat near some New Zealand couples who were attending a Pharmacists Convention. "Have the lectures and seminars been useful?" I asked.

"Well, the only one I have attended was 'How to fill in your Income Tax Form", chuckled a tanned contented neighbour as he quaffed his Steinlager. I've been playing golf or deep sea fishing every day. I think most of us have. You can't come to an island like this and spend your time sitting in a lecture hall."

All New Zealanders are interested in sailing. They have the most boats per capita of any country in the world. Before the evening was over we had swapped yarns and addresses and promised to visit them when we got to Nelson on New Zealand's South Island.

Rarotonga seemed a Garden of Eden as we hiked through the fertile valleys and forest and up Needle Mountain for a glorious view down to the sea the other side. A Sunday school group were planting gardenias by the roadside and making flower crowns. They gave me one. Huge trees shaded our way. A road tunnelled through one enormous banyan tree and its hanging aerial roots.

We were loath to leave, but the Harbour Master was firm. After applying for, and obtaining New Zealand visas, on Monday October 15th we motored out into the wide, deep, violet ocean. It was rough and windy as we headed north to Atutaki. With the reefed main and working jib up, we just slept, read and hung on. Before night fell,

A dark blue starfish

Peter took down the mainsail, we were going too fast.

At 02.00 Atutaki's light confirmed our position. Down came the jib and we motored around until the sun came up. WOODWIND was anchored inside the reef. Ken came out in their dinghy to guide us in. The lagoon was emptying fast, very fast. CLYPEUS touched bottom, grounded and was swung around by the current until she lay almost across the pass, held up on either side by sandbanks. Water swirled around her bow and stern.

"No point in worrying until the tide comes in again," said Peter, "I'll put the anchor out while you cook breakfast."

Ken joined us for eggs and bacon. When the tide turned we followed the narrow channel up into the lagoon basin and anchored behind Canadian LORCHA.

Atutaki became one of our favourite inhabited places. The snorkelling was fabulous in the clear warm water. I saw my first blue starfish. Nellie the baker, gave us bananas, papaya and tomatoes when we went to her house to buy bread. In the evening we watched the local dance show at 'Big Jays' and enjoyed good fish and chips. Then walked back to the dinghy in warm torrential rain and rowed home with water streaming down our faces dripping from our chins onto our knees.

Next day, Peter's 54th birthday, we hired a Suzuki 100 motor bike for the day; there being no cars to rent, and tootled around trying to find John and his wreck. As

We hired a Suzuki motor bike

I sat on the narrow pillion, my arms around Peter's waist and my cheek nuzzling his broad back, I reflected how few couples have the opportunity of re-living such youthful moments. I had forgotten the pleasure of feeling as-one as the bike laid over at the corners. The warm breeze ruffled our hair as we bumped along the mudpacked road around the perimeter of the island. The sensations were more like riding a horse than a motor-bike. I hadn't imagined seizing the day would turn out to be this good.

To our left, hazy in the morning mist, the sea frothed white as it hit the hundred metre wide reef and tumbled shorewards until it mildly rippled into the pale shallow lagoon. Many unpainted wooden houses were abandoned, their wooden shutters closed like sleeping eyes. Blossoming creepers crawled over the roofs and dripped from the eaves resembling tresses of be-decked hair. In patches of sunlight under the palms, piles of copra lay gradually yellowing and drying in the sun. The few people about were either tending their gardens or walking along the road. They raised their hand in greeting. The lonely villages slept under the soporific sun.

We watched a children's hula floor show, given by the local dancing school - charming! The children enjoyed it as much as we did and I chatted to one of the teenage dancers, Ngupoku.

As we toured the island next day, a rain shower thrashed down so we sheltered under a tree and Ngupoku appeared; we happened to be outside her mother's home. She invited us into the thatched wooden hut and made tea. Their house was clean, light and airy with running water but ever-present flies and mosquitoes. They let me hold Ngupoku's baby. The poor little thing, a year old, but really small with awful sores over her feet, legs and arm. Her huge brown eyes regarded me with little interest. There are clinics on the island, but running sores are part of the way of life, even on babies.

Island paradises don't stand up well to close scrutiny. Most suffer lack of sanitation, medical care and a restricted diet. We didn't ask whether Ngupoku was married and the subject wasn't mentioned. Her mother told us that more Atutaki men lived in New Zealand now than Atutaki. Tourism was their hope for the future. The main crops were coconuts and bananas which need very careful handling and had sensitive ripening times. Often, in the rough seas, banana boats couldn't get near enough to be loaded, so the bananas were ruined. Hopefully a dried banana industry was going to be started on the island.

Before leaving for Palmerston Island I went to buy bread and gave Nellie an embroidered hanky from Spain to thank her for her welcome and kindness.

She insisted on giving me fruit - oranges, papayas, breadfruit, taro, green peppers.

"Thank you but no. No, really no more. I didn't give you a little gift for anything in exchange."

"Do you like bananas?" she enquired.

"Er, yes," I faltered, "but really, you have given me too much already."

"I know, I know," she admonished. "My boy will bring you some bananas in half a hour. OK?"

"Thank you," I repeated. "We love Atutaki, we'll share the fruit. I hope we can come back one day."

As I joined Peter on board, a truck parked on the jetty and tooted. "Oh that's some bananas from Nellie," I said. "Will you row and get them or shall I?"

"I'll go," he said. "Stow those groceries carefully, it's going to be a bumpy ride again."

Peter sat in the dinghy, weighed down with two huge sticks of bananas

Next thing I heard was a shout and went on deck. Peter sat in the dinghy weighed down with two huge sticks of bananas. Hundreds of bananas, far too many for two people, even if we ate bananas for every meal.

Pass me a line," he called. Tying a rope around the cut end of the sticks he dunked them in the sea to rid them of cockroaches, tarantula spiders or anything else that might be hiding within the fruit. As I hauled them up on deck I calculated there must be a hundredweight of bananas. Some I wrapped in newspaper, a few hands in plastic bags and stored them in the forward cabin. Both sticks rested drunkenly in the corner taking up most of the cockpit.

In the sunshine with the wind behind us, the reefed main boomed out one side and the working jib the other. We rolled on west for two sparkling days, our schooner bow cleaving a rushing white spray. The sun twinkled on the droplets that splashed back to the cockpit. I went forward and stood on the bowsprit, at times mesmerised by the movement and glory of the day. At night phosphorescent curls streamed behind us like silver curlicues. Sometimes dolphins, in their tubes of silver, burst to the surface exploding into a bouquet of stars.

The lushness of the islands and the gentle Polynesian charm of Raratonga and Atutaki had beguiled us. The Cook Islanders like Tahitians, love music and dance, but with the bonus for us, that they speak English and enjoy a much lower cost of living.

As we sighted the palm tops of Palmerston, two sixteen-foot aluminium boats with powerful out boards plunged towards us through the

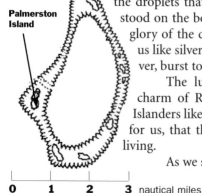

Palmerston Island

| 0 | 1 | 2 | 3 nautical miles |

Palmerston Atoll

heavy swell, each manned by five young Polynesian men of differing colours, from pale coffee to dark brown, all barefoot, but wearing shorts or cotton trousers and shirts.

"Welcome to our island," they called. The first launch came alongside and the young men scrambled aboard. One boy tied their boat so that it drifted astern. Another man shouted to the other boat, raised his clenched fists above his head in triumph and obviously told them to "Push off."

"No, no. They must come on board too". I gesticulated to the other boat to come alongside. In a seamanlike manner they climbed aboard and streamed their dinghy behind the other. I offered them all Coca Colas or beer.

"Wow! Beer please," the older boys said. "No beer for three months."

"And no bananas on Palmerston." One said as he eyed the two sticks of bananas stacked in the cockpit, while he found a place to sit. They settled themselves around the deck with a can each, and ate bananas.

"Well, this whole stick can be for your island. We dunked them well into the sea, so there should be no tarantulas or bugs in them." Peter added.

With huge grins, they introduced themselves in order of seniority: Tom Marsters, perhaps thirty years old, Jimmy Marsters, about 28, Hebrew Marsters, probably 18, Ahkim Manuka, exactly twelve and two months, and their friend Borneo, a slim dark woolly-haired young man. The other men, from the second launch, were strangely subdued, but they enjoyed their drinks and bananas. All were well-mannered, and spoke old-fashioned English as their first language.

As we cautiously approached the sandy shore in the calm lee of the atoll, we could see across the reef into the smooth aquamarine surface of the lagoon. On the far side, about four miles away, minuscule outlines of palm trees trembled, as though hovering above the sun-scorched coral. It was a perfect example of how atolls are formed over thousands of years by the tiny calcareous coral creatures gradually building up on top of the shallow rim of an extinct underwater volcano.

The young men in the second boat said, "Goodbye and thank you", jumped into the water, climbed into their dinghy and roared away through the shallow pass into the lagoon. There wasn't time to ask why they had gone, we were getting too close to the coral.

"Stop. Stop," Tom called from the bow to Peter at the wheel.

"Let go the anchor slowly," Tom shouted as the others jumped into the water. I

White tipped reef shark

followed them, marveling at the most beautiful coral garden, banked like a herbaceous border. Clusters of pink, purple, lavender, white, turquoise and indigo blue coral and verdant green clumps of seaweed sloped up towards the shore. Bright blue and green parrot fish; yellow and black angels; fluorescent blue gobies, and orange, white and black clown fish peeked out at us from waving anemones and coral fans. The boys took no notice of the metre-long white-tipped sharks cruising by. I pointed at them. The boys shrugged their shoulders implying 'no problem'..

A few yards away the reef dropped off into purple infinity. What creatures lurked down in those menacing depths? There would be nothing to stop CLYPEUS on her way to Australia if the anchor pulled out.

Jimmy Marsters swam down and caught hold of the anchor as it hung, suspended in the clear water, and guided it to a place where it wouldn't damage any coral. He carefully hooked it round a ledge, popped back to the surface and gave a thumbs up sign to Tom. Peter reversed the engine hard. The anchor held and looked as though it would have to tow the whole island if it wanted to escape.

Tom invited us ashore in their dinghy after explaining that the pass was only three feet deep; too shallow for CLYPEUS to enter.

"The first launch to reach visitors gets to have them as their guests," he explained. We were to be their guests every day for as long as we wished. They would pick us up before breakfast and return us after tea, before their evening prayers.

The men lowered one of the sticks of bananas into their aluminium dinghy. An exciting ride through the white water pass brought us onto Palmerston Island - a tiny pearl in the necklace of islands making up Palmerston Atoll. We were led across hot

palmerston Church built from wood cargo from a wrecked ship

white sand past a substantial, unpainted little church made of weather beaten planks.

"A vessel carrying wood was wrecked on our atoll," Tom explained "Our grandfather and fathers built the church themselves from the cargo."

Following a sandy track through yellow hibiscus and pink oleander bushes we came to their home. The handsome parents, Tuakana and Teinano Marsters, came out to welcome us into their crimson bougainvillea-covered concrete bungalow. They thanked us for the bananas and as we slipped off our sandals invited us to sit on the flowered chintz covered settee for tea and biscuits.

"Will you take milk in your tea?" Teinano graciously offered, as though we were at a tea party in Cheltenham. Her round frame was enveloped in a flower-patterned mumu, the full, yoked dress with puff sleeves introduced by the Missionaries all over the South Pacific to replace provocative grass skirts.

"Yes please. Do you have a cow then?" I asked, surprised.

Two slim brown young ladies in colourful sarongs, with red hibiscus blossoms tucked into their black hair, giggled behind their hands as they prepared a tea tray. Two other little girls, clutching a banana each, hid shyly round the corner watching our every movement.

"Oh no," Teinano's pleasant wide face creased into an even bigger smile. "It's coconut cream. We have no cows, but we do have two pigs and some chickens. The copra boat only comes once every three months. Sometimes it is too rough for them to land. Often we go six or nine months without supplies or a visitor."

"There are only 56 of us on the atoll, all on this island." Tuakana then told us the story of his great-grandfather, William Marsters from Gloucestershire, who arrived in a sailing ship in 1862, with his wife and two maids, to manage the coconut plantation for a French Company. After the first few years the French abandoned him and never made contact again. William wrote to Queen Victoria asking that the island be annexed to Great Britain with him as Governor. The British Government sent a formal document laying claim to the island and appointing him Chief Administrative Officer. Tuakana pointed to the framed Charter on the wall.

Teinano interrupted "Three families gradually evolved, the east, west and middle family. We are the middle family," she said proudly," but we have a problem." She nodded towards her husband, "Tuakana is the oldest grandson, and should be Chief Administrative Officer, but he had to spend six years in New Zealand for his tuberculosis to be cured. When we came back his young brother Bill had made himself Chief Officer and won't give back the official stamp. Now any visitors who come to the island have to be interviewed by him and he stamps their passports. You will have to go and see him soon. But mind you come back here directly. Tom will go with you."

We sipped our creamy tea from bone china cups and saucers. I noticed pictures of Queen Elizabeth in A.T.S. uniform when she was eighteen. Signed photos of the British Royal Family, including Princess Diana and Prince Charles, filled most picture frames.

"The Royal Family, do you know them?" I asked.

"Oh yes. The Royal Yacht Britannia has called here twice. The last time was only twelve years ago. Prince Philip stayed for over a week. We re-named our best bathing beach Elizabeth Bay." Teinano enthused about every incident of the royal visit as if it had happened yesterday.

Tom came in. "You have your passports and ship's papers?" He asked Peter.

"Yes," Peter patted his document case.

"Follow me."

"Thank you very much for the tea. Perhaps we will see you tomorrow." I said rising.

"Oh you must stay for a meal this evening. We are expecting you to join us. We have some minced turtle meat to make into a favourite meal for visitors and some fresh turtle eggs to make a cake. You are the ninth yacht to visit this year." Teinano clasped my hands between hers with friendly warmth.

"Thank you. We would like that very much indeed. Please can I see the turtles' eggs?"

"Variopanaa," Teinano called, and introduced her slim 30-year-old unmarried daughter who had that slightly pinched look of unrequited passion; the opportunities for meeting a suitable male were remote. She brought over a bowl of white spheres which looked like ping-pong balls. They were soft to touch, the thick skins dented as I poked them with my finger.

Tom and Jimmy led us out through the back door. We ducked under a tidy line of brown plastic sandals, similar to ours, which were strapped to a washing line in descending size to be shared by the family. Everyone west of Raratonga seemed to wear the same strong brown plastic sandals, made in New Zealand and riveted together with stainless steel fastenings, which were ideal for walking on the reef and hot sand. Dodging the bananas now hanging from a branch of a dense breadfruit tree, Jimmy said, "We'll lower the bananas every day at noon so that all the children can come and take one a day until they are all gone. They are a great treat. Many plants won't grow here as there is little soil, it's mostly sand."

"We will bring the other stick ashore tomorrow," Peter promised.

Our four male hosts escorted us along sandy paths beneath tall coconut palms. Small boys hid behind the tree trunks and shouted obviously rude words, which we couldn't understand. Some poked out their tongues.

"Take no notice," we were told.

In a small thatched shed, a handsome, round and kindly Bill T. Marsters sat at his desk, rubber stamp at the ready. We had a long chat. He explained that the New Zealand Government had appointed him as Chief Administrative Officer when his brother was away for so long, and that the appointment had not been rescinded.

There was another reason for a feud on the island. Somehow the teacher's house had been burnt down three years ago, and the teacher of the ten or eleven children had left. The New Zealand Government wouldn't send another teacher until peace had been agreed and a new house built, but the families couldn't decide where the money was coming from or who was to build the house. Consequently the children were receiving no formal education. Akhim, an intelligent lad of twelve still couldn't read. Later I took it upon myself to write to Buckingham Palace and ask if Prince Philip could cut through the red tape and have a teacher sent out from New Zealand. I received a letter from his Secretary thanking us for the information and saying that the matter would be looked into. A year later a letter from Teinano told us:

"Thank the good Lord we have a teacher for our children. The teacher came here early this year and our children is very please to be in school but there no teachers house yet. We are planning to build our church house next year."

On the way back to the house we were shown their little garden. A sole cucumber was nearly ready for picking.

"Is it big enough to pick now? How shall we eat it?" Ahkim asked. "We have never had a cucumber before."

"We usually eat it thinly sliced as part of a salad or in a sandwich with a little salt, pepper and vinegar." I hoped the taste wasn't too much of a disappointment after the weeks of anticipation. A great deal was expected of this poor cucumber, grown from seed, and hand watered every morning and evening.

We spent five days with these generous people, virtually kidnapped by them. No further opportunity arose to speak to Bill or to see the other young men. It seemed funny to be speaking good English and enjoying cups of milky tea in comfortable armchairs. Hearing the children being corrected to say "Please," "Thank you" and "Pardon" made it seem like home.

The house had running water, a toilet and shower, generators for light, a Hotpoint washing machine and some food freezers. They used these to store filleted parrot fish which would be taken to the Hotel on Rarotonga when the next supply boat came. Peter was able to mend some defunct freezers, and a Mercury outboard motor, so he was very popular.

Rowing across the lagoon in the early mornings was peaceful, the sea was so still and clear that the ripple made by our bow and oars showed us that we were actually floating on water and not suspended in space. Sometimes we rested at the edge in absolute silence to watch the rising sun cast long shadows between the tall, straight tree trunks. The only sound was the occasional plop of a fish or the sudden thud of a coconut landing. It was a joy to drift on the water and watch brightly-coloured fish dart beneath, or to gaze up and watch fleecy, wispy clouds float through a frame of coconut palms. The rasp of the dry palm leaves signaled the morning breeze was coming and it was time to row home and prepare for a day ashore.

One day the family took us to fish on the far side of the atoll. We were shown where to stand on the reef and hang baited hooks down holes in the coral, like Eskimos fishing over holes in the ice. The sea surged in and out through gaps and gullies. The family whipped fish out fairly regularly. Peter caught a small one, but I failed, so missed out on threading a wire through the gills of fish and out through their mouths as I had been carefully taught beforehand.

The picnic for the day was just coconuts, prepared in four different ways. For drinks we were handed large smooth green drinking nuts. Tom gave each nut three taps on the top and, with a slash of his machete, decapitated it with one blow. We drank the sweet, fresh water, then spooned out the delicate jelly lining. The main course was a brown and hairy inner nut which gave us the usual hard white coconut meat we knew. Also a big old yellowy-brown smooth nut with a sprout emerging. Jimmy pulled these apart with his bare hands. Each had a ball of white fibrous tissue inside, a new tree growing like a foetus. This soft spongy substance they called uto.

"Uto is pure protein," Variopanaa said. "It is the first food we give our babies. We have to taste a little first because sometimes it's poisonous."

We viewed dessert more cautiously! A smooth brown coconut that had been a green nut, baked in an earth oven. The insides had the delicious taste and texture of chocolate creme caramel.

In their home, the ladies made beautiful handicrafts including jewel boxes of polished yellow coconut shells, the lid hinged and decorated with fine basketwork. Teinano showed us complex patchwork bedspreads, plaited pandanus hats, and fans made of the same material. We followed her outside to watch white-haired and withered, Granny Masters, in her sarong, squatting beside a small fire of a few burning coconut husks. In an old tin, balanced on the husks, she carefully stirred a boiling red dye mixture into which she dipped the edges of woven fans until they became oleander pink. Before leaving Teinano gave me a delicately worked coconut jewel box which I will always treasure.

We didn't see many books in the house, and no TV. The youngest child on the island was five and Grandfather Tuakana took her on his knee each day to try and teach her to read. Naming of children was imaginative, they seemed to have run out of names: one girl was called 'Twenty-six', another 'Fifty-three', another older woman was named 'Painkiller'.

During the nights at anchor, flying fish often dropped on deck with a bump, fluttering their wings helplessly until they expired. We fried their bony bodies for breakfast, but were always given another breakfast ashore of curried fish pancakes, buns, bread or doughnuts, no matter what we said..

Teinano took me to look for shells, we didn't find any, but enjoyed walking and talking together. Women are so lucky, with empathy we share many common tasks and experiences no matter how different our backgrounds. Most of us have children, husbands, varied ways of cooking and washing to compare. A strange man landing on an island could be a threat, but an older woman on her own is usually greeted with grace and charm. I helped Teinano feed the pigs with taro root and broken coconuts

All the family came to visit our home on CLYPEUS one morning. We gave them orange squash, biscuits and freshly made shortbread. We found spare paper and pencils for the children to take ashore. I sliced an Atutaki melon to hand around and noticed that everyone kept the seeds, discreetly putting them into their pockets.

Some evenings, after their daily church service, the young men would come out to CLYPEUS for a beer. The sweet scent of tiare blossom drifted across the water as they sat around our cockpit softly strumming their guitars and singing. We made an audio tape of their songs and gave it to them and kept a copy for ourselves.

"Oh Palmerston, Oh Palmerston," Jimmy sang to his guitar while Tom plinked his banjo, Hebrew throbbed the beat on skin stretched over a coconut bole, Borneo rhythmically knocked coconut shells suspended from a bamboo stick, and Akhim played the spoons.

"William Marsters was a brave hero
He came to Palmerston long ago.
While on a ship he aspires.
To live as a merry king for the rest of his days

I listen to the tape now but cannot catch many of the words.

One song comes through loud and clear:

Take me back to dear old Palmerston
Put me on a ship for Palmerston
Take me over there, Drop me anywhere
As long as I return, I don't care
I should like to see my First* Mother
Diddle de aye di, diddle de aye di
Carry me back there
Palmerston's the place for me.

(First Mother would be the birth mother, second, third or fourth mother would be those aunts, or friends who looked after him elsewhere or if his first mother should go away.)

A bowdlerized rendition of 'Yes sir, *That's my baby*'" was followed by a Polynesian bump song played and sung with such vigour CLYPEUS must have been bouncing on the water. "Awe Awe,pa wa ete Mama Kae," they sang each vowel being separately pronounced.

"What does it mean? "

"Oh, nothing, it's just a play type song," said an embarrassed Jimmy.

But Hebrew interrupted "It's about old lady, she been making a fire near to the house and cooks something and burns the house."

"What does 'awe, awe', mean.?"

"Itchy, It means sore and itchy," they giggled and we didn't inquire further.
Jimmy said "Hold it boys. We must not waste Peter's batteries here. We only want to record nice things." He crooned into the microphone a love song which finished with

"But now I know I'll be true to you."

Then he announced into the microphone: "We have a dedication here from Akhim Marsters he'd like us to play a song to the people of Palmerston and especially to his Granny who is worrying about him and missing him a lot. But don't worry Granny he will be home in two hours to be together again and kiss you." They sang a gentle Maori song "Et tae kai kai yu ba tora" in which Akhim's young voice could just be heard and someone kept loudly shouting "Yes Granny!" through it.

The pink and purple glow of the sun cast a rose coloured spell as it finally sank into the darkening sea.

One morning the young men ferried Tuakana out for coffee so that he, and we, could listen to his audio tape as they had no batteries. It had been sent to him a few years previously by Commander Victor Clarke of Emsworth, Hampshire, who was skipper of Lord Cobham's yacht that had been wrecked on the atoll. The Marsters had rescued Cmdr Clarke and his crew; looked after and fed them for five weeks until the supply boat came. Listening to the tape brought tears to our eyes as the grateful captain spoke of the generosity and selflessness of the Masters family, who had clothed and fed them and shared unstintingly what little they had.

Goodbye Jimmy, Borneo, Akim, Bill, Tom and Hebrew

Before leaving, I made fudge for the children and we searched our home for suitable gifts: batteries, biscuits, perfumed soap, magazines, and a jar of Roses Lime Marmalade. Teinano crowned us with honey scented frangipani coronets and Tuakana placed fresh garlands around our necks. They took us to say goodbye to Granny Marsters who gave us three of the fans she had been dyeing. I have them displayed now on the wall and they smile down at me as I write.

The family gave us a celebration farewell meal in their home of a precious fresh roast chicken and rice with coconut sauce, followed by doughnuts. Then we trooped into the garden to sing together: songs and hymns. We said our fond farewells and sadly sailed away, rocking towards the west horizon pondering on the fact that the Marsters have clean air, sunshine and warm weather, lovely beaches, pretty shells, a perfect blue lagoon, good swimming and peace. but they have no radio, no television, no alcohol, no school, no potatoes, apples, oranges, lettuce or greens. They have no beef or lamb, but they do have pigs, fish, turtles, coconuts, mangoes, papayas, breadfruit, chickens and eggs.

With the ten yachts and the supply boat, visiting, hopefully four times a year, (but sometimes with a six or nine month gap if the weather is unkind), you have their whole life. I guess it would be pretty boring without the odd feud to liven things up.

CHAPTER FIFTEEN

Nuie
Lat 19°03'S Long 169°55'W
November - December 1985

For four blissful days the sun rose, peaked and set, one day gracefully making way for the next. Our own little universe cut its white frothy wake through the deep blue water. Sailing the sea under the sun and stars filled me with joy.

The tiny island of Nuie looked rather mundane as we approached - no golden sand, fringing reef or lagoon, no mountains or rivers, but what an exciting place it turned out to be. Volcanoes have lifted it twice out of the sea, once 100' and then another 60', so that all that was under the sea is now on top - caves, chasms, and coral grottoes are hidden in the tropical rain forest. Some glades look as though they have come from the pages of Grimms Fairy Tales with coral spires festooned with creepers and orchids.

Two American yachts were anchored, MAI KWAI and MOTLEE. We spoke on the VHF and Rose, Lee and I arranged to go into town to the market at 6am next morning. It was raining but we rowed ashore to look for the market.

"No market today, it's raining," a young woman called out from the door of her tiny wooden house.

Warm rain didn't bother us. We continued along the road and found two small supermarkets, a post office, a tourist office with a Philatelic Bureau, but no bank. At the only Hotel our men cleared customs and immigration. We all met at the Crab Inn for lunch. Fish in paper and eaten with fingers. "No chips as we have no potatoes, however, we do have chunks of boiled breadfruit instead!" The lumps of breadfruit made an excellent accompaniment to the fish.

As usual we asked our new friends about the names of their boats. Rose piped up, "Well you know the 60's Chinese song, 'Maikwai, oh Maikwai, Chinese Romeo sings'.' Well, 'Maikwai, oh Maikwai means Rose, Rose, I love you.

"Aaah! How romantic Bob", we all chorused in unison.

"I'm afraid MOTLEE isn't nearly as romantic," Tom sighed. "It's just a combination of Tom backwards with Lee's name added on. We are still thinking of calling her 'LITTLE SLOOP." Their boats were less than 25' (8.3m) and we admired both crews for crossing the Pacific safely in such small craft. CLYPEUS took on a whole new dimension as the largest boat in the fleet and became the party boat.

The local Australian dentist took us to The Golf Club for a drink, but; "Sorry no beer until the monthly boat comes in next Monday."

Canoe storage cave, 60ft above a very dangerous landing place. We explored caves and chasms, and couldn't have done this if we had waited to 65 to retire

Peter rented a motorbike for four days and we toured the island. Surprisingly deep, dark rain forest, grew between the scrub covered hills. We explored caves and chasms, letting ourselves down ropes and praying we would be able to climb up out again. (We couldn't have done this if we had waited to 65 to retire). It was so exciting. Fantastic stalagmites and stalactites, freshwater underground pools to swim in with the sun shining down through fissures in the rocks overhead. Thrilling it was! Never had we explored such exciting terrain completely alone.

At Uluvehi, a dilapidated fishing village on the cliff top, fishermen were mending nets. They took us down an old, worn, rock path to their precipitous landing place which looked impossible. From the sea they had to climb steep steps 100' up to a cave where their canoes were stored. We were told they kept their canoes hidden because in 1860 a Peruvian 'black birder' had taken slaves from here to work guano mines in Chile.

Snorkelling was different too. The reef was honeycombed with tall caves that enabled us to swim in one side and out of the other. Swimming through arches under water, opened up vistas of coral gardens fifty yards ahead. The only trouble was sea snakes. The locals insisted they were not dangerous as they had small mouths and couldn't really bite.

The New Zealand influence is very strong although Niue is completely independent. 2,000 Niueans live on Niue and 4,000 live in New Zealand; a similar situation to Atutaki.

One evening we visited THE hotel where Rose and Bob had taken up residence and, in the bar, were invited to enjoy a drink with the Premier. The next day by chance we met him at lunch in the cafe near Parliament House and were greeted like old friends. He told us they were trying to build up their tourist industry and had eleven tourists this week!

With Maikwai and Little Sloop we decided to cruise together to New Zealand

With MAI KWAI and MOTLEE, we decided to cruise together through the Tongan Archipelago towards New Zealand. It was the first time we had buddy boats and we found it added enormously to our pleasure. They had few charts and we had many, so usually led the way.

Speaking on the VHF every four hours and being able to rendezvous for barbecues on deserted beaches made our voyage seem safer and more fun. They nicknamed Peter 'The Admiral'.

Only 48 hours out of Nuie, but three

calendar days later, because of crossing the International Date Line; we sailed into the magnificent, deep harbour at Neiafu in Vavau, Northern Tonga. The new day starts here, or as they say, "Time begins in Tonga". (Actually they are 13 hours ahead of Greenwich; they wiggled the line a little so that they would be the same day and time as New Zealand their closest neighbour.)

There are 170 Tongan Islands, only 36 of which are inhabited. We managed to visit seven islands and found Tongans to be large, handsome people, proud of their Kingdom. Their 'hello' is 'malo e lelei' which translates into a gracious 'thank you for living'.

Everyone we met was friendly and generous in spite of having virtually no money. Each man is entitled to seven acres of bush to farm. From this he supports his family; perhaps taking some produce, mats or baskets his wife may have woven, to the market on one of the larger islands or try and sell them to tourists and yachties. Alofi was particularly persistent trying to make us buy wood carvings but did invite us to his home. The plaited coconut-frond home had no furniture or glass in the windows and only mats to sleep and sit on. The ladies cooked outside on open fires or in umus.

Feasts were popular and cheap to attend, but we found we quickly tired of umu baked food. Even though lobsters, fish and pork were offered, they were always wrapped in banana leaves which give a particular flavour.

Ladies and gentlemen wore woven pandanus mats, called ta'ovala, often tatty, tied around their waists as a sign of respect to their King and parents. Carvings, basket work and tapa, the cloth made from pounding the bark fibres of young manioc trees, were for sale very cheaply.

One place I really wanted to dive down and explore was Mariner's Cave which I had read about years ago in *Sailing All Seas in Idle Hour'* by Dwight Long. He told of a vast chasm under a small uninhabited island, the entrance to which was under the sea.

A legend told of *a Tongan Princess who, because her father would not allow her to marry her true love, had walked into the sea and drowned. Actually her lover had hidden her in this secret cave until her father, duly repentant, had been persuaded that, should she return from the dead, she would be allowed to marry whomever she wished. Her true love then magically produced her from the sea. All was forgiven and they lived happily ever after.*

The ultimate snorkel. It had fired my imagination to reach this subterranean cave and to swim down into it was a dream I wanted to live. We made enquiries as to its whereabouts and Alofi told us which island to go to and, on the northern cliff face, to look for a tatty palm tree over a smooth, slick rock.

With six guests on board CLYPEUS; our friends from MAI KWAI and MOTLEE and a New Zealand couple, Caroline and Noel, whom we had met while dining and dancing at the hotel the previous evening, we set off, bursting with

Woven Pandanus mats called ta 'ovalatied around the waist denote respect for King and parents

excitement. At last we found what could be the place. It was too deep to anchor, so Peter agreed to steer CLYPEUS around in circles and stand by.

A rainstorm couldn't dampen our enthusiasm. As soon as it abated, we jumped into the sea, a bit scared by the swell as it thumped and sucked around the cliff face. Bob and Tom had a trial look and then, as the sun shone again, the three of us took deep breaths and swam down through the dark underwater hole in the cliff face. The tunnel was about a metre deep and four metres long; the roof was lined with glistening bubbles. With lungs feeling as though they were tearing apart, we burst up into an eerily lit cavern. The sunlight from outside reflected on the white sand floor 40' below and sent up a ghostly glow that dimly lit the whole cave. Stalactites hung from the roof. A ledge, just above the surface, must have been where the poor princess sat, unhappy, damp and cold awaiting her father's forgiveness. As the ocean surge came in so our ears popped and the cave misted, at first I thought it was my goggles misting up, but as I was clearing them so it happened again. A perfect physics experiment explaining air pressure, humidity and mist.

Gulping air, we swam back down and out into the open sea with no problem. It was an experience of a lifetime. Lee overcame her caution and decided she wanted to swim down too. I accompanied her for pure joy at being privileged to do something so fantastic. This was well before scuba diving was an everyday sport.

Swallows' Cave was another thrilling spot. It was my turn to steer CLYPEUS around in circles while the others explored this magnificent cave in the rubber dinghy. A cathedral, with stalagmites reaching up from the deep white sand floor to the high ceiling. Swallows' Cave faces west and we were there at the right time for the glow of the late afternoon sun to shine into the cave and turn the stalagmites and stalactites into golden columns. Bats and swallows flitted and swooped around. Peter came back and rowed me into the cave while Bob took over CLYPEUS. Cautiously we explored as far back into the cave as we could and climbed up a cleft into a vast inner cavern. A shaft of light pierced the roof and shone down onto a skull?

"Is it a human skull? How old is it? Are there any other bones?" I whispered.

We crept closer to look,

"No it's only a coconut husk!"

"Thank God! Look how deep the cave goes, that crack in the wall makes it look as though there are caves going even further into the cliff."

"Let's go back now. We've done enough for one day and we want to get back into harbour before it gets dark. Come on." Peter pulled me back towards the light.

As we came out of the cave, the fruit bats (flying foxes) which we hadn't noticed hanging upside down from the trees, were beginning to stir and flap around, waking up for their night feeding flight. They swooped close overhead in the darkening sky.

My imagination took over, fangs sank into our unprotected necks and claws ripped us apart. "Do you thing they could be bloodsucking vampires? Can't you row any faster?"

As a teenager, Peter had frightened himself into continuous nightmares by reading 'Dracula' by Bram Stoker under the bedclothes with a quivering torch. Now he made that rubber dinghy skim across the water to CLYPEUS, as if all the bats in hell were after us. We climbed aboard, raised the dinghy, fired the engine and were off. Later we found that the flying foxes are kept as gentle pets or are a delicious tender meat when baked.

What a spectacular day! A day to remember for the rest of our lives.

Safely at anchor next day I wrote of our adventure in my 'letter to friends' but also added:

"I feel I should redress the balance a little as I have written of our voyage being mostly sweetness, light and a doddle. For us, so far, it has been. But here in Neiafu we heard that another yacht was missing: 'IZALIA' which left Rarotonga on October 30th, a couple of weeks after us, to sail to New Zealand hasn't been heard of since. Earlier in the year 'MAINSTAY', with a young NZ. couple on board, left the Galapagos Islands when we did, and has disappeared, even after a full scale search. To our knowledge three other yachts have gone up on the reefs or been dismasted, but with no loss of life. Couples are getting divorced, or have had accidents and had to fly home, or someone at home has demanded their return.

We have been so lucky. We are both remarkably fit and happy in what we are doing. CLYPEUS is proving a good boat for the course. Our equipment has stood up well. The self steering and Walker SatNav have taken so much of the strain and worry from our backs. Of course Peter being an engineer and able to maintain all our equipment is a great bonus."

On Lofanga Island in the Hapaii Group we actually had to borrow a wheelbarrow to take all their gifts of bananas, pineapples, coconuts and papayas to our boats. Rose, Lee and I arranged a visit to the primary school and the top class sang and danced for us. Their melodious singing in harmony was wonderful - no instruments of course, they don't even have enough paper and pencils for everyone to write every day. Their very positive and charismatic teacher William, hummed the starting note and the confident children sang their local songs but also *The Grand Old Duke of York, Amazing Grace,* and three groups sang three songs in harmony together - *Three Blind Mice, Frere Jacques* and *Row, Row, Row Your Boat.* It was special.

We took a world map (they didn't have one) and showed them our countries and sailing routes. They enjoyed our peanut butter and crackers, homemade fudge and

cookies. I was able to tell them how happily I remembered their Queen Salote riding and waving from an open carriage in the rain at Queen Elizabeth's coronation. I didn't tell them the Noel Coward quip, when Queen Salote entered the abbey, she was behind a very small man - a head of state - in the procession. Someone turned and asked Coward who was that in front of her? He replied, 'Her lunch.'

Next day best uniforms for a photo-shoot. Top two classes

We sang "*My Bonnie*" for them and I danced "*Halikidumpty*" (a Scots Reel) which left them open-mouthed. Apart from the unusual sight of a grinning 50 year old cavorting around in front of them, Tongans dance with their hands and heads, keeping their feet on the ground and knees together as the missionaries decreed. I had to explain that it was so cold in Scotland that dances made you jump about to keep warm.

The next island we landed on was not so happy or generous. We arrived on

Sunday morning and attended church where a fine, upstanding white-haired Tongan matron conducted the service with power and grace until it came to the prayers. With closed eyes and uplifted hands she wept to God to have pity on their poor island, they had so little. Which was of course true, although it was larger and had more varied vegetation than Lofanga. Whether this particular plea was for our benefit or not, we don't know. However the people were not as happy and proud as those on Lofanga and many people asked for gifts which we tried to satisfy. Somebody slashed a hole in our rubber dinghy too, so not everybody wanted to welcome us.

MAIKWAI, MOTLEE and CLYPEUS enjoyed a perfect few days stopping at uninhabited islands, cooking our morning-caught fish on the beach at lunch time. Often in the evenings Rose and Lee would bring a dish as part of our supper and we ate together on CLYPEUS. Sometimes we would lay our chequered cloth on the saloon table, light candles in bottles and hoist a sign

"Tongan Trattoria"
Spaghetti a speciality.

The others would bring wine and dessert and later we would sit in the cockpit cradling mugs of hot chocolate watching the silver moon dance on the black water before they rowed home.

Ata receded in the distance now uninhabited due to Blackbirders taking the men to slavery

Nuku'alofa, the capital, in the southern groups of islands, had the royal palace, an impressive new cathedral, a traffic warden, video shops full of gangster movies, cars, busses and a few tourists. The airport took major airlines and restaurants appeared to be mainly German. The Date-Line Hotel was sophisticated with an excellent cabaret of traditional local dancing. The market was busy with abundant fruit and vegetables and it all seemed such a hustle and bustle after the out islands. We stayed just a couple of days.

A whale spouted, and sounded, flicking his gigantic tail up in the air as we passed by uninhabited Ata, a dark, forbidding and lonely island. Evidently the King of Tonga had evacuated all the people from the island and brought them to Nukualofa early in the century, because slave traders kept raiding the island and carrying off the men-folk. We were sorry to leave Tonga for New Zealand and vowed to return next year.

On Saturday 7th December we made our best-ever day's run -147 miles from noon to noon. However it was really rough and water entered via the main hatch and made our bed sopping wet. As there was no way of drying it in the rough sea we took turns to sleep on the floor. There was a nip in the air and we started wearing proper clothes again, rather than just bathing costumes or sarongs. I caught a cold and felt lousy. Peter coped all one night on his own.

On 10th December a flaming angry sun rose at 6am, were we in for a bashing? We donned our oilskins and wellingtons, the first time since the Gulf of Mississippi. Our noon position was 33°33'S 175°15'E. only 128 miles to go to The Bay of Islands. For our last night at sea the weather softened and we celebrated with martinis and wine with a favourite dinner.

The next morning, after 927 miles, New Zealand glowed as the sun shone ahead on to the Island of the Long White Cloud.

A cannibal cooking pot?

So, at half way I wrote in my letter to friends:

'We have sailed over 20,000 to do the 12,000 actual miles to New Zealand, are brown as berries, fitter than we ever have been, seen so many extraordinary things and are having a wonderful adventure. However we feel almost satiated with all we have seen and done and are looking forward to four months in New Zealand to recoup, smarten up CLYPEUS *and have a bit of western living. (Peter says he has had enough "bongo food" for one year!)'*

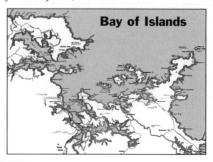

Bay of Islands

CHAPTER SIXTEEN

NEW ZEALAND
Lat 34°50' S
Long 174°26'E
Dec 85 - April 86

It was too rough to stop at Minerva Reef to see what wild life would be in the shallow patches of mid-Pacific coral. Ocean reefs provide protection from the swell but not the wind. At low tide there is coral to walk on and the fishing, lobstering and shelling are unspoiled. We had also heard that the lonely New Zealand weather forecasters on The Kermadec Islands would enjoy visitors. However, for most of the voyage the winds and water were in torment and we smashed along. Flaming orange angry sunrises made us wonder if the cyclone season might be early this year.

Entering the Bay of Islands was like sailing into a calm toy 'Noddyland'. Dark green forested hills rise above paler green fields dotted with white sheep and brown cows. The white-walled farms with red roofs are surrounded by meadows full of dandelions and daisies, cow parsley and clover. Small islands are scattered in the blue water of the many-faceted bay. Everything looked so fresh and green.

Friendly voices on the VHF advised us to stay on board until Customs, Immigration and the Agriculture Authorities had examined CLYPEUS, which they did very thoroughly. They were efficient and smart in their short-sleeved blue shirts, tailored navy shorts, white knee socks and highly polished black shoes. They were so charming they managed to make us happily sign a form guaranteeing $5,700 import tax if CLYPEUS stayed more than twelvemonths. Eggs, garlic and onions and an untouched melon were confiscated. Even the tropic bird tail feathers I had been given by the grateful fishermen on Mopihaa, were carried off to be fumigated. (They were returned unharmed by post two weeks later.)

What was on at the Yacht Club? We couldn't wait to socialise and talk but suddenly meeting so many people amongst so much chatter, was too much for us, and we crept back to CLYPEUS, and motored away to a quiet anchorage to readjust.

Taking our Radio Ham exam at Opua Yacht club

The cruising yachts had started arriving in November and were now well organised. Crews checked into an 8 am.

radio net on VHF each morning, gave announcements of events, 'for sale' notices, 'lost and found', and 'transport available or required', and any good buys that might be of use to other sailors. A class for Radio Hams had been set up in Opua Yacht Club where we were able to study for, and pass the tests for our U.S. Licences. We made arrangements for a transceiver to be brought out to Fiji.

Doyens of the cruising world, Eric and Susan Hiscock arrived from Australia on December 21st on WANDERER V. I rowed over and delivered a Christmas Card to our mentors, from whose books we had learned so much: 'Cruising Under Sail' and 'Beyond The West Horizon'. Not only had they inspired us, but they had made cruising respectable. We had encouraged our parents and children to read their exploits so that they would understand more of what we were doing and that sailing around the world wasn't anything mad or anti-social. The following day they rowed over, side by side in their dinghy, one oar each, and invited us on to WANDERER V for coffee and a glass of wine..

On board they seemed bright and full of beans in spite of being in their mid-seventies. We had a fascinating talk. Peter often quotes Eric's words, "I don't mind listening to the incredible sailing stories people tell me, as long as they don't expect me to believe them!"

Susan said she thought their last eight-month voyage to Australia and the islands would be their last as Eric's sight was failing. They didn't own a house and wanted to live on board as long as they could. Eric said he didn't intend sleeping ashore ever again. They kept a Mini Minor in a friend's garage and rowed ashore a couple of times a week to shop and visit. They proudly showed us "Cruising under Sail" which had just been published in paperback and were thrilled that their other books were being reprinted in paperback too. Eric had written a novel but the publishers had returned it saying they didn't think it would sell. "Probably not enough sex or violence in it," he muttered.

Lyn and Larry Pardey were in New Zealand as well, but we didn't meet them until Australia. What a small world the world sailing community seemed then.

On Christmas Eve carol singing by dinghy was arranged. Peter and I rendezvoused under the jetty at 6 p.m. with a cask of Australian Burgundy and glasses. American loner Carol was already waiting, so we had a little drink while we waited for the others who had promised to join us. Carol and I sat and sang "O Come all Ye Faithful."

No response, so we towed her to GUINEVERE who promised to come carolling with us, on condition we came on board for a drink first. We did. Gradually other dinghies rowed, or roared up, and we strung our craft out behind Marcia and Ted of RICOCHET as theirs was the most powerful outboard. In line, like ducklings, we wove our way between the anchored yachts. It wasn't altogether a musical success as the front carollers had often started the second verse before the tail-end-Charlies had finished the first verse. Socially it was a great evening, with generous libations offered down to over-worked throats - if some boat crews didn't join us we threatened to sing the 'Twelve Days of Christmas' just for them. It caused a riot when Carol and I requested they made it '144 days of Christmas' so that we would have time for a bathroom visit.

A howling gale blew on Christmas morning. Plans for a BBQ lunch on an island in the sun, then an evening Christmas dinner on board CLYPEUS, were abandoned. Our trio ended up rafting together near Pine Island for Christmas lunch. MAIKWAI had bought the turkey, MOTLEE cooked it and we carved and served in on CLYPEUS, together with traditional vegetables and bread sauce and then flaming, hollied Christmas Pudding with brandy butter and crackers. Our American friends had never had those particular trimmings so it was quite different for them. The little gold Christmas tree and many cards made the cabin very festive and we had a happy day although homesick for our family.

Later Don of SUNCHASER came and invited us all onto his boat for a party which was much enlivened by Paul and Emily Keller's suggestion that we each tell the story of how we met our 'loves'. Their story was one of the most touching: They told of how they met on the Oregon ski slopes when senior Dr. Emily was a pupil of Paul who, nearing retirement as a university lecturer, still spent his winter vacations as a ski instructor. Emily was his star pupil, who romantically dropped a glove. Paul kept it for a few days before returning it and they fell in love. He was working on his dream to sail himself around the world. The day after their wedding he sailed south and, after a short honeymoon in California, he sailed on his own to Hawaii while Emily sold her practice and then joined him there. They were a charming gentle couple delighting in each other in, as they put it, 'their golden years'.

The Bay of Islands is a wonderful cruising ground during New Zealand's mild summer. In February, I flew to West Australia to be with my parents celebrations of their 80th birthdays. Peter stayed in Opua and managed on his own: practising morse code, chipping off the sun-scorched deck paint, helping mend other boat's electrics and being entertained on other yachts.

On my return we were taken to visit Phil and Georgie Gardener at Waikare Inlet, a happy couple, who had 'seized the day' and made the life they want, where they want. They had sold their successful rose nursery, to buy 120 acres of virgin bush, to develop an experimental farm. Both are botanists and have earned the privilege of importing plants. With a government grant each year they visit Hawaii or other Pacific Islands for useful seeds and species that they think may flourish in the cooler New Zealand climate. Their valley is inaccessible by road, everything is hauled in by boat: building materials, fertilisers, food, and visitors, to the small quay they built.

They self-built their house to their own design with the help of one young man, a tractor with a grader blade, and buckets. In the corner of their wide verandah, which looks west out to the estuary, is a wooden jacuzzi tub. Most days they work twelve hours a day planting, pruning, grafting, digging and harvesting. As the sun sinks behind the far hills across the inlet, they sit and soak in their bubbling hot tub, she with a glass of brandy and green ginger, and he with a whisky and water and discuss their day's progress. We stayed overnight in the games room and helped around the farm. They showed us papaya, pears, peaches, plums, persimmon and passion fruit; loquats, lemons and tangelos; apples, oranges, grapefruit and figs; blueberries, cranberries, celery, potatoes, asparagus and tree tomatoes .

Georgie told us how they completed their water supply. After building a dam near the summit of the mountain behind the house, she had to climb up through the forest with a rope tied around her waist pulling up the black 1½"hosepipe attached to the rope, while Phil carefully unrolled it from below. When the pipe eventually reached the dam she had difficulty attaching it before it pulled her back down the hillside.

Phil had climbed Everest and as he led us on a tour up and down through their virgin forest at a fast pace, with no shoes on, we could believe it. He pointed out different fern spores; lichen, algae and fungi supporting each other. He explained that haemoglobin and chlorophyll are made up of virtually identical molecules except haemoglobin has iron, and chlorophyll has magnesium. Therefore the blood of plants is virtually the same as the blood of people. He also told an amusing story of when on Everest, after the climbers had relieved themselves behind rocks or bushes, the unworldly bearers would come to them, carefully folding the pieces of toilet paper and explaining that they had left this precious paper behind.

In March, with Lee and Tom, of MOTLEE, we rented a car for a four week tour of New Zealand's North and South islands. Sparse traffic sprinkled the roads and the scenery was magnificent. We borrowed a tent and camping gear, but actually only slept out under canvas twice. Usually we slept in cabins. All camp sites have them and they are cheap, dry and usually have two or four bunks. Clean communal stainless steel fitted kitchens, toilets and showers are provided for a cost of about $5 U.S. each per night. It gave us the opportunity to meet a varied cross-section of hikers, cyclists and caravanners from N.Z. Australia, America, Canada and Europe; mostly independent 'do it yourself' tourists.

The scenery is amazingly varied for such a small country with majestic snow covered mountain peaks, deep fiords, barely extinct volcanoes, hot sulphur springs and bubbling mud pools with steam vents and geysers. Beautiful sandy beaches and bays, untamed forests and bush and 30 million sheep grazing on green, green grass.

The hospitality and friendliness of the New Zealanders is legendary. One example was at a hot springs campsite where, outside each cabin, was a stainless steel lid opening into a natural steam oven. As we booked in the proprietress said: "Do you like trout?"

"Yes, we do."

She handed us a beautiful five pound (two and a half kilo) glistening, bright-eyed, rainbow trout.

"Have this then. Wrap it in aluminium foil and put it in a steam oven for half an hour. I'm sure you will find it delicious."

We did and it was.

The ferry-men between North and South Island were on strike so we had to fly over Marlborough Sound in a six-seater light aircraft. The view of the various peninsulars jutting out into Cook Strait was spectacular. On landing a similar hire-car wasn't available so we had to make do with an up-grade!

One particular stop on the way to Milford Sound was at Mirror Lakes and we walked a trail through cold primeval forest. The dank, dripping vegetation was a poisonous brilliant green. A few shafts of sunlight lit the moss and vines as moisture steadily dripped onto the squelching mossy path. Lichen grew like gangrenous mould on black-barked stunted trees. Subdued frogs croaked and gurgled. Small, slimy, black, leeches attached themselves to our long pants and shoes. It seemed an evil place.

What a contrast to the previous day's visit to Franz Joseph Glacier where, in strong sunlight, we had walked up the bare glacial valley for an hour and a half but appeared to get no closer to the glistening wall of ice. Eventually we saw that the white wall was mostly blue columns of ice with dirty, leaden melting crevasses slowly,

Franz Joseph glacier

The river carried down boulders of ice. We crossed that rope bridge

slowly, sliding down the valley. The air was so clear the glacier looked only yards away, but we were told it was still five miles distant on an unsafe path. Crossing a swaying suspension bridge we were able to climb down into a valley and watch the roaring milky-white river rolling boulders of ice over the rounded pebbles towards the sea.

Milford sound we took the Milford Haven boat tour and got wet

At Milford Sound we took THE boat ride on 'THE PEMBROKE'. The spectacular fiord had waterfalls crashing down, sending up plumes of mist and spume. It was particularly interesting for me, having spent most of my childhood in Milford Haven in Wales. The scenic names were all familiar - St. Anne's Lighthouse, Dale Bay, Lawrenny Peak, Cleddau River, even Pembroke Mountain. In 1820 a whaling /sealing skipper, Captain John Gronow from Milford Haven, had named them all. The weather was typically Welsh - it changed hourly from wet and windy to sunny and bright and back again. There was a two year waiting list to walk the Milford Track, the numbers allowed along it being strictly monitored.

On the way north, as we emerged into daylight from Homer's Tunnel through the mountain, and saw a sign to *'Murray Gunn's Museum and Camp Site.'* It sounded intriguing so, in the mist, we turned off the main road to follow the track to what had been the workers' cabins when the road tunnel was blasted through. Yellow wooden lapboard huts with flaking paint eventually appeared at the road side. A patient horse stood beneath a dripping porch. We entered the Museum where a pot bellied stove glowed with warmth and comfort.

"Cup of tea?" enquired a be-whiskered, check flannel-shirted old-timer.

Clutching our mugs of strong tea Murray Gunn himself showed us around the museum. Mangles, flat irons, shearing shears, branding irons, wooden buckets, butter churns, some implements only recently retrieved from daily use. Mr. Gunn still owned mines and dug for gold and rocks. A small selection of unique jewellry made from his own semi-precious stones were displayed. Peter bought me a pair of long, elegant, green ironstone earrings, quarried and fashioned by our host.

He directed us through the rain to a hut. A bedroom flanked each side of the living room with a wood stove. Dry paper, logs and matches sat ready. Soon a warm fire glowed alongside the oven and Tom lit the hurricane lamp. Nobody had visited, or cleaned the hut for a long time. We baked potatoes in the oven and fried lamb chops and onions on the fire.

Our tiny bedroom had a double bed below a small, squared, cob-webbed window. A somnolent bee buzzed against the dusty glass. It bumbled over the dead flies, legs up, on the black spotted windowsill. Lee found some small blue birds' eggs under her pillow.

It was too remote to find anywhere else to sleep. This was it for tonight. After supper we sat in front of the fire, reading and listening to the wind, than went to bed with the bugs. The rain drummed on the tin roof as we rolled our sleeping bags onto the lumpy bed and laid down fully clothed, wondering what would crawl out and over us.

The hum of flies and buzz of bees trying to escape through the closed windows, woke us. As it was still raining we abandoned our plans of walking some of the Routeburn Track and headed straight for Dunedin.

The Settlers Museum was of particular interest. Suspended on the wall was the original plan of the town drawn up in Scotland where the planners hadn't taken the hills into account. Many roads stopped at abrupt dead ends where the land rose steeply from the sheltered valley. Photographs of all the early settlers who had come ashore were up on the wall with the family trees of their descendants.

Don Peterson, a friend of a friend in USA, took us around Otago University's Medical School's Anatomy and Neurological Dept. Don was researching how nerve ends communicate for his Ph.D. We listened with rapt attention.

In another museum while following a school group around, I heard their guide say "of course the Polynesians who came in their canoes to The Land of the Long White Cloud, had a very difficult time. Why?"

The confident children called out: "It's colder than Tahiti and Hawaii?"

"They were homesick and couldn't sail back against the wind?"

"They had to find different food to eat?"

In an awed voice their teacher said. "Yes, all those things, but the worst thing was, there were no coconuts. In their old islands, the coconut palms provided their food and drink, their houses, clothes, dishes, cups, spoons and forks. Quickly they had to find substitutes for all their needs."

After our year in the islands, I could relate to that. The Islanders still depended on coconut palms for all their basic needs. The Maoris must have been strong and intelligent pioneers to learn a completely new way of living and source of essentials.

Over the Southern Alps we explored old gold fields, glaciers, tramped some Walks, climbed The Remarkables for a breathtaking view across to Queenstown.

The wizard and his silent heckler

Attended a performance of the Royal New Zealand Ballet in Wellington, and while staying with my Aunt and Uncle in Christchurch, went to Cathedral Square at lunch time to listen to "The Wizard" expound from his stepladder. (He is an outspoken University Lecturer, a political 'devil's advocate' who offers outrageous opinions to cause thought and discussion.) He succeeds, in spite of an elderly gentleman distracting the audience by standing nearby quietly calling down the pigeons and seagulls to swoop and take their lunch from his hand.

At Hawkes Bay we found a friend in deep depression in his vineyard. Because of predicted over-production, the Government had ordered him to grub up his fine vines, now dripping with a good harvest of grapes. It was such a waste. Although he would be compensated for the lost crop, it seemed criminal to be destroying good food and the years of stock improvement. We later heard on the radio that a major Californian vintner came to New Zealand, looking for white grapes to supplement his not-so-good harvest, only to find all their excess had been destroyed the previous week.

We visited Art Galleries and Museums, Maori exhibits and dancing, even a performing sheep display at the Agradome where 19 varieties of sheep were shown and blue-eyed sheep dogs raced across their backs in the paddock.

The Waitomo Caves were breathtaking. The boat we sat in was silently pulled along in the dark beneath a tunnel of stars which were actually glow worms, millions of glow worms.

New Zealanders are articulate, kind and friendly. Everybody had an opinion on both local and international affairs and could justify them coherently. They are convinced that there should be a nuclear free zone and they are in the best place to promote it. Having a population of only three million (less than Birmingham) it is amazing how influential their voice has been.

The food was excellent, super meat and vegetables, fruit and dairy products. The home dinners to which we were invited were totally superior to mine - Claire's Chateaubriand, Glen's 'Fillet de Boeuf en Croute' and the seafood crepes were perfect. The Restaurants we were recommended to visit were all good and inexpensive, especially the ones with "B.Y.O.B." displayed - (bring your own bottle).

April '86 saw CLYPEUS hauled out for a major five week refit at Deemings Yard in Opua. We had invited my nephew from Christchurch to come sailing with us during his University break. However, Deemings kept putting our haul-out date back, and by the time Keiron arrived we were still up on the hard with much work to do. He lent a hand but we felt very guilty that his sailing holiday turned into an unpaid working vacation. We tried to encourage him to go tramping around the lovely hills and bays, but that wasn't what he had set out to do. Inviting guests to a yacht is always hazardous, arrival dates and times are dependent on wind and weather, and on land you are at the mercy of the boatyard.

Cleaning the hull ready for the professionals

The boat work was well done by the craftsmen who were used to small boat care and maintenance. The motor mechanic Lee and his charming wife Philippa, took me on holiday with them to visit old friends. I felt privileged to be welcomed into homes as a friend rather than a tourist. The New Zealanders don't stand on ceremony, if you have a sleeping bag and there is room on the floor, please stay. Their hospitality was overwhelming and I enjoyed staying on a hill sheep farm and on a deer farm as well as with city friends.

The only sad memory was that on returning from our tour, WANDERER V was in Auckland whilst the legendary Eric attended hospital for radio therapy. The prognosis was not good and he never did return to Opua. I later received a hand written note from Susan (she must have answered thousands) telling of those last weeks and saying that Eric spent his last days on board WANDERER V where he wanted to be. I hope I can be as good and supportive a wife as she was throughout their long married life.

The refit was well done by craftsmen used to working on small boats

Samoa

CHAPTER SEVENTEEN

April in New Zealand was getting cold. Bitter southerly winds blew up from Antarctica. It was time to move north into the sunshine again. Some of our guilt at not being in England to share the national sorrows of Libyan reprisals and Chernobyl nuclear fallout, was ameliorated by the rotten, rough, wet voyage back to Tonga. On arrival in Nuku'alofa, no customs or immigration officials could be found.

The rugby test match . College students in white with mats around the waists

"They're all at the Rugby Test Match," called out Greg on NANNOOK, an Australian yacht anchored nearby. "It won't matter if you go ashore. Come with us. It's Tonga versus Wales." Greg and Ann, both teachers, with their three children were taking a sabbatical year to cruise the South Pacific.

The match had already started, Wales in their familiar red jerseys played fast and furiously but were being hammered into the ground, literally, by the huge Tongan's. Wales won the game, but Tonga won the fight. Three Welshmen finished up in hospital.

Apart from that, it was lovely to be in quiet, melodious Tonga again. We re-visited our friends on Lofanga and took them clothes, and paper and pencils for the school. They welcomed us enthusiastically preparing feasts and inviting us into their homes. The Tongas have no furniture just woven mats to sit and sleep on. Shoes are left outside. They cook in thatched outhouses with an open fire and umu earth oven. It is the responsibility of the older women to keep embers of a coconut husk fire always alight for the rest of the village to come and light their torches.

Moses, an earnest friend of last year, invited us to a feast. Laid out beneath a fabric canopy in his garden was a long banana leaf, with coconut fronds spread on either side for our seats. The meal consisted of a glistening brown, spit-roasted, suckling pig (nice crisp skin, a thick layer of jelly fat, then delicious tender pork), together with fish, yams, breadfruit and dried octopus in coconut milk, all wrapped in taro leaves and baked in the umu. The suckling pig took pride of place in the centre with a banana in his mouth surrounded by little parcels of leaf-wrapped food decorated with frangipani and hibiscus blossoms. The family pierced and handed us young green drinking coconuts.

They only had one knife

We sat cross-legged and ate with our fingers (they only had one knife) whilst the family sat nearby and watched. Moses made a speech of welcome and said prayers (in Tongan). William, the school teacher, stood and spoke in English. Then Peter stood saying we were honoured to be welcomed back so generously. Then Greg made a speech. The family, who had spent all day preparing the feast, still hadn't had a bite. After we had eaten as much as we could, we moved to sit on a mat and watched as they fell upon the food and demolished the remains. When the banana leaf table was empty the family rose and the dogs, pigs and chickens moved in. Nothing was wasted.

There was however an underlying reason for the generosity of Moses and his family. He later asked if Greg could sponsor his eldest son to attend school in Australia. Greg did his best to explain the difficulties and promised to correspond further.

During our first visit I had made friends with Louise, a pleasant woman of thirty or so. She attended courses on the main island in First Aid, contraception and maternity care, and was the only person with any medical training on the island. For this return visit I had brought good second hand clothes for the older, larger women, which I gave her to distribute, as well as clothes for the children. The older women had been very shy when we came before, partly because they often wore little more than a tatty mat around their waists.

Loiuse and her father showed a touching tenderness to each other

Louise was pleased with copies of the general photos we had taken last year. Later she approached me nervously to ask if I would come the next day and take photographs of her father and herself as he wouldn't live much longer. Father lived on his own in a little hut near Louise. It had no windows, was dark and hardly large enough for him to lie down. Since his wife had died he spent his days sitting on his mat contemplating nature - no work, no books, no radio. When I arrived he was dressed in a clean lava lava, shirt, tie and best brown jacket. He and Louise posed for photographs and showed a touching tenderness towards each other. Father's illness wasn't obvious and I got the impression that he had decided it was time to go and would just sit and wait for his final breath. I would have liked to find out more but it was a subject not easily broached.

Nobody else had been to Lofanga since our visit last November. We re-visited the school where the top classes sang and danced for us again. Greg and Ann's children came with us. Thirteen year old Paul took his saxophone to show and play. It was the first musical instrument the children had seen and they were fascinated. Paul, Joanna and Lia were equally fascinated by the fact that the students sang so well and in harmony never having seen a piano, violin, a film, car, or a television set. The teacher of the top class of ten and eleven year-olds, William, had a very positive outlook and the children proudly sang happy songs of their country and their King who studied at Oxford, and also a song in preparation for their impending school-life on another larger island. To the tune of *"It's a long way to Tipperary"* they sang:

"It's a long way from here to my school
It's a long way to go,
It's a long way from here to my school
Where the children play and sing.
Goodbye my little sister
I will be with you soon
It's a long way from here to my school
But I will be there."

The boys scoured the beach for our supper

William and Moses decided to teach us how to cook in an umu -we may need the skill in an emergency. On the beach at the appointed time we found Moses had been fishing for our supper for eight hours and had only caught one fish. Some ladies scouring the beach for their meal kindly gave us an octopus to supplement the menu.

A hole was dug and filled with coconut husks which were lit with a burning stick from the village. When going well, William laid large stones on top. The girls taught us how to grate coconut by sitting on a special stool with a sharp metal grater on the end. We were shown how to prepare the food, smearing it with coconut cream and wrapping it up in palm, taro or banana leaves. William peeled ripe, yellowing, papayas, cut them into chunks covered them in cream and

Moses and William decided to teach us to cook in An Unu. Some ladies gave us an octopus to cook

made them into parcels with banana leaves. Everything was laid on the hot stones then covered with more banana leaves, palm fronds and topped off with dry sand.

During the two hours of cooking the girls taught Tongan dances. Moses kept busy grating unripe papayas and mixing them with lime juice for our green vegetable. We sat eating under the stars, contemplating our yachts floating silently in the moon's silvery path and enjoyed the delicious feast made from natural ingredients. Nothing was wasted, the dogs came and licked up any remains.

Next day we sadly parted company with the islanders and Nanook as they headed back towards Australia and we continued northward. Anchored off another Tongan island a young fisherman came by in his canoe to chat. Offa was intrigued with Peter's Hawaiian spear - a barbed spear with an elastic thong that stretched to add force to the thrust. Offa suggested he tried it out to catch us some fish and to give me some hints. Donning mask and fins I enjoyed a wonderful couple of hours' snorkelling, watching how he hid behind coral heads underwater until a fish swam nearby. He efficiently speared many fish. I followed behind him with the line threaded through their gills and mouths. At last, water-logged, it was time to climb out. Offa indicated a suitable level place on the reef. The next surge deposited us gently on the coral and I waddled shorewards. My fins were getting in the way so I sat down with my back to the sea to take them off.

Suddenly a shout, and a roar of water as a three foot white wall of foam hit me and rolled me over and over on the sharp coral. As I tumbled, I can remember thinking 'Oh dear! I have known all my life not to sit with my back to the sea. It isn't hurting that much, perhaps I'll be all right.' But then, horror, the king wave was receding and I was being sucked down a crevasse and under the coral shelf. I grabbed the sharp coral around the edge of the chasm, but my fingers couldn't hold against the weight of water flowing out. I was about to give up and accept death, when strong hands were thrust under my armpits. Offa had run back and managed to hold me as the torrent swept back down under the coral until the next surge lifted me again. He hauled me out dripping blood and shreds of bathing costume. He supported me back to the beach near CLYPEUS and shouted.

Peter nearly had a fit as he looked at us through the binoculars, jumped into the dinghy and rowed to us. Offa was apologetic, I was in shock. Peter called on the VHF and a nurse on one of the other yachts came and washed out my cuts and grazes with hydrogen-peroxide, broke up anti-biotic capsules and sprinkled the powder on the worst places, bandaged me lightly and told me to stay in bed. There were no major wounds but every day for a week Susan came and scrubbed the painful lesions and sprinkled antibiotic powder into them. I was very lucky. No cuts turned septic in spite of the staphylococcal bacteria in the tropical warm water. With rest and no swimming most of the scars gradually faded. Shamefacedly I continuously scolded myself for stupidly worrying about sharks and all the new dangers, while forgetting the danger of the seventh king wave of which I had been aware and cautious about all my life.

The scars gradually faded. But I'd never wear that costume again

We continued north to Niuatoputapu, the

most northerly of the Tongan Islands and at dusk, couldn't see the entrance to the pass in a harsh rain squall. After a rough and worrying night, the blue lagoon was unbelievably calm.

On the seven-mile long, flat island, a five mile track allowed one car, two trucks and a tractor to ply between the three villages. There were a few wooden houses but most homes were earth-floored coconut-leaf plaited huts with thatched roofs and just mats and mosquitoes inside. There was no electricity so a coconut-husk fire was kept alight in each kitchen area. Once again we were invited to eat in homes, to a kava ceremony and also to a wedding. (Our gifts of sugar, biscuits, canned meat or fish, etc. and sent-back colour photographs were always graciously accepted.)

At the kava party we sat cross-legged (it is impolite to stretch your legs out in

A bridesmaid finishes off her dress for tomorrow's wedding

front of you) in a circle whilst a young man smashed dried kava root between two rocks until powdered (in olden days the women chewed it and then spat it into a bowl). He mixed it with water in a large carved wooden bowl and with elaborate gestures stirred it with his hands. Then he mulched the grey watery mixture through his fingers and strained it by twisting the liquid through coconut fibres. The Chief called the name of the senior guest who had to clap twice, accept with both hands the coconut shell full of kava and drink it in one go. The shell was handed back to the Chief for refilling for the next-named guest. The slightly narcotic kava, which looks and tastes like dirty washing-up water, made our lips and tongue tingle and had a peppery flavour. By the third ceremony I was actually acquiring a taste for it. A guitarist and choir sat outside on the ground singing softly for our entertainment.

The Tongan government does not discourage kava drinking. It is considered less anti-social than beer and spirits as the ritual means that nobody drinks quickly or alone. Kava also makes the drinker sleepy rather than aggressive.

Our party host invited us to the wedding of his sister. It was a grand affair. First we assembled at the bride's home where she was emotionally saying goodbye to her family. Through her tears, the beautiful young bride told us she would now have to live away from her village. (Her new home was only a mile down the road.) Her wedding dress was a finely woven mat wrapped around her body from her armpits to her knees and she had a new pair of thongs on her feet. Her brown skin glistened with

The bride and groom in theit mat wedding-suits which denote their wealth and social position

coconut oil and her smooth hair smelled of fresh frangipani blossom. Her handsome, but formidably muscled husband also wore a mat, short-sleeved white shirt and leather sandals. He sported a shock of curly black hair.

The church ceremony seemed similar to an Anglican Christian service, but of course spoken in Tongan. Then the grand feast: lobsters, suckling pigs, crabs, fish, prawns, vegetables and fruit. Peter was made guest of honour and placed next to the bride. Speeches and prayers went on during the whole meal.

It was explained that the two young bridesmaids had been chosen because their father had been lost at sea a few years ago, along with a dozen other island men who had canoed to the main island to see a rugby match. Coming home a storm had risen and they were never seen again. A quarter of the male population was lost. It was thought that the canoe had probably been blown off course and they had missed their island in the vast Pacific Ocean and couldn't get back against the wind. They carry no navigational instruments but rely on the stars and traditional signs.

In 1986 the Trade Winds were very fickle and brought many storms. It was hard work sailing to Pago Pago on American Samoa as we tacked through bullying seas. Twice we gave up and changed course to Apia on Western Samoa but on rounding the eastern end of Upolu at dawn, the island was suddenly enveloped in a towering black thundercloud with lightning sparking and flashing out of the blackness. The wind changed again to westerly so we gave up, turned round, and in three hours retraced that 36 hours of hard sailing. Sleeping and being ill alternately, we kept the mountains of American Samoa to port and eventually at 7 p m, in the dark, made our way into Pago Pago's enormous harbour.

What a culture shock awaited us. Brick and cement two story houses, paved roads, street lights, police cars with sirens and flashing lights. Finding our way into the harbour was difficult because of the confusion of lights, which seemed ridiculous after seeing no electric lights ashore for a month.

Arriving in a metropolis after weeks of sea and simple small islands, people seemed to speak so quickly we couldn't understand them. The fast-talking operator confused Peter as he tried to telephone Customs from the kiosk on the quay.

Samoans are very large people and when the team of five Customs officers came on board dressed in their brown lava lavas with revolvers stuck in their belts, we were overwhelmed. Fourteen knees filled the cockpit as they fired questions at us and we realised how slow our responses were. Air conditioned supermarkets were full of USA foods: Pringles, ketchup, 15 kinds of coffee, 20 kinds of salad dressing, paper towels and tissues. It was such a contrast to Tonga where most of the islands still didn't have a shop, people lived off the land and sea. "

Somerset Maugham's title *"Rain"* is very appropriate for his story, set in Pago Pago. It was incredibly hot and humid. Three or four times a day the sky opened and a deluge fell as though someone was emptying an enormous bucket of water. When it stopped, steam rose from drying surfaces and it felt like being in a hot-house, with everything growing maniacally like Triffids.

Christianity is very strong on the Samoan islands. Family prayers are said morning and evening and everybody (even tourists) must keep still whilst they are going on. Relatives are buried in house gardens under elaborate tombs or headstones. It must be tricky if you decide to sell up and move on.

Americans Susan and Ted on TYCHE had spent the cyclone season working in Pago Pago and had some interesting stories for us: At the high school where Susan was teaching, the faculty were asked to choose the Graduation Queen. Their choice was turned down.

"But why?" they asked. "We think she is the most beautiful girl with poise and charm."

"Because you can't vote him as the Beauty Queen." was the reply. The American teachers had no idea that many of the young girls were actually boys, designated from birth to be girls by their families if there were not enough females to do the chores.

Once we knew this, we saw many instances of men, dressed in blouses and lava

A 'Fatufeene' crossing the road in Apia

lavas, doing the washing or cradling babies in their arms. At a night club one evening, a party of ladies were celebrating a 50th birthday. It was a very friendly occasion and slices of birthday cake were passed to us. Some of the celebrating guests performed dances and sang on stage with the band and they did have rather chunky calves and large feet, but Samoans are big people and we thought no more about it. However as we were leaving, after an exceptionally happy evening, an expatriate whispered in our ears "They're all men you know."

No, we didn't know, but had admiration for the 'ladies' with the way they had coped with the gender forced upon them. We would like to know more details of the hows and whys, but have never managed to find out. The 'ladies' are known as 'fatufeenees'.

Large American purse seiner fishing boats were for sale tied against the quay; beautiful modern ships, like millionaire's yachts, complete with helicopter and landing pad. Seven had been operating out of Pago Pago but now three boats were laid up as their owners are in receivership. A watchman showed us over one of the splendid vessels which had proved so efficient that they had fished out the W. Pacific. We saw virtually no ocean life in this area.

The Sir Walter Raleigh from Hull - A charity funded ship researching and helping in the islands

We were very cautious about anchoring in bays around Samoa as we didn't know the procedures. First, one needs official permission, and then each Matai (chief) demands payment - anything up to $30 or $40 U.S. and gifts of kava root, so we were wary. Friendly expats told us that in the early 80's the U.S. poured $80,000,000 a year to 30,000 people to make sure the strategically well placed harbour would be available to the U.S. Navy. However very little of the money reached the people or projects for which it was donated. The Matai retain a feudal system. They collect all wages and then redistribute it around the village as they think fit. The ordinary Samoan has no redress and no bargaining power against the Matai, so there is little incentive to get promoted, or even work at all.

Many men had extensive traditional patterned tattooing from the knees up. They looked as though they were wearing tight cycling shorts beneath their lava lavas. The higher up their torso the tattooing extended, the higher their place in the social hierarchy.

Western Samoans lived a quieter and more rural life, although many worked in the tuna canning factories in American Samoa. Their green undulating land had a quiet charm, not as dramatic as American Samoa. The houses (fales) were thatched with round ends (so that devils can't hide in the corners) their plaited palm frond walls roll up during the day for sea breezes to waft through. Whitewashed stones surrounded immaculate gardens and an aura of park land pervaded.

Men had extensive tattooing - the higher it rose up the body, the higher their social position

In the Marquesa Islands we had met a Columbian millionaire (so he said) who had a romantic looking wooden 70' schooner. At various ports across the Pacific we had met and he enjoyed talking to Peter. Here Peter learned a little of the problems of blue water voyaging in a large yacht. In the mens' concrete ablution block close to the anchorage in Apia, the millionaire confessed how lonely he was. How he had to sleep with a gun under his pillow because he didn't trust his Colombian crew. His dynamic wife told me how she wasn't even allowed to go to the fridge and get herself a snack because the cook complained. Always there was the problem of maintenance, seamanship, and cleaning not being done properly. It made us realise how lucky we are to have the health, and competence to sail our own small boat without any crew.

The climb up to the grave of Robert Louis Stevenson was long and hot, and once we had left the shade of his pale grey house with its wide verandahs behind, the path was slippery with red mud. Flies bothered us. They bit our arms and legs and buzzed about our heads. The oppressive sweet smell of decaying vegetation hung thick on the air. At last the tangle of bushes rustled in the wind and our heads felt the cool sea breeze. On a small clearing on the hilltop stood the grey stone tomb looking down to the sea. The air was fresh and cool as we read the engraved stone:

> *'Under the wide and starry sky*
> *Dig the grave and let me lie*
> *Glad did I live and gladly die,*
> *And I laid me down with a will.*
> *This is the verse that you grave for me:*
> *'Here he lies where he longed to be;*
> *Home is the sailor, home from the sea.*
> *And the hunter home from the hill.'*

R.L.S.

CHAPTER EIGHTEEN

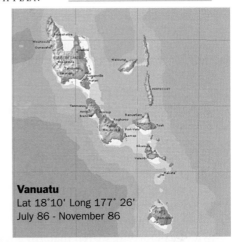

Vanuatu
Lat 18°10' Long 177° 26'
July 86 - November 86

Wallis lagoon finding our way between coral heads

At the South Pacific Arts Festival in Tahiti I had admired the dance team from Wallis and Futuna Islands. "Please can we go?" I asked Peter. "No reason why not," was the reply.

In Wallis lagoon, the water was so clear it was uncanny diving from the boat. It required courage as there appeared to be nothing between me and the sand thirty feet below. The French do appear to have acquired the most beautiful Pacific islands. Wallis radiated a greenness that sparkled from the varnished fronds of palm trees down to the tangle of bush. Flowering vines spread out onto the sand. The whole world - land, sky and shimmering sea, looked so fresh and new that it brought to mind Genesis, when after the Sixth Day, God looked at His creation and saw that "it was good".

The local gendarme, Pierre, and his wife Monique, befriended us and drove us round the well-cultivated island and took us to a motu for a picnic in their motor boat. The locals were tall, good-looking Polynesians, who walked with dignity. Their greeting was a pleasant and friendly: "B'jour M'ssieur, M'dam".

Pretty little round-ended fales, one room, with only mats, pillows and no furniture, were surrounded b green and red-leafed hedges. Pigs snuffled along the beach and on the reef at low tide. They catch and eat crabs to supplement their diet of coconut.

Monique said that the last humans were eaten only 45 years ago. Not a white man, but a brave warrior killed in inter-tribal warfare - they hoped to ingest his courage as well as his protein. However, the French Procurateur of the island told us how, at a local party, he had gone to the freezer for more ice and been shocked to see a human hand protruding from under the frozen butter and fish. He didn't investigate or talk of his discovery. Pierre told us that if there was an important football game or a particularly good programme on TV, he would bring the prisoners into his home to watch and then lock them up again afterwards.

A celebration Mass was being held in the crowded cathedral, each pillar covered with a colourfully woven mat. An abundance of flowers filled the area and everyone wore traditional dress of grass skirts, sarongs or lava lavas. The French authorities invited us to a Palace annexe to join them for breakfast. It consisted of warm roast pig, baked fish, taro and bananas.

A complicated kava ceremony followed on the lawn in front of the royal residence with the King and French dignitaries being honoured in order of

Note huge pig

precedence. Forty huge half-roasted pigs rested on piles of yams and taro awaiting distribution; the two largest going to the King. Wearing flowers and grass skirts four groups performed sitting-dances of hand and head gestures. One row stood behind doing the same gestures but moving their feet and hips a little. It made Tongan dancing and singing seem very sophisticated, imaginative and precise, and Tahitian dancing   positively indecent!

A Regatta followed the feast. The traditional Wallis single-outrigger canoe is the same at both ends. Fast, but the mast has to be taken down and refitted at the other end to change tack.

We had to tear ourselves away from this paradise as we wanted to be in Fiji in time for the Fun Race to Vanuatu.

Suva is a sunny city, with parks and gardens left from British Colonial days. More than half the population are Indian, originally brought over to help in the sugar and banana plantations. Our first meal ashore was in a restaurant where no cutlery was provided. Kneading the rice into a ball with my right hand and then dipping it into the curries and sauces was messy, but we improved with practice. Here we picked up our new ham radio receiver.

New Zealand friends had given us gifts to deliver to Ono in the Astrolabe Archipelago. We anchored in the wrong place but a local man took us home to meet his wife before guiding us to the correct bay. She welcomed me inside. It was a revelation, much more comfortable than imagined. In Ono village, grass thatched huts surrounded the ruins of their concrete church which, together with the school,

Traditional Wallis out-rigger canoes raced. Masts had to be removed to tack

Happy family outside their thatched home

Inside was a relevation very comfortable

had been destroyed in the previous season's cyclone. Now, each Sunday afternoon, a parent couple walked the children seven miles to another school with dormitories. The couple cooked and cared for them until it was time to walk home on Friday afternoon. The next week another pair of parents, took on the duty.

Then we hastily made for Musket Cove on the island of Malolo Lai Lai, a short distance from Nadi (Nandi) Airport to join in the Fiji to Vanuatu Fun Regatta.

In 1860 Musket Cove was bought for one musket from the native people. Australian entrepreneur, Dick Smith, had established a resort and yacht club for which the life-membership fee is one dollar. Yacht's names are carved into the wooden beam above the bar as a permanent record of membership. Musket Cove and Vanuatu Cruising Yacht Club, organise the Regatta. Fixed radio schedules on VHF, SSB and Ham bands provided us with our first caring cocoon for 540 miles of our 50,000 mile voyage.

Forty yachts filled the lagoon when we arrived. It was the Rules of the Race that

Panorama of ......

had attracted us. They included:

1. Penalties for superior yachts with a rating certificate or rod rigging, bloopers, bow thrusters, etc
2. Matching oilskins, Sperry topsider yachting shoes, sails less than four years old, or trouble-free refrigeration.
3. Handicap allowances would be given to yachts carrying children, pot plants, a washing machine or photo-copied charts.
4   Each yacht should be floating at least 6" below her waterline. The use of engines was definitely encouraged.
5. Prizes for everybody: oldest skipper, youngest crew, biggest fish, first and last boat across the line.

Our effort was 'Musket Cove's' entry for the America's Cup

During Regatta week competition was fierce in rowing, outboard dinghy, board-sailing and swimming races, and on land, a children's Olympics. We raced on a sleek 14m New Zealand sloop "A PLACE IN THE SUN".

It was good to be at the front of the fleet for a change. CLYPEUS is no racing machine, especially with five years of cruising gear on board; we hoped we wouldn't be left too far behind.

A highlight was the live figurehead competition. The winner, AMUONA, suspended his stoic Australian wife bare-breasted from the bowsprit, while above Captain Bligh roared "Ah ha! My proud beauty" and

.........*Musket cove lagoon*

prodded her with his whip. A tomato-sauced Mr. Christian suffered, tied to the mast. Our effort was 'Musket Cove's entry for the America's Cup' The boat was festooned with Fiji Bitter beer boxes and a laundry basket, covered in foil to look like the Cup, on the bow. The 'Pig Feast' on Saturday night completed a fun week with dancing on the beach.

Feverish preparations ensued on Sunday morning for the midday start. Customs and immigration officials were flown from Nadi Airport. We were the only British boat.

Once beyond the reef the wind picked up and a fine sailing breeze kept us all moving fast for four hours when the lead boats disappeared beyond the horizon. After a rough night the wind died and the seas stayed lumpy. From then on, it was light winds, calmer seas and much motoring. The sun shone. The blue Pacific lived up to its name. Porpoise played around our bow. We sighted a whale and caught a 50" Mahi Mahi landed it, measured, photographed, cleaned and filleted it. Bottled some, pickled some, and as we have no refrigerator, ate a lot.

The ham radio added a new dimension as we joined the radio skeds to give our position and hear how others were faring. By Wednesday afternoon the first boats arrived at Port Vila. We were still 170 miles out with no wind, so motored all night and most of the next day and night. We crossed the finish line at 0602 on Saturday morning, 22nd out of 32 yachts. Club officers, in their launch, welcomed us with a gift carton of fresh French bread, wine, beer, pate and ham. Customs and Immigration came out to clear us and take our shotgun. We anchored in front of the Waterfront Restaurant to shouts of "What kept you?" and "We've drunk all the cold beer."

The President of Vanuatu awarded the prizes that evening. Our prize, donated by the Bank of Hong Kong, was a three-tiered black lacquer box - perfect for storing my prized cowrie shells. It bore a plaque for 'The yacht that had sailed the greatest distance to join the race".

The following week of parties ended with a race to Havannah Harbour; where the entire American Pacific Fleet anchored in World War II. After a barbeque on the beach and al fresco breakfast, a lady helms-persons race back to Port Vila, completed the festivities. It was a cruiser's dream come true.

Sailing to the outer islands was like going through a time warp back to the Stone Age. The best gifts we could give were empty, glass screw-top jars. The islanders have no way of keeping ants and bugs out of their food. Plastic bags were another 'miracle' in which they could hang food on a branch away from ground animals.

One Sunday, three canoes landed in our lonely anchorage by a remote island. The women wore mumus, and the only man, grey slacks with a white short sleeved shirt.

"Are you going to Church?" I called. "Can I come with you?"

They nodded. They spoke little English but as we walked through the jungle for a couple of miles, I learned they were Presbyterians from Awok, making their once-a-month visit to hold a communion service in a remote village. Emerging on a wide beach we followed the shore-line into the jungle again and eventually arrived at a small village where the sound of moaning and keening filled the air. A villager came to meet us and told that a young mother had died and they were mourning her on the beach.

"Did I want to come with the ladies?" I declined feeling it would be an intrusion and sat on a bench beside a hut playing with young children until my 'family' returned. I've since regretted not seizing the opportunity to witness the rituals.

It seemed that life expectancy is only 40 years, particularly for women who may have given birth to ten piccaninnies in a grass hut with no medicine or doctor. On some islands where Missionaries lived, the people are better educated and can radio for a helicopter. However, this particular village had no phone, radio or road, it would take a three mile run through the jungle and a five mile canoe paddle to reach a telephone. Since independence in 1981 the Vanuatuans have thrown out most of the English and French, so the medical care is going to become worse before it gets better. It was sobering to be with a crowd of friendly women chatting and exchanging gifts to realise most of them will have died of natural causes before they reach my age.

After Church I was invited to help make the communal meal of lap lap, and sat on a mat with the women grating green bananas with the edge of a serrated cockle shell. We mixed the brown pulp with tapioca and coconut milk on wide banana leaves, then patted it all into a four-foot-wide flat pancake. Pieces of raw octopus and fish were carefully placed on top, then more banana leaves to cover the mixture. Flat stones, heated by a fire of coconut husks, were lifted between split bamboo rods and carefully placed to receive the flat cake. They had no metal pots.

We sang familiar hymns while we worked, and while the meal was cooking, danced. They learned "Halikidumpty" a Scots reel from The Mull of Kintyre and said there were going to dance it for their Christmas party. Vanuatu custom dancing is mostly stamping, chanting, banging spears on the ground and raising clouds of dust. The women didn't have any dances or songs to teach me as the men are in charge of dancing, and it wasn't really allowed on Sundays anyway.

Time for lunch. We sat on the earth floor around the slab of lap lap in semi darkness, as their huts have no windows, just gaps in the bamboo walls to let the breeze through. They un-wrapped the thick and heavy solidified jelly, with lumps of chewy octopus in it and demonstrated how to tear pieces off with my fingers and feed it into my mouth. With no salt, pepper or spices, it was bland and boring, but not really unpleasant and probably very nutritious.

"Is this a meal for a special occasion or do you have it every day?" I asked.

"Every day " was the cheerful reply.

"Mmmm Lovely!" was my answer, but thought 'Peter wouldn't have enjoyed this.' He really doesn't like having to make suitable conversation and eat unfamiliar, bland food.

We sailed on north, between islands covered with coconut palm plantations. Those in good order had line upon line of tall trees, each with a shiny tin collar to stop rats climbing to the coconuts, with tidy trim lawns beneath. Pyramids of coconuts waited in the shade ready to be processed. Other plantations looked abandoned and unkempt with straggly palms poking above tangled bushes, broken fronds and brown coconuts scattered untidily across clearings. We met a young Australian planter who had bought a rundown plantation. There were many wild cattle on the estate, so many, he was able to sell the surplus bulls for more than he paid for the plantation.

100,000 American soldiers were stationed at Luganville on Esperito Santo during WWII. Then there were seven telephone exchanges. Now it's a ghost town with wide deserted streets. A few Chinese shops were open. All stocked up to the ceilings with knives, nails, hinges, T shirts, thongs, onions, machetes, and fish hooks, but as all the shops stocked the same items and there was no-one to sell them to, it was difficult to see how they made a living. A little brown man without shoes, wearing nothing but a penis sheath, held high in place by a thong around his waist and between his buttocks, walked nonchalantly on the other side of the road.

Million Dollar Point, is worth mentioning. At the end of the war when the Americans moved out, they tried to sell their equipment to the English or French but nobody could agree on price, so the Yanks bulldozed all the new equipment over the cliff into the sea. Now it's a divers' paradise as they swim between mountains of 1947 unused trucks, graders, jeeps and cranes all piled high under the water. There's also a sunken American warship nearby and many yachts gave pride of place to original Coca Cola bottles and souvenirs they had recovered from the deep.

'God works in mysterious ways': On Uripiv Island we happened to go ashore on a Sunday and, at a loss for a gift to take, took a spare paperback modern New Testament we had been given in the USA. A crowd of small boys awaited. Two were blonde, the oldest of whom, who was probably five, insisted I followed them through the coconut palms to their home to meet his Daddy. Ross and Elizabeth, a young New Zealand couple, were living in a bamboo hut with their three small boys. Ross was translating the New Testament from the original Greek into Uripiv language, working with the village elders who were using the English King James version. They had reached an impasse in translation and needed further input. A modern language New Testament was exactly what they needed!

Ross typed on a Sharp 5000 word processor that ran off one solar panel. He and Elizabeth were the only white people on the island. The doors of their small thatched home were left open. Local children wandered in and out, squatted in front of the toy box and played for a while with a plastic car or truck, but as they had never seen the real thing, it didn't hold their attention for long. I was particularly impressed with Elizabeth's gentle and patient mien, keeping her family well fed and happy under such primitive conditions

On our way to New Caledonia we tried to visit volcanic Tanna Island to climb Mount Yasur to look down into the hot, red, bubbling, molten inside of the active crater. After two days and nights of slamming into wind and waves we gave up, but our friends continued and said it was well worth the effort.

Instead we headed off downwind to the beautiful white-sanded, lapis lazuli coloured waters around the island of Uvea. There were so many pretty white shells on the beach you could shovel them up. Administered by France, it resembled French Polynesia. Attractive young people with flowers in their hair sang as they swam in the lagoon. Actually, they were happily stoned out of their minds; they had flown from Noumea for a local wedding and hadn't finished partying.

Strolling along the beach I met two English girls: Polly and Mary from Greenwich. I remarked on how many fish there were in the lagoon.

"Yes," said cockney Polly, "every time I go swimming my knickers fill up with bloody fish."

During the night, on the way to New Caledonia we were frightened out of our wits. It was a particularly dark night and at the helm I called to sleeping Peter that there was an unidentified light approaching. He came, looked, said "It's a planet," and went back to bed.

A few minutes later I called back "Your planet has got red and green moons around it, and is approaching fast."

He came up and agreed. "I'll call on VHF to find out who it is," and went below.

The lights came closer; I turned to the left full throttle; the lights followed. I turned to the right, the lights followed. Who was it? Pirates? Kanak revolutionaries who were opposing the French in New Caledonia? Gun runners? Drug dealers? Whoever it was, what did they want with us? If it was French Coast Guard why didn't they identify themselves on the radio? I concentrated on weaving our course ahead. Thinking 'don't panic, don't panic,' but where was our gun? Where were the bullets? What could we do if attacked?

Worried Peter came into the cockpit. "They don't answer. Keep weaving," while I attach our search light."

He blazed our 'million candle power lamp' at the approaching vessel and we saw the high grey sides of a destroyer with white numbers on the bow. As he was just saying in a relieved voice, "it's OK. It's the French Navy" so they turned on their 20 million candle search light and almost burnt us out of the water it was so bright. We heard our radio crackle and a French voice say

"Yacht CLYPEEUS, Yacht CLYPEEUS, zis is ze French Navy. Where are you headed?"

Peter went down and answered "French Navy this is British Yacht CLYPEUS on course to book into Noumea. Why didn't you answer our identification call, you frightened us."

"Sorry, but we 'ad to find someone who spoke Eenglish. Continue to Noumea. Bon chance."

"Merci, bon nuit."

The powerful vessel roared away and we had a whisky each to calm our nerves.

Noumea is a fine Riviera-type city, sophisticated, with beautiful harbours and beaches, backed by high red mountains of nickel and iron ore. Baguettes, butter, pate and plonk, were readily available, as in all French dependencies.

We attended a rodeo up in the mountain organised by Noumea Junior Chamber of Commerce. It probably sounds racist, but I don't mean it to be, it was just such a surprise that all the handsome young Jaycee volunteers manning the stalls and barbecues, were black-skinned Noumeans speaking French. The Rodeo ground had fine newly erected, fresh smelling, wooden stockyards and corrals. The event was between three Australian cowboys versus the local Kanak stockmen. They all tried very hard to entertain and raced around yelling and lassooing, but the cattle were just not interested. It was too hot. It took more effort to get the cows and bulls running, than to catch them and tie them up.

Here, the ladies danced traditional dances, mainly stamping and chanting to complex rhythms. We felt, if they continued, they could easily work themselves into a trance. Some of the yachts' people who sailed to volcanic Tanna did get caught up in a traditional sacrificial pig ceremony. They were escorted to a central tree to watch the celebrations. Hundreds of dancers around them gradually stamped and chanted themselves up into a frenzied climax and although the visitors had been told they would be safe, they were not too sure.

In retrospect they called it a wonderful experience, but at the time they felt it would have only taken one person to shout 'kill" and all would be lost. Part of the celebration was to club sixty pigs to death the following day - so the locals were already in the mood. White men are known as "long pig". They don't eat women - as we are unclean. In the Fiji Museum we had seen many relics of cannibalism, especially the three pronged forks reserved for ritual human feasts.

In Vanuatu, stories circulated of telepathy and thought transference. The Minister of Tourism told of his father, who as a youth, had been isolated for months in a cave on an uninhabited island to further his sensitivity. He could describe accurately many islands and places he had never visited. Old people can will themselves to die, and place curses on others. In one village it was still possible to buy a carved stone, take it to an old man to have a personalised curse/blessing put on it. It will then bring you good luck and keep you well, but should you lose it, you will die. We decided not to get involved and never came across anybody malicious, they were all friendly, well mannered and very shy.

From Noumea we set sail with great excitement for Australia. It seemed like a dream to actually be approaching the wide, brown land I loved .

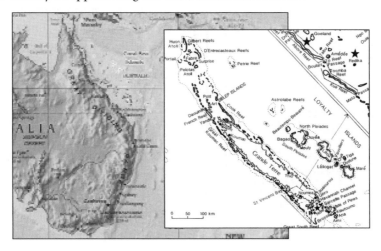

Australia
November 1986 - June 1987

CHAPTER NINETEEN

CLYPEUS jolted and jarred her way through rough lumpy seas for nine days to Australia. Huge warm waves broke into the cockpit. Peter wrote in the log: "Wheee! Going like a train!" We felt bruised and battered when we arrived in Coffs Harbour on Sunday 16th November 1986, wet, weary, and ready for a rest.

Officials told us to anchor until the doctor had been to inspect to ensure we were not infectious. He arrived in a couple of hours. While we waited, I was on a real high having reached 'the lucky country' again, but to Peter it seemed just another anchorage. I wanted to take a "We're in Australia at last" photo of him sitting on the bow enjoying a can of Fosters with Coffs Harbour in the background. He didn't want to stop reading his book. I felt like dragging him out of the cabin by the scruff of his neck. Verbally I think I did.

After a thorough inspection one friendly Customs officer kindly volunteered to take us on a quick tour of the town in his car to show us the bank, post office, launderette and supermarket. It all looked clean, bright and prosperous. He loaned us some dollars to make phone calls and buy fresh bread and milk. In the supermarket the splendid variety of fruit and foods brought tears to my eyes as I thought of the islands we had visited. The contrast was too much - what we take for granted in a Western society and what islanders actually exist on. They are not unhappy with their way of life - they have no idea this abundance exists, but I was aware of the simplicity of their diet - perhaps six fruits, six vegetables, fish, pork and occasional turtle.

A surf carnival was in progress on the beach. Healthy, strong, blonde children raced into the surf, watched by affluent families sitting under the umbrellas; dipping into Eskies full of food and drink. Polished cars parked behind the beach sparkled and twinkled. Bronzed life guard teams, wearing little cotton caps tied under their chins, furiously paddled their surf canoes, defying the surf as the bows of

A surf carnival was in progress

The surf boats rose vertically up the incoming waves

their boats rose vertically up the oncoming waves.

Back on board, the 'head' was full of wet, salt-laden clothes, so our first trip was to the launderette. As we trudged back with pillowcases full of lovely dry, folded linen, a brand new Mitsubishi Pajero four wheel drive, pulled to a stop beside us.

"Are you walking to the Marina?" enquired a cultured Australian voice.

"Yes."

"Well hop in. I'm on my way to check my boat. Where are you from?" We gave Clive a quick run down on our lives and invited him on board for coffee and a look around. After a pleasant hour, he suggested we had an evening meal with him. He would pick us up at 7 p.m. We phoned my parents in W. Australia. It was so good to hear their happy voices and let them know we were safe and would be seeing them soon. Then we phoned our children in England and USA. All was well, but my heart was torn between my far-flung family.

That evening we experienced the best kind of culture shock.

As promised, Clive picked us up and drove us to his apartment attached to the modest Motel he owned. He invited us into his dining room where, the warm glow of genuine Sheraton furniture shone beneath Georgian silver candlesticks. Serving dishes groaned under a fantastic display of lobsters, king prawns, Moreton Bay bugs, caviar and colourful salads. Mozart gentled on the sound system. Clive, a wine buff, insisted we sampled many of his best wines. With his charming lady friend we talked of sailing and our mutual love of 'the wide brown land'.

At midnight with effusive thanks we said we must go.

"Well I can't drive," he said, "and it's too far for you to walk. Take the car."

"We couldn't possibly," said Peter "I noticed it only has 4,000 miles on the clock."

"Take it, take it. Normally you could stay here but all the rooms are full."

"We..ell, if you insist."

"I insist, I insist. Have another cup of coffee."

An hour later he led us to the door. "And I don't need it tomorrow. Keep the car for another day."

"No, we will return it by nine and thank you very much." We were overwhelmed by his generosity and trust.

The engine purred into life and we slowly tootled home in the moonlight down the coast road; the sea gleaming on our left and the peaks of the Great Dividing Range rising dark and high on our right.

"It's too good a chance to miss. What about packing a thermos of coffee and our sleeping bags and sleeping in the mountains," I suggested. "We could wake up to actual bird song".

"OK,'" said Peter and we did just that. Parked in a wood on a bluff overlooking the lights of Coffs Harbour we watched the moon's glow rippling on the swell of the black Pacific Ocean. What a lot had happened since those first days out of Panama when I had voiced my fear that El Pacifico was going to swallow us up if we made a mistake. I reflected that there was still time.

We awoke to birdsong as a misty sun rose and its watery warmth filtered down through the gum trees. 'Perhaps I'll see a kangaroo or a lyre bird', I thought as I quietly opened the door and stepped down onto the dawn-damp grass. Bell birds chimed and kookaburras laughed, welcoming a perfect day. I truly felt 'my cup runneth over.'

Long lost letters were waiting for us. Royce, the postmistress was so helpful

We returned the car and strolled home to a friendly boating community in the Marina via the Post Office where a load of letters had eventually caught up with us. No more sailing this year, the rest of our journeying would be by road. CLYPEUS was hauled out in November.

Travelling by coach we visited Sydney where we had lived in the 60's. Old friends made us welcome and invited many of our old mates around for a champagne breakfast beside their swimming pool. Life seemed even more affluent now.

It took 54 hours in the bus to cover the 2,500 miles across the Nullarbor Plain to Perth to see my family and the America's Cup. Only 54 hours? It had taken us five days in 1967 when we drove across with the three children. It was our first real adventure with no paved road and three to four hundred miles between petrol stations. Each night, before camping, Peter ensured the car was facing the right direction in case the sun being on our right, rather than our left, confused us and we drove east instead of west. The bull dust track jittered and vibrated the car until we thought our teeth would fall out. A smooth bus ride was no problem.

The America's Cup was well organised as the world saw on television. As one journalist wrote 'The mating dance of the lead bottomed money gobblers'. The wall to wall blue sky stayed with us for the whole three months of our stay. A fresh afternoon wind from the sea, takes away the worst of the heat. Perth and environs are one of the brightest, cleanest, least polluted urban places to live in the world.

My sister Hilary and her husband were members of Fremantle Sailing Club where the big event was being held. They were involved in hosting and adjudicating at the marks. Pleasant days were spent anchored near the buoys scrutinising the action. The New Zealanders appeared the expert team right up until the final races when Connors got it all together at precisely the right time - clever man.

For a few years I'd had female problems. The local doctor quickly scheduled me for investigation and then immediate surgery.

The night before going into hospital Peter booked a table at THE restaurant 'where it was all happening,' to make sure we would have a table in the midst of the international crews. We were excited and arrived about 7 p.m. Not a soul was in the restaurant but we saw it was a B.Y.O. The receptionist suggested a bottle-shop nearby where we could buy our wine and expected something to be happening by the time we returned. A bottle of Wolfe Blas Yellow Label was recommended and it has become our special red wine. No people were on the streets as we returned to the restaurant which was still deserted.

This was the night the Americans had won their third successive race and won the CUP. Australia was in deep mourning. The Americans were quietly keeping in training. For the whole evening we had, what we had been assured was the 'swinging place', all to ourselves. Even the owner came and sat with us and talked for half an hour, then the chef. We had a few dances in front of the bored band, an excellent dinner and actually thoroughly enjoyed our quiet evening, although we had expected the rave up of our lives.

Next day we went to the hospital very worried about the probable cost. Peter left as the admissions clerk led me away to fill in the admittance forms. One question was: 'Who is responsible for payment?' I asked her, "Who shall I put? Me or my husband? After all, I may kick the bucket."

She said "But you're British aren't you?"

"Yes."

"And you are here on a current tourist visa?"

"Yes"

"Then with the reciprocal arrangement that visiting Australians get free treatment in England, you will receive free treatment here. Just enter your tourist visa number."

"That's great. Thank you. What a relief."

Later I phoned Peter. "It's all right about payment, they only asked for my visa number."

"What! They took your Barclaycard Visa Number?" he asked in horror.

"No, no, only my tourist visa number."

"Phew! That's good news. Everything OK?"

"Yes," I replied everything is wonderful. Everybody's so friendly, even the doctors call me Shirley. It's all very informal. They seem to be my friends already and give the impression they will do their best for me." A welcome contrast to the more formal reception we are used to in British hospitals.

After six weeks' rest, we carried our first computer back to CLYPEUS - a Compaq portable, almost as big as a medium-sized suitcase. My articles, with Peter's photographs, had been published, so we felt justified in the investment. It was a good decision of Peter's as it enabled us to become computer literate and rejoin the workforce later.

Back in Coffs Harbour as we prepared CLYPEUS for sea, fledgling shearwaters (mutton birds) on their test flights kept crashing into the rigging. We made little tunnels with sail bags and equipment on the foredeck so that the dazed birds could hide until they recovered. They lived in burrows on Mutton Bird Island, the outer limit of Coffs Harbour Marina. The twang of birds bumping into rigging as they practised circuits and bumps, awoke many sailors. Nearby a 40' Swanson SUTAMON was being worked on, and lived in, by a happy family who were intending to sail to Europe. They had a television and invited us to join them to watch "Howard's Way" a

Tao aged 9 and Monique aged 5 take a break

Sutanon's invited us to join them to watch 'Howards Way'

mini-series about sailing families filmed on the Hamble and South Coast of England, familiar ground and water to us. A close friendship developed. SUTAMON was launched with usual celebrations. We admired the way the little family of Theo, Sue, Tao 9, and Monique 5, were working together, all helping to make Theo's dream, to sail his family back to Amsterdam where he was born, come true. *(Years later they told us the moving story of their arrival in Amsterdam. While waiting for the lifting bridge into the City, to open, Sue was holding their lines to a bollard. She mentioned to the bridge-keeper that they had sailed their children from Australia to introduce them to the land of their father. It seemed a long wait but, when the bridge did open and they passed further into the canal, children and adults ran along the canal side, waving Dutch flags and shouting "Velcom, velcom." Theo admitted he couldn't see where he was steering, tears of relief and gratitude blinded his vision as Tao and Monique stood on either side of him with their arms around his waist).*

In Coffs Harbour I attended Fitness classes daily, frenetically exercising to throbbing disco music to get myself ready for sea. On Sunday evenings we walked to the Catholic Sports Club where a delicious roast dinner and then ballroom dancing to a live band was enjoyed for a very modest cost.

Our six month visitors' visas had almost expired. This year we planned an easy cruise; back to New Caledonia and Vanuatu and up to the Banks and Torres Islands and perhaps The Solomon Islands. No long ocean passages, no crises. Huh!

On the June 11th SUTAMON accompanied us out of Coffs Harbour to bid us good-bye. As they turned back to shore so the sun was setting behind the Great Dividing Range bathing her sails in a rosy glow and outlining the dark mountainous skyline. I felt very emotional. Australia has been so kind to us.

As usual, heading back north-east, we thrashed over, under and through the waves, hard on the wind for nine days. We rediscovered the bliss of heaving-to for our meals. The motion doesn't cease but much of the noise and violence does. By pure chance we achieved a perfect landfall right on the Amadee lighthouse and entered Noumea Harbour in the sunshine at lunch-time. Nick and Susie of PETA LYNN had heard us call Harbour Control and were waiting to take our lines and share cold beers and French bread. We sat on the dockside waiting for Customs and Immigration and caught up on eighteen months of adventures since we had last seen them in New Zealand.

We sailed off to Ile des Pins, 60 miles south east of Noumea. Isolated coral reefs meant we could only day-sail and it was half way, at Ile Ouen, where we received a radio message:

"I GOT MARRIED THIS AFTERNOON AND I'M SO HAPPY,
    LOVE ANDREA."

A toast to our daughter. 'I got married this afternoon and I'm so happy'. - Who to?

What a surprise! Who to? Had she married Rupert? Why hadn't she told us more? This island was uninhabited. Where was the nearest telephone? We opened a bottle of champagne to celebrate our daughter's wedding, sorry not to have been there to support her and give her 'the works' if she had wanted it. I felt very guilty and had never imagined her getting married without us being there.

Once again there was a spectacular sunset as the red globe sank beneath the stark bare hills of red nickel ore and I reflected on the choices life offers. We had anticipated being home in three years and never considered sons or daughter getting married or grandchildren being born, and growing up, without us. Here we were, already four years out and only just over halfway. Not old enough to claim a state pension and with very little prospect of getting jobs if we did rush home. While out here, we were living very happily on £5,000 a year - no inescapable taxes, insurance, car, telephone, water or electricity bills

Underwater coral cliffs rising just below the surface to two feet in as many yards, made finding our way out of the bay at dawn hazardous. We hurried to the Isle of Pines, landed and walked three miles to the telephone box, which was next to a gendarme post, the only building in sight. From this coin box, in the middle of nowhere, we were able to direct dial Andrea and speak to her in her new home. A tearful joy.

With a happy party of Australian, Canadian and American yachties we climbed the hill and looked around an old prison where the French evidently deported their 'criminals' in the 19th Century. It made us feel less apologetic to know the French had the same system as Britain for deporting undesirables.

To celebrate Andrea's wedding, we organised a beach BBQ. Peter laid our mullet net and caught sufficient fish to put on the grill, with salads, potatoes, and pumpkin pieces wrapped in foil, toasted on the ashes, it was a feast to remember. The moon and stars shone above the palm trees reflected in the bay and with congenial company we felt we must seize the day and make the most of it.

With mixed emotions, I had to be positive and spent time constructing a poem:

Warm winds waft the driftwood fire
Instant friends gather round the glow
Bright eyed fish glisten on the grill
Where from? Where bound? What winds will blow?

Starlight and moonshine reflected in the bay
White sand meets the coral strand.
Rigging taps as mastheads slowly sway
Beneath palm fronds, warm ripples lap this land.

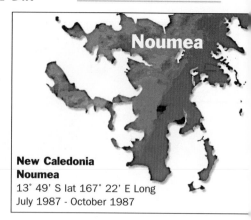

New Caledonia
Noumea
13° 49' S lat 167° 22' E Long
July 1987 - October 1987

CHAPTER TWENTY

We booked out of Noumea on 18th July 1987 and motored on a calm sunny day through Canal Woodin. Five bottle-nosed dolphins played around the bow for over half an hour, squeaking and swimming on their backs so they could keep eye contact with us as they flipped along in front of CLYPEUS. Their long noses were well-worn and tinged with orange. We anchored in a bay to await the wind. It was glassy calm in the morning with sea eagles hovering overhead. Whilst I cooked breakfast, Peter popped the fishing line over the side and caught lunch.

On the way to Vanuatu the new Genoa was hoisted for the first time. The shining white sail billowed, glistening in the sun and freshening wind. We hung on and raced at 6-7 knots anchoring for lunch at the Customs Buoy in Port Vila to await the Authorities.

The 'Independens Selebresen', the seventh anniversary of Vanuatu's Independence, from France and Great Britain, was about to start. An impressive flag-raising ceremony and marching opened the proceedings on the greensward in front of the Parliament. The "Force" in white tunics, black trousers and red belts looked impeccable. The band was good, loud, and in time, but, from then on the published programme bore no resemblance to events which were sometimes an hour, or a day, late.

For four days on the grass sea-front there were bamboo-plaited stalls around an arena and stage. Western pop music played day and night and it sounded as if a riotous time was being had, but it was all very gentle. The stalls sold food: kebabs, lap-lap, rice, fish, and steaks. Lemonade or green coconuts were for sale (no beer or spirits). Four popular gambling stalls, where up to 100 vatu ($1) could be placed for a bet on a turn of the wheel, was all the 'vice' we found. Shy, well-mannered people packed the area day and night. They patiently sat on the grass and waited for the programmed event to happen, and when it didn't, eventually got up and wandered around the stalls again. The custom dancing was primitive. Fuzzy-haired men in short grass skirts stomped around in circles to different rhythms, gesturing with spears, bows and arrows. No women danced.

The main event was a Race Meeting. Only the second horse race ever held in the

Racing was fast and furious

French race goers

country. It was organised by the Kiwanis (like Rotarians) with an expert from the Australian Jockey Club who brought over silks and hard hats. The horses were all working horses from the plantations, ranches and a riding school. The jockeys were Vanuatuan-born stockmen or expatriate businessmen and wives. Racing was fast and furious in clouds of dust after the leaders had passed. The local stockmen won most of the races wearing their borrowed silks, cotton trousers and trainers. They were almost too shy to receive their trophies and hid their faces behind their hands at the presentation.

A Fashion Prize encouraged some elegant Parisienne outfits and hats. Champagne corks popped under garden umbrellas. Hordes of children of all nationalities played together and raced around. At one stage, they were near the emergency helicopter and the radio commentator called over the microphone in pidgin English: "Hey you piccaninnies. You no touchem him mixmaster blong Jesus Christ!"

I bought a Bislama (Vanuatuan pidgin) dictionary. A few amusing extracts: guess what a titti -basket is? - a bra! If read phonetically most words can be understood by English speakers:-

Yurpin		European,
Blong yufala	-	yours,
pulumdaon	-	to pull down, demolish.
kambakambak	-	to return.

New school

We planned to weave our way north through the islands.

August 21st saw us back at Awok Island to a great welcome. We were proudly led up to the new schoolhouse. Each man from the village had given up one day a week to build the plaited hut for the five to eight year olds. Previously the children had to leave their homes to board at a school on another island where a different language was spoken and some of the

The classroom was built. The teacher in residence with the promised blackboard, table and chalk

We started off their library with books and a first aid box

children just couldn't cope, so had returned home, and were not receiving any tuition. The parents had told us last year, that if the villagers built the school and a teacher's house, the Government would provide a teacher, a table, blackboard and chalk.

Now the classroom was finished and the teacher in residence. We started off their library with a set of children's' encyclopedias about different countries and peoples which we had bought with donations from talks I had given in West Australia. A Coffs Harbour pharmacist had given me advice and donated a simple first aid kit for playground wounds. At an emotional evening presentation, the Chief gave us fishing spears and beautifully woven bags and mats.

The girls taught me how to catch, kill and cook octopus: place small clay pots, in which they like to hide, between rocks. Pull the body inside-out which kills it. Cut away the ink sac, chop the tentacles into pieces and spread with coconut cream before wrapping in a banana leaf and baking in the umu, Ten year old Jeni demonstrated with the octopus crawling up her arm as she pulled and pushed to get it inside-out. The islanders have few technological skills or ideas of maintenance. However they are quick and clever socially, most speak three or four languages and although their skills and knowledge are not sophisticated, when pollution overtakes the northern-hemisphere, or the 'big bang' comes, they will survive. They DO survive with no electricity, no imported food, fuel etc. and live fulfilling and happy lives.

The most dramatic island we visited was Ambrym with three smoking volcanoes clouding the sun. At night we anchored beneath the red glow from craters reflected back down from the clouds. After I had been snorkelling in the clear water over a black sand beach, it was casually mentioned that there were many sharks and three people were taken last year. No more swimming here.

The neighbouring island of Pentecost had many rivers, waterfalls and mountains but no roads, just tracks. Distance is measured by how long it takes to walk along jungle paths - from sunrise to sunset, or sunrise to noon. Some boys brought me a gift of a baby parrot, which again I didn't accept. It seemed churlish but what do you feed to a baby parrot? Where would we leave him if we went on a land trip?

String Bands were all the rage. Every village had one. They consist of six or seven young men with a couple of guitars, a ukulele, a rattle, bongo drums and a tea chest

The boys gave me a baby parrot

with a 3' long broom handle to which a string is attached and held taut and played like a double bass. They enthusiastically compose their own songs. We expressed interest while in Wali village and that evening, whilst having dinner, heard music floating across the water. On the beach "The Seven Stars" serenaded us by moonlight. Next day Peter recorded them and gave them the cassette.

Pentecost is the original Land Diving Island where they have been bungy-jumping for centuries. To ensure a good yam harvest and the approval of their gods, the men construct a 75 metre tower around a tall tree trunk and dive with the correct length of liana creeper attached to their ankles. The clever ones just skim the ground with their heads before the fully extended creeper contracts again. Not for them the safety of water beneath, these guys do it for real. The diving only takes place in April to June when the creepers are most elastic.

I visited the local hospital, which consisted of

Pentecost. The original Bungy jumpers

Kava house

four six-bedded wards: a hut each for men, women, children and maternity cases. The men's and children's wards were empty. Each had a concrete floor and six black iron bedsteads with stained striped mattresses, unswept floors with leaves and spiders in the corners and the windows had neither glass or mosquito nets. The maternity unit had three mothers with two babies. They were pathetically grateful for the little baby clothes. Two lady visitors were sitting cross-legged on the floor pulling a slab of lap lap apart with their hands to share amongst the patients for Sunday lunch. The women's ward had two TB cases and a malaria patient under a mosquito net. The staff said they were usually very busy during April to June with land-dive casualties and malaria cases. Malaria is endemic and we found taking the recommended prophylactics for four months made us feel continuously nauseous, particularly when sailing.

The villagers were hospitable, kind, honest and generous, as only the really poor can be, inviting us to take kava with the men in a long dark thatched meeting hut. We climbed in through the window/door-hole and sat in the gloom around a small fire.

An elderly man hacked up kava root with a machete, putting the bits in a hollow tree trunk then a young man rammed and mashed them with a heavy pole. The resultant mush was transferred onto a large ancient board and kneaded while an assistant slowly added water. With elaborate gestures the kneading continued until it could absorb no more. The mush was squeezed by hand and juice ran into two coconut cups. Each cupful was filtered through a piece of sacking into another coconut half and offered to us. There appeared to be no complicated ceremony as in Tonga or Fiji. We were told to just pick it up and drink the peppery, grey milky-thick liquid, which again made our tongues and cheeks tingle. We would like to have stayed and chatted longer but it was getting dark and CLYPEUS was a long walk away.

A week later we blew across to Luganville to book out of Vanuatu, bought our duty free and excellent vegetables from the covered market. After a few days in Palekulo Harbour sailed on up to white-sand Champagne Beach, where cruise ships call. Port Olry was en fete as the Pope's Representative, Cardinal Gintan, was visiting the French Catholic Mission. We were invited to join their feast and custom dancing. Tribal dancers had been brought down from the hills for this occasion and they really were unworldly. Small men and women wearing just 6" grass skirts slung low, with feathers stuck in their fuzzy hair and babies slung across their backs. Other ladies carried their possessions in string bags on their backs with the string handle across their forehead taking most of the weight. Peter stayed on CLYPEUS as usual.

Cross-legged, I sat on the ground for the feast spread out before me on banana leaves. When everyone else started I copied them and tore off lumps of unsalted pork, baked breadfruit and taro with my fingers. We smiled and I tried to talk to the little woman from the hills opposite me, but she stuffed the food into her mouth so fast she couldn't even smile. It must have been the feast of her life, the way she downed the delicacies. The local ladies were very superior in their attitude to these 'primitive people from the mountains'.

This gentleman still hunted with a bow and arrow

We had an idyllic sail from Santa Maria to Vanua Levu: blue sky, sparkling sea, and porpoises. I spent blissfull moments on the bowsprit with my legs dangling, contemplating CLYPEUS's billowing white bow wave tumbling over my feet as we overtook wave crests. I watched flecks of foam fly away and was conscious of ripples rustling along the hull. The wind breathed into our curving sails. I couldn't ask for more.

However, Peter was insular and miserable. Why wasn't he enjoying himself? Wasn't this what he really wanted to do after all? He said, "you don't have to smile and look happy, to be content", but he certainly wasn't a bundle of fun. Trying to talk to him was difficult, he found it hard to say what he wanted. He admitted that he missed not designing equipment, and being with other engineers, he wasn't having a chance to be creative. Keeping CLYPEUS maintained and on course wasn't enough. However, realistically, there wasn't much call for 57 year old electrical engineers during the world-wide recession now being experienced. I decided to mention in my next 'letter to friends' that he felt he would like to have another opportunity in the work force.

The Admiralty Pilot spoke of Waterfall Bay. There it was, a waterfall sparkling in the sun as it fell into a pool and overflowed down the beach. Carefully we edged into a wide sandy bay, anchored, then rowed ashore to the deep pool beneath the cascading water. I took a towel and a pair of men's shorts for a gift and presented them to an elderly local couple who walked down the beach to meet us, Victor and his wife Rose. Victor immediately donned the brown shorts over his loin cloth. I asked if

Victor took us to a secret cave. 'What did these people do wrong? I asked.'They came'.

I could do my laundry in a side-pool. They nodded happily. As we laid the washing out to dry on the flat stones they pointed out the deep grooves worn into them where their ancestors had sharpened their stone axes and weapons.

Victor, a slim, brown sixty-year old, and his family were the only inhabitants. They lived in two wood-and-palm-leaf huts. Rose, her sister Adele and Victor in one; their daughter Marion, husband Issor, and two small children in the other. The first evening, we took my Walkman tape recorder ashore to record their songs. Peter tested it: "One, two, three, four, testing,

testing." Victor snatched the Walkman from him, said: "Five, four, three, two, one, testing, testing," grinned, and handed it back.

This gentleman, who still hunted with a bow and arrow, had been an observer for the American and Australian armies during WWII, reporting on Japanese shipping in the channels. He sang with great vigour *"Tipperary"*, *"Waltzing Matilda"* and *"Deep in the Heart of Texas."* He asked if England had been in the War? He wore a crucifix around his neck and said they were Anglicans although they no longer had the opportunity to go to church.

He taught us how to kill and eat coconut crab

They had a pet turtle they had raised from an egg. The children fed it with hibiscus flowers, shell fish and hermit crabs. Issor did not appear until the third day - he had walked for four days to buy a can of paraffin.

We stayed a week with these lovely people. One day Victor captained CLYPEUS to take us to a secret cave where human bones and skulls rested on a shelf. Skulls and signs were carved into the stone surfaces.

"Why did you kill these people? What did they do wrong?" We asked him.

"They came." He said.

He continued thoughtfully. "We killed any man or woman who came on our land. We were heathens then. They would only come to take our food or our women." The canoe had come from Ureparapara, the occupants were massacred as soon as they landed, and then eaten.

Marion and Issor took us up into the hills above the waterfall to spear fresh water prawns (you have to be very quick). We had as much success there as we did later, on the reef in the dark, learning to catch crayfish (lobsters without big claws). 'Nil points' on both occasions. Issor made the following suggestions to catch reef lobsters: choose a very dark night, before the moon rises. Wear strong sandals and gloves and carry a torch and a sack. When you see the red eyes of the cray, stomp your foot on it to hold it then pick it up by the back of its head, tip it sharply into the sack, tail first.

He also taught us where to look for and how to kill coconut crabs. Tying up their huge claws studded with large white molars for grinding coconut shells, while they were still alive and struggling, was another skill we didn't master! If they hid in a hole where their back was still accessible, a jungle knife could be thrust in between head and carapace. We did manage to hunt and cook a few and their delicious white meat resembled crab, tasting of coconut rather than sea salt. The family showed us wild yams, nuts, fruits and plants we could eat, healing leaves to rub on stings, bites or sores. Marion and Issor spoke excellent English, as well as their own island language, and Bislama.

We took ashore home-made biscuits and fudge for them. At the farewell party they gave for us of coconut crab, sweet potato, yams and lap lap with coconut cream, they sang and we danced a stamp dance together. It was a wonderful happy time until we had to part. An American yacht arrived and joined in the feast. After we had toasted each other raising our green coconuts, they sang a goodbye song composed by themselves. Then they walked down the beach with us singing:

"Goodbye, Goodbye, for ever more,
May you live a happy life and God be with you always."
Rose, Adele and I, all cried. The brave little family stood on the beach and waved us out of sight.

Ureparapara Island looked an ideal anchorage with a long horseshoe bay but it was rolly and rough. Many villagers came out through the surf in their canoes to visit us for popcorn and to have tea and biscuits. Chief Philip came with his visitor's book for us to sign and asked for batteries, earrings and tobacco. Before we left, we managed to find him what he wanted, together with a towel for a new baby, and pencils for the many children who brought shells for my collection.

We were invited to join their Sunday celebrations. Peter stayed on board, but once again I enjoyed helping to prepare a Sunday feast and sat with the ladies grating and squeezing manioc (tapioca) for lap lap. At 4 p.m. I returned to the Meeting House to watch twenty men all pounding tapioca with ceremonial clubs. One big glutinous lump was placed on a huge wooden dish and cooked. Then they added cooked nuts into a hole in the centre. It was now called 'skooner" and when cooked was ceremoniously cut and presented after church. They asked me to choose a hymn and sang *"Jesus shall reign where'ere the sun"* in Bislama for me

After three days we couldn't stand the rolling any longer and set sail for Tikopia. We really wanted to see this Polynesian outpost which is a link in the Polynesian chain from Asia to Tahiti. Friends encouraged us on the radio to come and once again enjoy the Polynesian life style. Unfortunately it was too rough. We were both very seasick and eventually gave up and skidded back to Ureparapara.

The weather was unsettled and the sea, horrible, so we decided it was time to head back to Australia and made for Saddle Island in the Torres Group. After another rotten, bouncy, night we left at first light and sailed fast to Tegua. and enjoyed a sheltered anchorage for four days while the wind continued to howl. Ashore we explored through the woods and actually hunted, killed and cooked a large coconut crab. During our expedition on this seemingly uninhabited tropical island we came across a notice saying:

"KEEP OUT. NO TRESPASSING."

We did meet one inhabitant, 'Selwyn', who offered us a bush turkey he had just shot with a bow and arrow. We politely refused saying we couldn't pluck and gut it, not knowing whether he was the owner, the game-keeper, or a poacher.

This corner of the Pacific was very troubled at that time. Fiji had undergone a coup, the Kanaks were revolting again and had shot two French Gendarmes in New Caledonia. We considered sailing on to Honiara in the Solomons, but the light wind was against us and in the rough sea we knew we would use too much diesel. Instead we rocked and rolled, being seasick, towards Australia via the Entrecasteaux Reefs just north of New Caledonia. Thirty tropic birds twittered and chattered around us all one afternoon.

In the evening Peter was miserable yet again. We talked and tried to come to an understanding of what? If we were not happy now would we ever be? This was our one life and we were more than half-way through it. What did he want if it wasn't this? He was living the dream of so many people Was it turning into a nightmare for him?. Did he really want to go back to work?

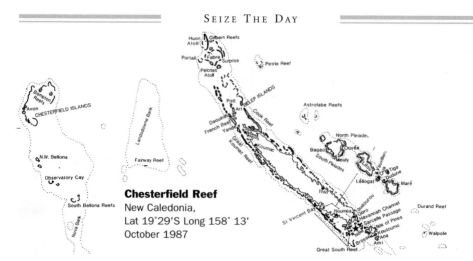

Chesterfield Reef
New Caledonia,
Lat 19°29'S Long 158° 13'
October 1987

CHAPTER TWENTY ONE

Light wind, no wind, strong wind, bringing delights and dangers as usual. The experiencing of heaven or hell sometimes separated by just a few minutes, when a squall stirs the wind and water into a frenzy, or coral heads are spotted a few yards ahead in seemingly deep water.

The ocean was all ours, but the blue cloudless sky belonged to white twittering tropic birds, swooping streamlined terns, and what we thought were albatrosses, but later turned out to be masked boobies. Fluttering, dipping, storm petrels and flying fish skimmed the sea surface.

On the fourth day out a blue-footed booby kept us laughing as he tried to land on the mast. He kept zooming in and circling; his blue-webbed claws extended ready to hold on to the swaying mast-head light. Each time, as he approached from afar, I flapped my arms in rhythm with his wing beat . He was fascinated. We continued our 'conversation' for almost an hour.

On Saturday 3rd October
the log reads: *17° 09'N, 162°48W. Rough day hard on the wind. Hove-to for tea. Shirley seasick again. Changed course to try and get to the Entrecasteaux Reefs.*

Sunday 4th October.
13.00. Entered blissful blue lagoon 18°07'N 162°49'W14.00. Anchored off Huron Island. Turtles crawling up beach to lay eggs, Masked boobies and terns nesting. Super swim of N. coast. Whilst walking round island found and picked up turtle eggs in line on the beach, some poor reptile didn't quite make it to her nest. Made bread and then chocolate cake with turtle eggs. Big thunder clouds around.

Turtles crawled up the beach to lay their eggs

After dinner we took rugs and torches ashore to wait for the turtles to come and lay their eggs. They took no notice of us as we lay under the full moon and watched CLYPEUS gently rolling in the swell, her golden masts glistening in the moonlight. To me, it was paradise, but Peter wanted something more, although he didn't know what. Lying still, we watched a turtle laboriously approach and slowly dig her hole. It was almost dawn before she had flicked the sand back over the eggs with her flippers, then slowly, drag herself back to the water's edge.

When swimming I held onto a turtle's back and tried to ride it, but she was too fast for me underwater and I soon lost my grip. It was a perfect day on our own uninhabited island, swarming with wildlife, birds and fish.

As we sat in the cockpit having our evening cocktail and peering over the side following the antics of the fish in the coral beneath us, a military jet roared in out of nowhere, zoomed down close to our mast heads and buzzed us. The noise was indescribable. The whole earth reverberated with the power of the small plane. It came back three times; so low, we feared it would hit the masts. The French Authorities obviously didn't want stray boats in their territory in northern New Caledonia.

Peter was very apprehensive. Perhaps they would send a gunboat and soldiers would come stomping all over the deck? It was too late to dodge the coral tonight. We would leave first thing in the morning.

Recklessly, at dawn, before we could see clearly what was beneath us, we eyeballed our careful way across nine miles of lagoon and out through the Pass. The jet didn't come back. They probably assumed they had frightened us off. They had!

We set course for Bampton Reef. Three days and 276 miles later we anchored off a sand islet. The anchor disappeared between coral heads. Would we be able to get it out when we were ready to leave? Peter pumped up the inflatable for me and pushed me off to explore this scrub covered sandy plateau. As I stepped ashore, clouds of shrieking terns flew into the air abandoning their nests and eggs to this strange creature. Few, if any, humans have landed in this particular spot. Perhaps mine were the first female feet to make imprints in the white sand.

There were masked boobies feeding full-grown fluffy chicks, naked fledglings and whole eggs in some nests. Also blue, brown and red-footed boobies, frigate birds with brown-headed young ones peering at me through the low bushes. Roseate terns, bridled terns and black terns, white-capped, and brown noddies, turtles, and magnificent shells were just lying on the beach waiting to be picked up.

As we sailed on towards Chesterfield Reef the huge round white moon set in the west; just before the round red sun rose in the east. The sea was calm as we tried to solve the problem of how to enter Chesterfield Lagoon in daylight through the SW pass. Our chart had no details of a pass from the east; as it had never been surveyed, the area had just been left blank - a 'here be dragons area'. We decided caution was needed and hove-to north of the reef to wait and calculate. Our charts were very old as this area was last surveyed in the 1870s. Being of no strategic, commercial or military use, nobody has bothered to survey or print charts of the area in the 20th Century. The most up-to-date British Admiralty Pilot we had been able to buy was 1969.

The entrance into Chesterfield lagoon was 40 miles south. It would take at least eight hours, and when we got to the entrance, another three or four hours of daylight to thread our way through the coral to the Anchorage Islands where whalers from New Zealand used to stop and rest. We couldn't do it all in daylight. Hopefully our Aussie friends would be there.

At 01.30 on a calm and balmy night with a full moon it was time to set sail again and carefully make our way down the reef keeping five miles off and be at the entrance at 10a.m..

Peter was on watch trailing the fishing line. At 03.15 I suddenly woke up to the scream of the fishing reel running out, a shout from Peter, a twang, a bang and a crunch. Jumping out of my bunk I rushed up into the cockpit.

White-faced Peter was clenching the wheel.

"Look behind," he whispered.

I looked behind and saw two slim coral towers almost meeting at their base.

"We went between those coral heads", he croaked.

"We did what? How on earth did we get through?"

"I don't know, but there wasn't time to take the sails down or even un-rig the self-steering. We just ploughed straight between them. I thought there was a fish on the line but the hook must have snagged on coral. The line broke and when I looked up, there they were, dead ahead."

Once through, which accounted for the bang and crunch, he had automatically turned right, away from the reef. He handed over the wheel to take the mainsail down. My teeth chattered as we slowly left the reef behind keeping a good lookout for any more uncharted coral.

He took the wheel again and I put my arms around his shaking shoulders. "Well luckily we seem to be OK. I'll go and make us a hot drink and write our position and what happened in the log."

As I stepped down into the cabin and turned on the light, a cascade of white water was tumbling down from the forward cabin. It bubbled over the cabin sill, ran along the floor and disappeared into the bilges.

"Peter, Peter" I shouted. "Come quickly. We're holed."

"Hang on while I set the self steering away from the reef."

I ran forward to try and see where the water was coming in.

"Oh my God! I didn't think we could possibly have got away with it." He groaned as he saw the water bubbling up under the bunk. "Quick start the engine, we must make sure the pumps work and the starter motor doesn't go under water." Immediately he pulled up the floorboards. The little 'Taiwan takeaway' automatic electric pump was doing its best, but it wasn't enough.

"Bucket" he shouted, "and start pumping in the cockpit."

In the cockpit I bent to the pump, the sea was calm beneath the unperturbed silver moon.

Forward and back, forward and back I pumped as hard as I could. The noise of water tumbling into the cabin kept on. Peter was sloshing buckets of water out through the door where the cockpit drains funnelled it back into the sea.

He came up. "OK. I'll take over here. You go and pump the toilet bilge pump. I've changed the valves over. We're not keeping up with the inflow yet. The water's still rising."

Pump, pump, pump, the two of us heaved back and forth at the pump handles sending feeble little squirts of water back into the ocean. As I pumped, sitting on the closed toilet seat, I watched the water gurgling past in the passage-way and realised we were not succeeding. Nobody was mending the hole, nobody was looking out, nobody was navigating. What the hell were we going to do?

A shout, "I think we're holding it. See if you can find the hole."

The main hole was obviously somewhere under the starboard 'V' berth which was piled high with books, sails, vegetables, letters, files, oilskins. Frantically I threw them all back onto our bed, pulled off the squab, lifted the lid and then started pulling everything out of the bin beneath: spare oilskins, blankets, sail material, sewing things, knitting gear, jars of shells, spare depth sounder, spare VHF.

Now I could see it. There it was. Not so big, only as big as a fist but with a star of cracks around it, through which the sea spurted each time the bow dipped.

"Found it. It isn't that big."

"OK. You take over here and pump and I'll come and look."

We changed places.

"God I hope that Taiwanese electric pump doesn't give up, we've had it if it does," Peter muttered as he passed me. "I'll pump down here in the bathroom while I think what to do."

As I stayed pumping in the cockpit he jammed rags into the hole but the outside pressure pushed them back. Then he found the bag of cement, and gallon can of Sika quick-setting-fluid. "Where are the rubber gloves? I'm going to try and fill the hole. Keep pumping."

Ten minutes later he came back, "It's not working. The glove fingers split every time I put them on. I've slopped Sika everywhere and it seems very corrosive. Each time I mix a little in my hand and hold it over the hole the sea spurts through. What does stick on is OK and sets well. Let's inflate the Avon and try from the outside."

He took over to give my arms a rest while I undid the semi-inflated Avon and foot-pumped-up the back half. He launched it and disappeared over the side while I continued to pump.

Suddenly we were in rough water. The dinghy was alternately above or below deck, with a rise and fall of about six feet. I was so frightened and couldn't stop my chattering teeth. I didn't like him being out there, in the dark, on the ocean, without me. Why was it suddenly so rough? The minutes dragged on as I kept pumping: two thousand,eight hundred and one, eight hundred and two, eight hundred and three. Oh my back!

A hand and yellow cuff appeared over the rail. "It's no good I can't keep my hand with the cement in it over the hole because the dinghy and boat are going up and down against each other too far. Why is it so rough now? Help me aboard."

I helped him aboard and carried on pumping.

"OK. Where are the rags? I'm going to fill the hole with rags and put a board against it. I'll chisel the rags into the cracks. Seen anything?"

"Nothing, but my back is breaking and my arms aren't as strong now. The rags are under the bathroom basin,"

"OK. give me a turn pumping."

"No. You go and fill the hole or our situation won't get any better."

"I'm so sorry, sorry"

"Sorry, sorry too. Go on. Mend the hole and pray the electric pump keeps going." I listened to the suck and swallow of the sea and then to him banging away; finding a piece of marine-ply; plugging the cracks with chisel and hammer. As I pumped I kept looking out, but there was nothing to see except the moon shining on the water, which was calm again.

Peter came up. "There must be other holes somewhere but I've stopped the main flow. OK. I'll take over. You make us a 'cup-a-soup'."

Back down in the cabin, the steady mutter of the engine and warm glow from the gas ring comforted me. Water still trickled down from under both forward bunks but we could cope with it.

"I'll drink mine first, and then I'll pump while you drink yours." I called to him.

"Thank goodness for the electric pump. It's done a wonderful job. Oh! my arms, will they ever recover?" He gasped.

"Here have your soup while I pump."

"Dawn's coming." He sat back and relaxed. I'll fix a larger outlet pipe that will get rid of the water quicker. We'll try and sail and keep the starboard hull above the surface. You know," he said conversationally, "if we were sinking, we'd never have gone down for the EPRIB (Emergency radio beacon). It's in the wrong place on the ceiling amidships isn't it?"

"I hadn't even thought about it. Just hoped, and knew you would think of something in time. I'm surprised we didn't even think of abandoning ship." I said. "Keeping the boat afloat took all our energies and thoughts, didn't it?"

"Well, we still aren't OK if the pump stops. There should be a fix coming up soon. I'll go and find out our position and we'll decide on a course."

The sun rose. The water was calm. I looked over the side.

Oh my God! There it was! the bottom, crowded with coral heads only a few feet beneath us. I screeched in shock "Peter. Come quickly. Come and look. We must be inside the lagoon."

"How can we be? How do you know?"

"Look over the side."

"Crumbs! Undo the self-steering. Take the wheel. Look ahead. We've got to get CLYPEUS heeling to port and we've got to set a course to the islands so that we can beach her."

"No we can't. Somebody's got to keep pumping."

"You're right. OK, I'll reset the self-steering and we will just have to hope no coral heads get in the way. I've no idea where we are, or what course to steer. Keep pumping and I'll be as quick as I can."

As I continued pushing the handle back and fore with a quick peep over the side every now and then, it seemed impossible that CLYPEUS could find her way through the coral heads, and I just waited for the scrape and bang. It never came. (Sometimes it seems quite obvious that our boat cares about survival just as much as we do, and is part of our team.)

Peter came up smiling grimly. "The uninhabited Anchorage Islands are to the south and the wind is from the same direction so we won't get any help in keeping the hole out of the water." He hoisted the mainsail and we kept pumping alternately. Every time the bow dipped so the inflow of water increased. We still couldn't relax.

He found and fixed a fatter piece of tubing which emptied the bilge water directly over the side. At noon, by careful monitoring, we found that we could now stop pumping. Peter took the wheel. "Bring up the binoculars, it looks like low islands ahead. See if you can see a likely place to beach CLYPEUS."

I peered ahead. "I can see the islands and I can see six masts as well."

"What?"

"Six masts, they're here. NUAGES and TATTLER must be here."

"Give me the binoculars." He scanned the horizon. "I wonder if anyone has their VHF on? Go and call them."

I rushed below. "This is CLYPEUS, CLYPEUS, we have had some trouble and need to beach her. Is anybody there who can suggest a good place?"

"CLYPEUS CLYPEUS this is TARA II. G'day. Sorry about the trouble mate. Yes, we can find somewhere for you. Most of us have our dinghies in the water and hand-helds, we'll scout around."

Peter came down and took over. "Great to hear you TARA II. We're holed just below the waterline on the starboard bow and have been pumping for eight hours. We would like a sandy beach where I can make repairs. We draw 5' 9". When is high tide?"

"High tide's now, at noon. No worries. I can see you. Keep heading towards us all and keep your VHF on. Cheers.

"Cheers. CLYPEUS standing by."

We went up into the cockpit and holding hands watched the red Zodiac and grey Avon inflatables zoom off to find our resting place. We were going to survive.

"CLYPEUS CLYPEUS" the VHF crackled

"Yes, TARA II"

"Head south east. I'll come and lead you in."

A few minutes later we greeted Jeff in his dinghy and slowly followed him between coral heads to a sandy beach on a scrub-covered sand bank. Willing hands took our

They pulled us into shallow water

Filling up sandbags to prop up our hull

anchor chain and pulled us into shallow water until our keel rested on the sand.

"I've got some polypropylene sugar sacks on board, shouted South African Jack as he zoomed off in his dinghy.

Sugar sacks? sugar sacks? what did he mean?

Our friends waded out, we bent to hold their hands and make contact and quickly tell what had happened. No time for stories now, somehow we must hold CLYPEUS upright so that she didn't fall over when the tide went out.

Jack returned. "OK. you guys, come and help me fill these sacks with sand and we will make a wall under the hull so that she can lean on them."

They set to, filled the sacks with the soft white sand and as soon CLYPEUS decided which way she would lean, banked them beneath her. She gently settled and seemed safe.

We climbed down, hugged and kissed our dear friends and all crowded round to examine the hole. How insignificant it looked from the outside, only as big as a fist. How had so much water come in?

The hole - how insignificant it looked from the outside

Peter set to work knocking out the loose concrete, he wanted to fill the hole and have it set before the tide came back in ten hours. As he worked waist deep, I emptied all the wet things onto the deck to dry in the sunshine. It was a perfect day in the fantastic blues of the lagoon

He managed to cement in the hole before dark when our friends called us to a barbecue on the beach. As dusk fell they plied us with consolation, food and drink. We sat around the glowing fire enjoying their companionship and hearing their stories while trying to stop little sand crabs committing suicide. The transparent crabs were fascinated by the flames and, unheeding of the heat, dashed into it to instant combustion. Pete of TATTLER, in true Australian humour, christened our sand cay: "Pyre Island".

Pam and John offered us a horizontal bed on NUAGE but we preferred to sleep together on dear CLYPEUS at an angle of 45°, just in case something went wrong as the tide came in.

All was well. Peter was waist deep at dawn putting an epoxy resin and a fibreglass patch over the new cement before the water rose again.

At noon when we refloated, they towed CLYPEUS to an anchorage alongside TARA II, The engine wouldn't start because water had entered the starter motor. Peter immediately dismantled it and dried it out.

Pete and Jack took me snorkelling and we caught a large multi-coloured coral

Drying out

crayfish which was delicious for the evening barbeque, together with the fish caught in our mullet net. Pam and John's offer of a peaceful night on dry, clean, sweet-smelling Nuage enabled us to have an untroubled sleep before leaving for Australia the next day.

However, we had to retrieve our mullet net. During the night it had trapped three sharks, all now dead from drowning. The largest was over six feet, Pete couldn't clear its head from the ground as he lifted its tail as high as he could. The other two sharks were a mere three and four feet long, but all were tangled in the net which had to be cut to extricate their fins and tails.

In company with NUAGE and TATTLER we left via Long Island passage, an uncharted way into the lagoon which they had heard about. We noted with joy that no water was seeping in through the repaired hole. There must be cracks somewhere else as a trickle was still coming in from behind the port bunk. However when hauled out later we discovered no further damage. The water must have been the residue gradually draining. In retrospect the easiest temporary repair would have been to place a cushion over the hole, cover it with the wooden chopping board and jamb a plank against it and the far side of the hull. We had both read how to do this but at 4am, in crisis conditions, didn't remember.

Our mullet net had trapped three sharks

For three days and nights we cautiously sailed or motored towards remote Kenn Reef. Two basking whales with just their fins showing lazed near the surface. At Kenn Reef we anchored, hoping to snorkel over the coral, but the north westerly wind made the anchorage rough and rolly.

I baked and iced a sponge birthday cake for Peter's 57th birthday. NUAGE and TATTLER dinghied over for a celebration dinner. How we enjoyed our confident self-deprecating Australian friends.

One of Pete's jokes was: "Why do Australian Diggers' hats have the brim turned up one side?"

"Don't know. Why?"

"To make room for the chip on their shoulder."

THE BALLAD OF CHESTERFIELD REEF

by Shirley Billing

The night was dark. The sea was still,
The wind it did not blow.
Below the deck the Watch did sleep
Our fate he could not know.

The sea was black, the moon shone high
The yacht it slid along.
They cannot see the reef below
It lurks where fishes throng.

A scream of line, a fish, he thought,
But as he glanced ahead,
Two spires of white rose from the deep
"Oh God! For sure we're dead."

A twang, a crunch, a bump and then
Silence,… not a sound.
The boat scraped through, momentum won
Over the coral mound.

"Thank God," he cried in great relief,
His tongue licked round his lips
But down below the hull was holed
The fate of countless ships.

The sea it bubbled up and ran
Along the cabin floor
The crew looked down, cascading foam
Came tumbling through the door.

"Quick start the motor, Man the pump
We have so little time
Quick, bring a bucket. Raise the floor
Our fate is on the line".

They lift and bale, out through the door
A steady rhythm flows
No panic, but a fevered pace
Ensures the flooding goes.

Priority to find the hole
Which gurgles 'neath a bunk
"Throw off the mattress, cushions, books ,
Quick, quick, or else we're sunk."

Now pumping, pumping, back and forth
They pumped for hours near nine.
Who could repair, look out, or steer
When pumping took their time?

.*"At last we're winning, level's down"*
The skipper cried with glee
"With wet cement I'll mend the hole,
We'll beat this greedy sea".

Cement quick setting he applied
But as he held it there
Each wave burst through his fingers wide
And crumbled. Oh! Despair!

And then a plank of wood he found
And jammed it 'gainst the side
With cushion to absorb the waves
The sea, it was defied.

Repair, it lasted all that day
A sandy isle appeared
Ashore they ground without a sound
Alive, not drowned as feared.

A good repair was now achieved
As lobsters, crabs looked on
A feast by firelight soothed their souls
Above a full moon shone.

Oh fare ye well, ye sailors brave
Remember our sad fate
To sail near reefs on any night
Is tempting Heaven's gate.

* * * * * *

CHAPTER TWENTY TWO

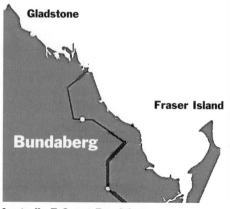

Gladstone

Fraser Island

Bundaberg

Australia E Coast Bundaberg:
October 1987 - September 1988
Lat 2°22' Long 152°34'

S andy Cape lighthouse hove into view, after a smooth ride from Kenn Reef. As a huge red sun heralded the 21st of October we headed for Bundaberg up the Burnett River. At 5 p.m. we passed through the outer marks and anchored in the fantastically calm and peaceful river above the sugar sheds and wharf. White pelicans perched on navigation marker posts, cormorants, sea eagles, terns, swooped and dived for their dinner. Curlews sauntered and sanderlings scurried along the sand banks. Oh! what a blissful peaceful night we had with land on either side.

The voyage south was pleasant and uneventful. Fraser Island

We motored up river, through the morning mist to Bundaberg and tied up to await Customs and Immigration. The Health Officer took away all our remaining vegetables, and tins of meat and salmon. The Customs officers apologetically gave Peter a large orange decal number to stick on each side of the hull to identify us as a foreign vessel. On the radio we had heard from other yachtsmen of this new bureaucratic game, and how, when you tried to remove the decals on leaving Australia, the numbers took the paint off with them.

As Peter pointed out, there is little point in identifying all the 'good guys' who have checked in officially, when the 'bad guys' can creep into Australia unnoticed. He would NOT stick large orange numbers on his boat and called at the Tourist Office to complain. The Tourist Department sympathised, photo-copied and sent off the letters that Peter and other international yacht captains composed to The Federal Prime Minister, The Minister of Tourism, and the Prime Minister of Queensland, asking that they re-consider the situation.

While the men were fighting bureaucracy, the ladies wallowed in the clean hot showers and watched load after load of salty linen tumble around in the washing machines while we chatted, did each others' hair, wrote letters, or read up-to-date magazines.

Peter and I gradually recovered our egos and appreciated each new day, having so nearly lost our lives. We bought a small 12 volt colour TV with a 5" screen which consumed less than one amp and ran happily off the batteries.

Some time later the Authorities notified us we wouldn't have to stick the decals on our hulls and came to retrieve them. Politics seem very direct in Australia. You complain directly to a Minister, somebody answers, a decision is taken, you are notified.

As Bundaberg is in the cyclone belt we decided to return south. The sugar cane was being fired prior to cutting and great clouds of thick black sweet -smelling smoke and fine ash rolled over CLYPEUS. The voyage south to Coffs Harbour was pleasant and uneventful. CLYPEUS was hauled out and we set off by coach to Sydney and the airport.

For five months we delighted in family and friends in England and USA. How we enjoyed their welcome and hospitality. We don't know how we can ever repay them but hope that sharing our experiences will be a contribution. It was lovely to see our children, all happily married and bringing up their families their way. Our new grand-daughter Emily arrived on schedule in February and Andrea and Rupert were expecting a baby in October. Paul and Alice's baby Owen was a chuckling, chubby delight.

The rise in house prices was a great shock - we had expected rises of perhaps hundreds or even thousands of pounds, but not hundreds of thousands of pounds. Would we ever be able to afford a house again? The house we had sold five years previously for £84,000, was now advertised for sale at £250,000.

Living and shopping in Australia, USA and England for five consecutive months was fascinating. Australia had by far the lowest cost of living, especially at the latitude of Coff's Harbour where neither heating nor air conditioning are needed.

December and April were spent on Paul's 56' steel yacht, DEO GRATIS, which he had designed and made single-handed. Moored in a Mississippi backwater in Louisiana Cajun country near Baton Rouge, each weekend we watched camouflaged hunters proudly land beautiful dead deer, some with great antlers. At a wedding on a Mississippi Steamboat we danced to a Trad Jazz Band and on deck listened to the calliope steam whistle play *"Ole Man River"* while the stern paddle wheel splashed round.

We enjoyed a crawfish boil under the portico of a white-pillared plantation home surrounded by magnolias and live oaks festooned with Spanish moss. Heaps of steaming red crawfish and small potatoes boiled in their jackets, covered a trestle table. Everyone helped themselves using fingers - delicious! Dignified peacocks displayed around us but were not too proud to peck up any dropped tidbits.

Live oaks festooned with spanish moss - a family picnic

We had decided that should an opportunity arise for Peter to return to work; he would take it. We rented a car and drove to Atlanta for a job interview that didn't materialise. The dogwood trees bloomed amongst springtime fluttering aspens. Driving to visit friends in Austin and Houston, spectacular Texan spring wild flowers covered fields with bluebonnets and red-indian paintbrush flowers. Galveston looked similar to Coff's Harbour with the same sky colours and fishing boats looking like giant butterflies, their blue and brown nets hanging to dry from the hinged trawl arms.

Only once did we have to scrape ice from the car windscreen

England seemed green and quaint after the vast expanses of USA and Australia. It was a mild winter . Only once did we have to scrape ice from the car windscreen and feel our way through fog. Snowdrops, primroses and a few hardy daffodils were about near Andrea's Herefordshire home. We toured to see friends. How precious our old friendships are to us now.

It was hard to say goodbye again. Sydney sparkled and looked freshly laundered as we touched down at 6 a.m. The friendly Italian driver of the Airport shuttle-bus treated like us taxi fares because we had so much luggage. He diverted the bus to take us to the left-luggage room at Central Station.

CLYPEUS was lowered back into the water on Friday 3rd of June 1988, the fourth official day of winter, but warm enough for us to wear shorts and sandals in a north easterly gale. Huge waves were breaking into the harbour. A dozen teenage boys in

Coffs NE gale

In the NE gale - Coff's harbour

their wet suits had forsaken their surfboards to strut along the top of the sea wall. They squealed with delight as a 'big one' approached and ran to crouch behind the protective rocks as the foaming wave erupted and flew right over them to crash on the road and cascade into the Marina. Exciting!

I had spent time thinking about how to improve my method of doing the washing by hand. Stomping it in a bucket appealed. A trip into town to find Cinderella a pair of buckets to fit her feet caused some giggles. But I left Coffs Harbour fitted out with a twin tub - a bucket for each foot!

Our sail north to Surfers Paradise took 36 hours of squalls, rain and calms over a rough following sea. Poor Peter was sick most of the way. Running downwind in the dark towards a lee shore whilst looking for the entrance to the Gold Coast Seaway seemed very foolish, despite the welcoming shimmering lights of the Casino, hotels and high rise apartments. The Volunteer Coastguards talked us in on VHF Radio, then showed us where to anchor and offered hot showers and coffee in their sumptuous Control Tower - all built with donated money and all volunteers; ladies and men doing a 24 hour weekend shift.

Andrea had given me a long-stitch tapestry kit of *'The Owl and the Pussy Cat'* for Christmas which I was enjoying embroidering. Monique (6) and Tao (10) were interested, so when I saw quince for sale in Southport market they came to supper and we 'dined on mince and slices of quince', which of course we ate with runcible spoons. (special spoons I made with sea shells stuck on the handles.)

A tortuous inland route wound to Moreton Bay and Brisbane, dodging between mangrove covered islands and sand banks. With SUTAMON we vied who would go aground next in the mud. Lonely anchorages were hosts to wild kangaroos, wallabies, ibis, black and white pelicans, crested terns, sea eagles and ospreys. It seems incredible that unspoilt nature is still so accessible and there are so few people around to enjoy it.

World Expo 88 was happening in Brisbane. Moored within the Botanic Gardens in the middle of the city, we walked to smart shops, Art Gallery, Expo site, Museum, Theatre, and Cinema. The clean, cosmopolitan city centre impressed us, as did the friendly crowds at Expo. Our Brisbane friends, who had helped us in our hours of need on Chesterfield Reef, all came for drinks on board then took us to a converted Anglican Church for a pancake dinner.

The East Australian coast is a sailing paradise. Sometimes the need to share a perfect day was overwhelming:

"Tonight we are anchored off a ten-mile white-sand beach on Fraser Island. No one else is here. The lights on the mainland sparkle in the distance, the crescent moon and a million stars twinkle above. The spaghetti bolognaise is almost ready whilst we sip our boxed "Burgundy" and watch the News on our tiny TV.

Yesterday, after a rough and rolly night at sea, we crossed Wide Bay Bar at the recommended time and place, and were still tossed around like a tiny cork.

The calm and serenity of our anchorage amongst the mangroves was blissful.
After a nap I explored the creek in the rubber dinghy and watched hundreds of fiddler and soldier crabs feeding on the uncovered mud/sand banks. A whiskered snout rose above the water, to snort and toss a few fish around, but I never discovered what sort of body it had: a dugong or a seal?

Kookaburras, currawongs and parakeets cackled and cried sleepily as the sun went down into a crimson sky and the reflection of the gum trees gradually faded in the silent creek."

It is all so wonderful and yet we constantly feel guilty. Is it just human nature? We know we are not doing enough for our parents, but it isn't always easy to share this responsibility, one couple living in Australia and the other in England. We have no outstanding bills, electricity, rates or gas charges accumulating, no mortgage or HP. We owe no money and can live simply on the income of under £7,000 pounds a year from our house investment. Yet we feel it is too good; something must be wrong. Why?

If we were at home working and spending all our income, everyone would consider we were normal and we certainly couldn't have found the time or money to visit my parents in West Australia as we have. We have paid into the National Health Service for 30 odd years and still are, so hope to have a small pension when the time comes to really retire. Our only worry is the cost of finding a house near our children. We have seen and learned how few material possessions are actually needed for happiness (but I would still like to own a small home with central heating, a fridge, washing machine and a car!)"

Peter noted some boat details for our sailing friends:-

"Our war on rust and flaking paint continues in the tropics. New anchor chain was needed this year. At the London Boat Show in January we bought a new Mercury outboard motor and Avon 8 since our 17 year old Redstart finally gave up. We carried both new items on the planes and were lucky enough not to have to pay any duty or excess baggage charges. Here in Australia we bought two new deep cycle batteries, an additional electric bilge pump, new lifebuoy light, charts and pilots - there are excellent cruising guides to the E. Australian coast.

The Kenwood ham radio spent six months with the makers and has recovered and now our computer is down and in intensive care!"

Easy sailing up Australia's East coast

The Whitsunday Islands provide magnificent cruising grounds and Clive, our Motel friend from Coff's Harbour, joined us for a week. We have always thought Australia 'the lucky country' but sailing the Queensland coast confirmed it. Beautiful coral atolls with sandy cays only 50 miles from Bundaberg. High mountainous islands and remote sheltered fiord-like anchorages on the mainland where the mountains meet the sea. An abundance of fish, oysters, crabs. We watched a pair of sea eagles courting, spiralling down with their beaks touching. It was easy sailing on the calm inside passage sheltered by the Great Barrier Reef with the SE Trades blowing freshly to speed us on our way.

One small island was special - Middle Percy. An Englishman called Andrew Martin has lived there, on his own, for 25 years. He lives in an old house up in the hills but has built a tree house, and an 'A' frame house adjoining the beach, for the yachties. It has hammocks and tables; water, sink and draining board; barbecue and seats; a shower and a place to do laundry with lines to hang the washing on. Everyone is welcome and no charge is made. Andy is an idealist with a sense of humour too. There are little notices posted on trees:-

Middles Percy the resident Emu fell in love with our outboard

"Please understand that the bi-ped living on Percy is extremely camera shy and could become extinct if you persist in observing his comic behaviour through your lenses."

"AXES - Simpletons have successfully used axes for centuries, but yachties, despite their prowess in things nautical, mechanical and technical, seem incapable of chopping wood properly. Split the wood along the grain, with the sharpened edge of the axe head"

Visiting yachts have left souvenirs including an artificial leg

Visiting yachts have left their names and dates carved or painted on boards, plates and bottles. Sundowner left his pink artificial leg hanging from the ceiling with "the best leg of the voyage" painted on it! I put a line drawing of CLYPEUS with our itinerary typed on it, in a screw top jar, and my parents actually saw it on a TV sailing programme as some filming cruisers read out our message.

We arrived in Townsville for the last two weeks of the South Pacific Arts Festival. Once again a superb celebration of island dances, chants, drums, paintings, crafts, films and all FREE.

If you remember, last time in Tahiti, seats for performances were

South Pacific arts festival

expensive so I had sat behind the dancers. This time it was really good to see the smiling faces rather than just the wiggling bottoms!

The Hawaiians set up a romantic traditional wedding on Magnetic Island. Once again we enjoyed swaying wahines, their dark long tresses crowned with a ring of flowers, as they danced to the drums, the drums. A walking-on-fire ceremony took place. After much hocus pocus the Hawaiians demonstrated walking across the hot coals. Then officials invited some of the audience to have a try. I joined the queue. They asked "have you been drinking alcohol?" and ladies, "are you having your monthly period?" Those who said yes were asked to leave the line. Waiting to walk across the fire was scary as we watched the shimmering heat rise from red-hot coals. They told us to "Step carefully on the smooth black stones." The black stones were only warm but it was wise concentrate on keeping your balance and a relief to reach the other side.

The Government Aboriginal Settlement on Palm Island seemed a well-run community but the Aborigines didn't necessarily want to be there. They were busy trying to catch enough turtles to provide a traditional feast for Festival Visitors and were disappointed not to be able to provide turtle meat and complained about laws which stopped them catching their traditional food.

CHAPTER TWENTY THREE

Papua New Guinea Lat 11°01' Long 150°34'E
September to December 1988

The social life at Townsville Marina was lively. We enjoyed having authors Lyn and Larry Pardy on board for dinner. They were good raconteurs and told of life on their famous wooden, un-motorised, and un-electrified yacht TALESIN. It made me realise what luxury I have on CLYPEUS, no electric light for them, or the assistance of a motor when clawing off a lee shore.

With SUTAMON, our Australian buddy-boat, we set off to Papua New Guinea, 650 miles north north east. Once again it was a rotten rough, tough, six day sail hard on the wind - banging our heads against a brick wall would have made a pleasant change!. Heaving-to for meals and for one night to sleep, was the only respite.

Milne Bay Province was shrouded in mist as we made our landfall across the submerged reef - a landfall with no visible land but the depth sounder suddenly lifted from a thousand fathoms to about forty feet. Gradually mountain-tops appeared and ephemeral fingers of vapour explored the dark green valleys. Beneath rain-darkened clouds we steered in through the reef to China Strait and Samarai Island.

SUTAMON had anchored ahead of us and had cold champagne waiting to celebrate the end of their first ocean voyage. They couldn't believe how awful it had been. They hadn't eaten for five days and Tao and Monique had made do with fruit, bread and biscuits. However, traumas of diesel tank and deck leaks were soon forgotten in the excitement of meeting new people and exploring the mountainous island in the hot, humid climate.

Samarai used to be the white, manicured, Government town before the Australians left on Independence in 1965. Now there are only three white men, one woman, and a couple of hundred local people. White ants and creeping jungle are gradually overtaking the rotting buildings. The locals are small, brown, gentle, friendly and indolent. They were kicked and humiliated by the white administrators and their wives, had a separate poor native hospital and were not allowed to live on the island or walk in front of white people. However, they appear not to bear any grudges or to resent white visitors. Most speak English and there are trained nurses, teachers and a doctor, thanks to efforts of an English Missionary: Charles W. Abel of the London Missionary Society. Unfortunately, the locals haven't been able to maintain the self-supporting educational, boat building, printing and medical training establishment he and his family built up over the last hundred years and it too, is decomposing.

The people have little reason to do formal work. The land is lush and fertile and their wants simple. They talk freely of their grandparents being cannibals, who, they say, were ready for Christianity as they were tired of the fear, mystery and magic of their former religions, but magic is still powerful. Although relatives are given a formal Christian burial, it is still considered that bad magic killed them, not illness.

Before leaving Wokingham I had read *'Forty Years in Darkest Papua"* by R. Abel (son of Charles) and now, here we were on Kwato, where he had built his Mission. Two young Leicester University graduates, Mark and Ruth, were enjoying their voluntary service overseas, revitalising the training centre. Mark was trying to get the boat building shed going again - two 35 foot wooden work/fishing boat keels were laid. Ruth was teaching the pre-schoolers. Both accept that whatever influence they now have, will only last a few years.

The locals try hard to please and always answer with a smiling "yes", or "may be", but life gently continues in the old ways. They sit in the shade endlessly chewing betel nut, their smiling mouths looking like black caves stained with red. Discoloured tooth stumps are all that remain of their childhood gleaming white teeth. Betel nut is a narcotic that has a soporific effect and pleasant taste when chewed with powdered lime and mustard catkins. The Government consider it is a lesser evil than alcohol so doesn't actively discourage it and there are no dentists.

We were invited to a splendid native wedding in European style at Kwato Church and subsequent feast on a nearby island. The bride in her white gown and veil had to take off her satin shoes and hoist her long dress up around her waist to sit in a dugout canoe to be ferried ashore for the village reception. The groom, with his trousers rolled up around his knees, carried her ashore. At the reception I took a surreptitious look under the table to see the bride- still wearing her white gloves, but having discarded her pretty, uncomfortable, shoes.

An octogenarian German watchmaker had a "tide-o-meter" in his lagoon-side kitchen: a tidal well in which he measured the rise and fall of the tide each day then sent the information to weather forecasters in Australia. He also enjoyed some pet geckos (lizards) for whom he had made a tiny golden goblet, which he filled with port after dinner each night. The geckos would scramble down from the walls and, standing on their hind legs, sip the port from the golden goblet while he drank his port from a crystal glass.

In 1988, to use THE telephone in Samarai - it was on the counter of the post agency - the Postmaster demanded silence and refused to serve anybody else. So, everyone had to listen to the person speaking, in fact people came in off the street just to listen. The 'phone didn't work very often. Whilst waiting to buy stamps one morning, a dog fight started in the street. The Postmaster came from behind the counter, shooed us into the road, locked the door behind him so that he too could watch the fight and brouhaha. When the dogs had gone their separate ways he unlocked the door and we all trooped back to business as usual.

A week later we left for the really remote islands in the Louisiade Archipelago where there would be no shops, brick buildings or telephones until we arrived in Misima two months ahead.

Those two months in the Louisiade Archipelago were a happy sojourn into a gentle Christian Stone Age. We visited 16 of the 400 islands and met only friendship and hospitality.

It felt a great privilege to be amongst the first visitors who were not administrators, traders, or missionaries. We arrived as friends and were accepted as such. Electronic navigation has made the difference. No way would we have attempted these coral- infested waters under constant cloud cover with just sextants.

So few visitors have been to these Islands that toddlers, who hadn't seen white people before, cried with fright when I approached. Many of the older people hid inside their houses, but the younger people are keen to talk in English and visit CLYPEUS. On most mornings a few silent canoes paddled around us. Nobody intruded or knocked on our hull, but a discreet cough let us know that somebody was out there waiting to visit. They say P.N.G has 700 languages. English is the lingua franca and in schools after Class One, all teaching is in English, so it was easy to converse.

On October 3rd a radio message told us that Andrea had 8lb Alexander on September 30th. Mother and baby were well. We were delighted, but so sorry not to be near her.

On the islands we visited, the people were happy, resourceful, clever craftspeople and pleased to see us. We traded children's clothes, towels, sugar, and sticks of chewing tobacco, for pumpkins, papayas, pineapples, greens, crayfish, shells, and carvings. They are accustomed to trading and still use special money (bagi) and an ancient language within the centuries-old, still flourishing canoe-trading ring.

Pots are left to dry for three days.

Warri Islanders make and trade pots; Panaete Islanders - canoes; Basilaki Islanders - sago; Hummock Islanders - pigs and vegetables; Misima Islanders - betel nut, pigs, vegetables and boat building wood; Wanim and Bageman Islanders - make bagi. They still use bagi and pigs to pay for brides, canoes, pots and food, and live as their ancestors have done for thousands of years. Copra, beche de mer and

Hummock island

trochus shells are sold to the outside world for cash, which is used to buy rice, hurricane lamps, oil and clothes.

Western clothes mean washing, whereas traditional grass skirts and leaf G strings are easy to replace. Many ladies wore just short grass skirts, no tops. However, it is shameful to show any thigh. The skirt made for me wasn't big enough when I tried it on, so it had to be enlarged amid a crowd of bare-breasted ladies all "tut tutting" at my inch of bare thigh!

Unfortunately Theo, skipper of SUTAMON caught malaria, in spite of taking Fansidar tablets which their doctor in Townsville had insisted were sufficient protection. Three weeks after arriving in Papua and twelve hours after anchoring off the perfect little uninhabited island of Ita Marina where Theo had rowed ashore and said, "it's perfect. Too good to be true. It can't last". Next day he succumbed to fever, shivering and delirium. We thought he was suffering from heatstroke as he had been on the foredeck eyeballing through the shallows all the previous day, and after all, we were all religiously taking the recommended anti-malaria drugs. However most evenings Theo walked to a waterfall to collect water, wearing only his bathing trunks. For five days Sue cooled and bathed him, and kept notes of his condition. The children came to CLYPEUS each morning to do their school work.

The enforced stop gave us time to enjoy our little paradise island. Peter and I swam and snorkelled in the aquamarine lagoon, looked for shells, read, had barbecues. One night we slept out on the beach there being no mosquitoes as there was no fresh water.

Fire and barbeque most nights

The dinghy singers

Three other yachts arrived, one with a nurse, and one whose radio was more powerful than ours. Australia transmits excellent radio medi-care via their coastal stations. Sue spoke to Brisbane Hospital who diagnosed malaria. The nurse had a malaria treatment pack which was administered immediately and we heeded the radio advice to return to Samarai and doctor. By that time Theo was well enough to direct operations lying in the cockpit so Sue and children motor-sailed following us for the journey back to Samarai. Consultations and blood samples, which Sue took by ferry to the mainland for testing, confirmed the whole family fit.

We returned to the remote islands where the attractive and friendly children would be on the beach to greet us speaking good English. Near naked, they would swim out and climb in our rubber dinghies and sing. hymns; tuneful island legend songs and *'London's Burning'* and *'The Minstrel Boy To the War has Gone'*, which we assume they learned from BBC Schools Broadcasts audio tapes.

In the lagoon at Panapompom a Japanese Zero plane, a relic from W.W.2.was lying in about 10' of clear water, amazingly clean with just a little coral in the pilot's seat and around the tail plane. The propeller blades were still attached to the big radial engine.

The Islanders told us how difficult it was for them to understand our white men's war, where, in the evening, soldiers go back to camp to eat and enjoy a drink at the bar, watch movies and go to bed. Then get up in the morning to go and kill indiscriminately some more people. Their wars are for hate, revenge or territory and they fight until they have won or lost. Only minimal warriors are killed and eaten as the final triumph. Women and children are left alone. Makes you think!

One evening we sat on SUTAMON's after deck, anchored just inside the pass into a blue lagoon, watching the sun go down. As we sipped our evening beer, Monique pointed to a large black triangular fin slowly circling the boat. They had caught a small shark, tied a rope noose around its tail, attached it to a stanchion, and hung it over the side to bleed so the flesh would be white for their evening meal. As we calmly watched the triangular fin approach from the stern, the shark suddenly emerged like 'Jaws' and with fantastic power and acceleration, rose and ripped the shark from the stanchion and dived. It was unbelievable. It was as if a nuclear submarine had emerged from nowhere at full power. A show of such energy and force was incredible. Peter and I waited a while before rowing home in our vulnerable little rubber dinghy. We remembered the couple who left their small red rubber dinghy floating astern with the oars akimbo. A shark suddenly bit a great lump out of the side, obviously thinking it was a big fish.

Meri preparing filters

The men on Warri gathered clay for the women to clean and roll into long worms. They coil pots which they decorate before firing on coconut husk fires on the beach. When the dark brown clay turns orange, it's done.

We watched a family on Basilaki prepare sago, their staple diet. While Grandad fashioned a bowl and funnels from the outside fibres of a sago palm, his two sons-in-law chopped the palm and with stone axes hacked out the core. One wife carried the sago and buckets of water to another wife Meri who had made plaited filters from pandanus leaves. Meri squished the sago in water and pushed it down the funnel and filters where the mush settled out and was dried in the sun to crumble into flour. The next morning she kindly brought us a cake each. Having no sugar or yeast the cakes looked like rough cardboard and tasted the same.

Ebora Bay and village

The villagers at Ebora, on the larger island of Misima, shared their way of life for a few days. We were only the second pair of yachts that had ever visited. Later, TIMSHELL from Australia arrived with their two young daughters on board. Every Thursday at the school, pupils wear traditional dress and learn traditional skills and dancing. The friendly dancing teacher showed me a few steps. The morning flag-raising ceremony in the playground brought tears to the eyes as the children enthusiastically sang their National Anthem as the flag was hoisted.

In the afternoon we watched the dress rehearsal for a display they were to perform at the gold mine, twenty miles away. There was no way of communicating except by canoe, and later, when we arrived at the mine landing stage, we mentioned that the children were looking forward to performing. "That's a pity," said an official. "The ceremony was held last week."

After school the headmaster guided us up to the village gardens on the cliff top. The only tools they have are sticks, no spades or garden forks. On the way he stopped by an old tree, thrust his hand into a hole and nonchalantly pulled out a skull. "This would be somebody my grandparents ate," he said as he threw it back. "Invaders were not buried, we just scattered their bones after the feast."

When we returned to his house a crowd of villagers were already standing outside the windows. Evidently he had recently purchased a generator and television set. While his family sat inside, the rest of the village fought for a place at the glassless windows to watch the programmes.

At a jungle mountain stream not far from the large scar of Misima gold mine, we playfully panned for gold, swirling some of the sandy stream-bed around in large leaves. Yes, we could make out gold dust, little flecks of gold gradually collected as we swirled the water away. Some young men in loin-cloths standing holding their spears watched us, so, being cowards, we put it all back like naughty schoolboys. However they were friendly and told us of some boys who picked up a large nugget and dragged it in a sack to the assay office at the gold mine. They were rewarded with the full value. Villagers sometimes charted helicopters to go and find the lumps of yellow rock referred to in the stories that have been handed down orally through the generations.

Some young men carrying spears watched us pan for gold

We had a slow, but amusing voyage, back to Australia. After four days our little fleet of three yachts were becalmed in the Coral Sea. Engines were turned off to ensure we had enough diesel to get back through the Great Barrier Reef. Smooth slopes of dark blue water advanced, rocked us gently and then continued on their way north-west. Bio-degradable rubbish accumulated on the surface around us - banana skins, paper and coconut shells. A morning radio programme was started between us on low power VHF radio: Radio Coral Sea with music requests, weather and fishing reports and jokes from The Australian Children's Joke Book. The hot pale blue sky shimmered above us, the decks burned our feet. The striped awning over the cockpit gave a modicum of shade. Until, at last, water chuckled under the stern and we glided through the blue. Our green and yellow cruising chute flew for days and nights with a light easterly wind pushing us back to The Great Barrier Reef.

CHAPTER
TWENTY FOUR

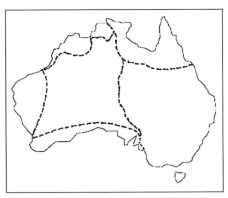

Australia with land route **Townsville:**
October '88 to June 1989
Lat 19°11'S Long 147°23'E

Back in Townsville it was HOT: over 85° in the cabin day and night, in spite of additional awnings and a sea breeze during the day. Two electric fans helped to move the air around. Across the park from the Marina was an excellent outdoor swimming pool. I enjoyed taking over the aqua aerobics class three mornings a week when the American Instructor sailed away.

We planned our voyage home, collected charts, applied for visas, wrote to Embassies. I wrote to our family and friends:

"This year has been so good I can't see how or why we should stop cruising. We were very unsettled on our return from "home" but this seasons cruising has re-affirmed our conviction that the sacrifices are worth the freedom to travel and explore where and when we please. We enjoy the loving togetherness and understanding that seems to get better all the time. We delight in the satisfaction of keeping our life support systems working unaided and living so close to nature. We rejoice in the peace, the unpolluted areas we cruise, the simple life with few worries: survival, our families and long term money.

In the seven years since we started living on board we have sailed 31,000 miles and travelled another 84,000 by air or road. After Christmas I'm coaching over to Perth to see my parents, which will be 11,000 miles round trip. That's 95,000 miles that were not in our original plan at all. Peter prefers to stay on CLYPEUS to get her ready for the homeward voyage and protect her from cyclones. Locals are very apprehensive this year as the sea is hot and the rains heavy already - 18" rain fell in 24 hours last week. He is subsidising our Marina fees by doing electrical repairs. So far this week he has mended two Autohelms, one "Navicohelm" and rebuilt an auxiliary charging system. Luckily there is a good local components' stockist. I'm giving ladies and gentlemen haircuts, teaching Aqua-aerobics and writing articles to supplement our reduced investment income.

A letter arrived from Peter's former employers. "Would he consider re-joining the company for two years to assist in the formation of a joint venture manufacturing

Family wedding in Perth

enterprise in Taiwan?" The financial crisis in 1987 had severely reduced our income.

We seized the opportunity to restore our capital.

Peter encouraged me to take the opportunity to visit my family again for a family wedding. He would correspond with the Company about terms and how to fit it into our route.

Northern Queensland life is very laid back. Doctors (in the hospital), dentists, policemen, Customs Officers, and bank employees wear smart tailored shorts, short sleeved shirts and long socks. Customers walk into banks, shopping malls, and the post office wearing no shoes or shirts but a Crocodile Dundee type hat, shorts with perhaps a vest, T shirts or sun tops. If Peter wore a tie to go out to supper, it caused hoots of derisive laughter. We warned those sailing to Europe they will need a tie and blazer to socialise in Yacht Clubs but they didn't believe us.

After sharing a happy social Christmas in the Marina, on December 27th I left to back-pack my way around Australia. I enjoyed the long bus ride with the chatty drivers and films on TV. Once again the navigation was superb and not a single wave broke over the coach!

We passed emus and brumbies (wild horses), spiralling williwaws twisting the red dust up and along the scrub plain. The air was clear and the countryside so flat around Richmond, you could almost see the curvature of the earth. The driver mentioned that all the town and farm water comes out of a bore at 127°F. Roadside hoardings were pierced with bullet and shot holes. They advertised 'TOOHEYS ON TAP', 'MOBIL', 'MOTEL', and 'MEATPIES'

The northern route to Perth via Broome was spectacular during the 'wet'. We suddenly entered country where the grass was a brilliant Irish green, freshly sprouting out of the red earth after the first rain for five years. Against clear blue skies, pink and grey galahs and red and green parakeets squawked and wheeled round coolabah trees surrounding the full billabongs. Flood debris hung high in the trees. Along the roadside lay drowned cattle, the brown skin sagging between the bones. Sometimes just a bleached white bovine rib cage and tail bones laid on the verge. Brolgas flew low, their grey bodies heavy behind their slender necks and bulbous heads.

At Threeways, the junction of roads from Adelaide, Townsville and Darwin (all at least 1,000 miles away), it was necessary to change coaches. In the middle of the night we were deposited at the lone filling station, with an attached (but closed) café and had to sit on the kerbside for an hour until the connecting bus arrived. There was an interesting mural painted on the wall.

At Mataranka where *"We of the Never Never"* was written and filmed, I jogged between the tropical palms to the clear thermal pool and had a delicious swim while the other passengers had lunch. The homestead was visible through the trees along with aboriginal humpies made of bark, twigs and grass, between tall brown termite mounds.

After a day, a night and a morning we arrived in Katherine in the Northern Territory. The tourist information bureau recommended a backpackers' hostel with air conditioning and swimming pool for $12 a night in the five-bed dormitory.

On New Year's Eve I took a boat trip up Katherine Gorge, south west of Kakadu National Park. The tall Akubra-hatted Ranger, Alex, drove the bus; gave us information; took the money; helped us aboard the flat-bottomed boat; untied the ropes; moved the gang plank; started the engines; drove the boat and guided our tour on land as well as the river. He was a gem!

Whilst cooling off in the swimming pool at the Hostel a New Year's Eve party was organised between all the young international travellers. The men bought the drinks and the girls bought the food. Fourteen of us shared a "Roast Chook Takeaway" in the girls' dormitory whilst watching the Nelson Mandella Birthday Concert on TV. At midnight everyone jumped into the pool and with glasses of champagne toasted 1989. They were charming young people from England, Sweden, Switzerland, Germany, and Australia, all well-behaved and sensitive to ethnic and religious differences. Nobody aggressive or pushy and I felt privileged to be included.

Next day we all went our different ways. The almost empty coach travelled hundreds of miles without passing any other traffic or seeing any towns. I watched videos, chatted to the coach captains, saw more emus, brumbies, kangaroos, brolgas, goannas and water buffalo. At dusk the crimson cliffs of the Kimberleys faded behind a purple haze before the stark white moon rose amidst a million stars: no people, no pollution.

On to Derby, Broome, Port Headland, Kalbarri, Denham - from where you can travel to Monkey Mia and wade into the sea to feed the wild dolphins. If only I had realised it would have made a memorable stop-over. But all my Australian family were already assembled for the wedding.

At my parents' home In Rockingham, the sun shone for two months. They were now 83 enjoying having their three daughters together again. Hilary took Sheila and I to play golf, hilarious hit and giggle games. Shouting "fore" to clear the kangaroos nibbling the greens made it different!

Ann and Don of SHOESTRING (chapter 4) arranged for me to spend a day in Bodhinyana Monastery. Rojena (heavenly light, light of life) was my companion for the day. A 30'sh lass from Nottingham who had trained as a nurse at 'Barts' Hospital in London and was now a shaven headed, white robed nun, the only female in the Monastery. She lived in a wood in her kuti - an eight by ten foot hut, with a bed, mat, candle, duvet, pillow and torch, and books. On the washing line outside hung a white skirt and top, like a judo outfit. The monks existed in their kutis with just a mat on the floor and a plate to hold their candle.

They rose at 4.30 to meditate and chant until 7.30. Chores were done until the only meal of the day at 10.30. The afternoon, evening and night is spent meditating, studying and sleeping. At 8 a.m. I was given the task of helping the supporters and novices prepare a lunch from donations. I sliced and buttered bread, then spread it with marmalade, Vegemite or peanut butter.

At 10.30 I was invited to join the shaven monks in their saffron robes who were sitting on mats around a large room with a shining polished wood floor. It was indicated I took the extreme left mat and sat down, in as near a lotus position as I could manage and followed their movements. A tall dark skinned novice brought in the food. Chanting started, we bowed three times to Buddha with our hands together. The Abbot was served first. He spooned a ladle-full of food into his bowl and passed the dish to his left. Sixteen dishes were served: curries, prawns, meat, salad, rice, pasta, potatoes, baked beans, prawns in batter, tiny spring rolls, melon and lychees, cake, cinnamon toast, (my) bread and butter, and a large platter of apples, oranges, grapes, and bananas. Everything was laid, one on top of the other, into each bowl.

Being the most humble, on the extreme left, every bowl and dish gradually became my responsibility. Not looking ahead, I had started putting the dishes down close around me. As I sat in excruciating discomfort, with my legs crossed, so I had to lean further and further away to put down the dishes and had nowhere to ease my legs. Eyes were closed for seven to ten minutes in further contemplation before the Abbot tinkled a bell to indicate 'eat' time. During the silence I furtively watched what was happening and, as my legs succumbed to agonizing cramps, tried to stretch them without clinking a dish or knocking something over. We ate from our bowls with spoons for nearly an hour, trying to pick out savoury morsels from under the cake and lychees. Lemonade or Pepsi was passed around, and later tea from a huge teapot circulated. Empty cans, teapot and milk jug joined the wide wall of dishes around me.

More meditation until the Abbot tinkled his bell and started chanting. The monks joined in the soft melodious chants and, after six kneeling bows to the Buddha statue, we de-kinked and dispersed. I helped clear away - my own particular 'merit' task.

During the afternoon, as I helped Rojena with her task of watering a tree, cupful by cupful, from a bucket of water, she told me her story. She had been backpacking with her boyfriend when she became involved with the Buddhists in Tibet. She pursued her 'call' in Australia. In July 1989 she expected to return to England but was very apprehensive about her mother's reaction to her shaven head in their little village outside Ilkeston in Derbyshire. Rojena hoped to join a monastery in Hertfordshire but worried how she would settle in a crowded establishment after the seclusion and privacy of a 12 monk monastery in fifty acres of woodland here. We meditated in the kuti for the rest of the afternoon until Ann and Don came to pick me up at 5 PM.

I travelled back to Townsville across the Nullabor Desert. Due to re-vitalised mining activity, Kalgoorlie had boomed in the three years since 1986 and now had a K Mart, Kentucky Fried, refurbished Hotels and new homes. At the Wudinna meal stop, I talked to Julie and her husband who were owners and drivers of a road train (a 62 wheeler articulated truck with two long wagons). They drove four hours on, four hours off. As they had so much invested in their vehicle they had to keep moving. They took turns to sleep on a little bunk at the back of the air-conditioned cab and

Outback transport 62 wheeler road train. The temprature was 120° F

their life seemed very similar to ours on the ocean - except they could get off if they felt like it. They carried no livestock, just general cargo from town to town in the outback and had a home in Adelaide where they spent spare days washing and servicing the truck. A labrador puppy with impossibly big paws accompanied them. In '67, when we crossed the Nullabor, pastel coloured flowers burst into a carpet of blossom after a night of rain. This time all was dry red dust sparsley covered with low grey-green scrub.

I spent a few days with friends and family in Adelaide and the Barossa Valley where they were just beginning to pick the autumnal wine grapes. My nephew Simon took me to the racing stable stud where there was a swimming pool for the horses!

The road through the Red Centre from Adelaide to Darwin had been finished the previous year so it was a smooth and comfortable ride. The coach arrived at pink, Coober Pedy, the desert opal-mining town, where everyone lives underground. At dawn, mounds of pink dust with glinting metal chimneys sticking up above ground showed where the homes were. The outskirts of the town resembled a lunar landscape: shafts and mullock heaps with trucks and windlasses stretched to the horizon. There was time to visit the underground church and underground four star hotel. Until last year water was scarce, scant rain fell and only a trickle could be raised from the salt water bore. Now a deep bore well and desalination plant had been installed and water was almost plentiful.

On top of Ayers rock

At Alice Springs I took a two day safari tour to Ayers Rock and The Olgas. It was wonderful sleeping in a swag under the stars. The Olgas are huge rounded outcrops of orange conglomerate stone. Ayers Rock wasn't a disappointment. Climbing it was far more difficult than I had imagined. 32 people have died from heart attacks or been blown off by the wind during the seven years it had been open to the public. As the dozen or so international safari guests jolted along in the big Land Rover type jeep we sang songs including Waltzing Matilda:

Once a jolly swagman, camped by a billabong,
Under the shade of a coolabah tree.
And he sang as he watched and waited till his billy boiled.
'Who'll come awaltzing Matilda with me.'

Down came a jumbuck drinking at the water-hole
Up jumped the swagman and grabbed him in glee
And he sang as he stowed him away in his tucker-bag,
'You'll come a-waltzing Matilda with me!'

Down came the Squatter a-riding his thoroughbred;
Down came the Trooper - one, two, three.
'Who's is the jumbuck that you've got in your tucker-bag?

You'll come awaltzing Matilda with me.

The swagman, he up and jumped into the water-hole,
Drowning himself by the Coolabah tree;
And his ghost may be heard as it sings in the Billabong,
'Who'll come a-waltzing Matilda with me?'
by: A.B. Paterson.

John, our Toddy's Outback Safari tour guide, was a mine of information. He explained the words. A jumbuck is a sheep. If a swagman (traveller) was starving, he was allowed to kill a sheep for food but must leave the skin, hide and wool for the squatter -(the owner who had leased Crown land). The Trooper 123 was a police sergeant with three stripes. John finished with a question -

"OK. What was the swagman's name?" We all shook our heads.

'How could we know that?" someone asked. "It isn't in the words."

"Listen," sang John " 'And 'e sat, and 'e watched, and' e waited till his billy boiled.' The swagman's name was Andy (Andrew) of course."

'The Alice' is a fine well-tree'd town and in the clean and pleasant Backpackers Hostel I was nick-named `the granny with the tranny' who slept in the top bunk in the unisex dormitory. Once again charming, sensible and interesting young people.

Mt. Isa, the mining town, was the only place of any size between Alice Springs and Townsville. (Mt. Isa's Town Council looks after an area greater than Holland.)

Peter was waiting for me, looking fit and well, with champagne on ice. He had worked hard on the boat and organised a chart exchange for all the boats travelling to Europe via the Red Sea.

He went into hospital for a hernia 'op'. On the day he was discharged, warnings of cyclone Aivu were announced giving us two days to batten down the boat and take off emergency bags: food, first aid kit, drinking water, clothes and sleeping gear; ship's papers, passports, credit cards, driving licences, valuables, electronic gear and any-thing else irreplaceable. We included all photographs and negatives but left books and souvenirs. Water tanks were filled in case there was a water shortage later and we bought extra tins of meat, vegetables, and rice as it may prove better to move on up the coast away from the aftermath of destruction. The locals were generous with advice like: "Raise your club burgee from your masthead so that you will know which is your boat under the water." Some local boat owners lowered their dinghies under-water to protect them.

It was scary, when the wind started whistling through the rigging, gusting over 50 m.p.h. One of the upstairs offices, in the marina administration block had been made available to yacht's people to set up camp. There were many offers from the locals to stay in their homes and government buildings were offered as an evacuation centre, if the Marina office became insecure. However all the boaters wanted to stay as close as possible to our boats and each other.

A great camaraderie developed and everybody assisted wherever possible. A young Israeli couple with their daughters came on board for a cup of tea. "The excite-ment and apprehension is rather like going into battle," said feminine little Prina.

"What do you mean?" I asked.

"Oh! Yoar and I were in the army. We were in the front line together." she added nonchalantly.

"You actually carried a gun and had to shoot it?" I asked.

"Of course." She delicately sipped her tea.

Yoar said ruminatively into his mug, "Yes, this is like going to war, but this enemy we cannot fight."

"Mummy, Mummy," Netta tugged her sleeve. "Can we go to the cyclone now?"

"You would think we were off to the cinema," Yoar grinned. "Come on then. Do you want any help Peter?"

"No, we've taken off all the sails and everything from the deck that we possibly can, and doubled and trebled up all the lines. Do you realise that if the two metre cyclone surge comes at high water all the pontoons will float off the top of the piles and the whole lot will be blown up the river, boats and all."

The wind howled and the rain thrashed us as we closed our brave little boat and gave her a pat and a prayer, wondering if we would see her whole again. Yoar and his little family held on to each other tightly, their oilskins blown flat against their backs, their dark hair whipping forward as they blew up the swaying gangplank from the rocking pontoon.

In the large upstairs room, families were organising their space. Radios relayed the storm warnings. Little children happily peeped out of 'cubbies' they had made from the stacked gear. For them it was great fun. It wasn't so bad for parents either, a party atmosphere prevailed. We had all done all we could. The eye of the storm would probably arrive in ten hour's time during the night, there was nothing more we could do except chat, play cards and have another glass of wine.

Periodically someone would force open the glass door and stand on the verandah assessing the oncoming storm. When they came back in and all the cards blew away there was criticism amongst the calls of "What's happening now mate?"

We took the opportunity for a long hot shower and shampoo; there may be no water or electricity for a while if flood damage destroyed services.

Happy children peeped out of their 'cubbies'

Fortunately for us, the storm deviated from its track and the eye passed about 50 miles south. As it was low water all the boats were well down in the Marina basin partially sheltered from the wind and we suffered no damage. A state of emergeny was called and where 'Aivu' did cross the coast the poor people had to rebuild their houses and re-tile roofs. The winds in the centre were over 140 mph. As Dorothy McKellar so aptly wrote of Australia: 'a wilful, lavish land'.

We had left CLYPEUS wondering how damaged she would be next time we saw her, but not a scar. We had been through far worse times together.

Then our time in Townsville raced away, filled with socialising and international dinner parties on board where we discussed 'punctuated equilibrism', 'philectic gradualism', fossils and inter-continental movement and animal migration'. International cruising sailors are a fantastic mix of professions and cultures, and when we can bear to stop talking boats, we discuss knowledge from our previous varied lives. We also made a small spray hood, which taxed our ingenuity and patience, new dodgers and a spinnaker sock and two wooden seats high on the stern, so that we could sit up in the breeze whilst sailing, or having a sundowner.

The Aqua Aerobics classes closed, more stores were purchased and packed, and emergency kits re-freshed, while Peter checked the rigging, engine, batteries, bilge pumps etc. and refitted the wind vane and solar panels.

A definite job offer for Peter to start work in October as consultant to a Taiwanese engineering company arrived before we left. He was really looking forward to it. We decided to follow our original plan, to be in Singapore by September where CLYPEUS would be hauled out and we would fly to Taiwan. The terms of employment were reasonable so we hoped to save and catch up on inflation. The company would fly us home to England each year, which was a great incentive for me. I missed my family so much.

We sailed north from Townsville on the 18th May. I wrote in the log:

"Sails up. Clothes off. Yippee!" We had a wonderful sense of freedom as land-based cares just fell away. That night, we could see the Southern Cross, Plough and Orion all visible at once.

The east coast of Australia provided fantastic, but rugged, sailing. It took a week to sail to Cairns via many islands with sandy bays. On the mainland, behind the golden beaches, the densely forested land rose steeply towards the Great Dividing Range that towered into the clouds. This area was still remote, without road access and only sparsely populated.

Cairns is an exciting resort with many tourists, but for the anchored yachts it was a long ride in the dinghy across the swiftly flowing river estuary to civilisation. The southern side of the river was still just mud and mangroves. We took the exciting Karoonda train trip up into the mountains to the Atherton Tablelands, built in 1888; a spectacular ascent passing through fifteen tunnels in tropical rain forest to the rolling famlands beyond Atherton.

My sister Sheila and Tony arranged a stopover in Cairns so together we swam on the Barrier Reef. The marine biologist from the tourist catamaran gave more information about the varied corals and fish in half an hour than I had managed to glean over seven years on my own.

We looked out for the stone ruins in Watson's Bay where in 1881 Mrs Watson was attacked by Aboriginals - their house had been built on a traditional ceremonial site. She escaped in a barrell but was ventually found on another island having died of thirst with her baby in her arms.

Cooktown, 70 miles further north was where Capt. Cook's ship ENDEAVOUR hit the reef in 1770 and was beached and repaired. We arrived in time for the annual re-enactment of his landing

Our hero Captain James Cook. Cooktown

and dressed up to join the celebrations. Stock hands had come in from the outback and the Pubs were open 24 hours a day. Comatose bodies, clutching beer bottles lay scattered on the streets in the mornings.

Cooktown, in 1890 had 60,000 people, now it would be difficult to assemble 600. It was the gateway to the Palmer Gold Fields, had a railway and, according to the museum, 193 hotels and brothels. It is in a beautiful river estuary between hills, but the sandflies and midges drove us mad. Their bites are unnoticed for 24 hours before they start itching, and then.

The road north from Cairns to Cooktown which had only been surfaced for two years stops here. It is a real frontier town.

As we sailed north we anchored in the evenings and watched our tiny TV screen. Between programmes were usual advertisements for detergents, and Japanese cars. Gradually they began to get a more regional flavour: rodeo boots, Akubra hats, Driback coats, The Flying Doctor Service, rifles for $585 (with ammunition), cattle dips and douches, and finally advertisements for Brahmin bull semen and embryos - surely they must have a very limited market?

It was a rush to cover the 1500 miles to Darwin in time for the Darwin to Ambon Race preparations, as it was only possible to sail when the sun was high because of the coral reefs. Peter (as Admiral again) painstakingly found and marked on the charts 22 anchorages, about 40 miles apart for our overnight stops. The SE trade winds were strong during the days but fairly still at night, which was perfect. John and Innes on QUALLEE OF SYDNEY made up our flotilla of three boats. SUTAMON had hauled out for antifouling in Cairns, but we hoped to beach and antifoul CLYPEUS in Gove.

During this time the Tiananmen Square massacre occurred so we didn't know whether Peter's Taiwan job was actually viable. We decided to stick to our plan until Singapore, and continued trying to learn Mandarin from BBC audio tapes.

Crocodile warning signs and their smooth slides down into the water were everywhere. At Hope Isles the fishing line wound itself around the propeller and I had to go over the side in 30 feet of murky water, to cut the line from around the propeller shaft. At Lizard Island's sandy beach the hull had to be snorkel scraped, in as shallow water as we dared. My adrenalin was getting plenty of exercise.

Research on crocodiles revealed that two types inhabit Australia: the salty estuarine or salt water crocodile and the (freshie) freshwater crocodile. Salties eat dogs and humans, freshies do not. Male salties can grow to six metres. The females grow to two or three metres, lay their eggs in earth mounds and guard them jealously. We mentally noted to run if we saw a three foot high mound of earth. (See Appendix 8)

From Lizard Island I sailed with Liza and Andy on Canadian yacht BAGHEERA to the Cod Hole in the outer reef to feed the massive, benign, potato cod by hand. Peter climbed Cook's Look, where Captain Cook stood to survey the reef and find a way back into the Pacific. It was worth the hard climb for the magnificent view.

Bathurst Bay had a monument somewhere? A sad place where all hands were lost when a fishing fleet was blown ashore in the late 19th Century. Amazing hills of great, grey, smooth boulders tumbled down to the beach. Where had they come from? There were no mountains nearby. We were so intrigued we forgot about the tide and found our boats were all aground on the soft sand. CLYPEUS managed to get off first and towed SUTAMON afloat. A rope was rushed to QUALLEE but it took a long time and much diesel to eventually pull her off. We were all ashamed of ourselves.

Coastwatch planes buzzed us every day and spoke over VHF to ask if we had seen anything unusual. We looked forward to exchanging words with the friendly pilots. The sea was full of "things". Many evenings we had beach barbecues together. Peter became fisher of the fleet catching Queensland school mackerel; a game fish with white firm flesh similar to turbot. Large tasty oysters abounded and in Owen Passage in the Flinders Islands we stopped to chat to some prawn trawler fishermen. We offered them a six pack of Fosters and politely asked if we could buy some prawns.

"Got a bucket mate?" the grey-haired skipper asked.

We did indeed have a plastic bucket. They handed it back filled with king prawns. SUTAMON, QUALLEE and we, each took our buckets of already-boiled pink prawns, cold cans of Fosters Lager, sat in the shade and 'pigged out'.

At Portland Roads Peter and I rowed ashore to post a letter. The five houses along the dirt road had no power, telephones or piped water. Ross Pope who was about to drive the 27 miles (two hours drive on the unmade road) in his Land Rover to Lauritown to post a letter. He kindly agreed to take ours. The post plane delivered and took letters to Cairns on Thursdays. Ross and his wife had lived in this tiny hamlet for thirteen years having previously been lighthouse keepers.

Drive 27 miles to post a letter

The next night we anchored in Margaret Bay along with eight prawn trawlers. The Bay was seething with birds and fish but sand flies and mosquitoes whined towards us as we tried to row ashore. I set the wire crab cage, baited with a mackerel head on the edge of the reef. In the morning it was a tangled useless mess having been savaged by a shark which had bitten a hole big enough to get his head in and then shaken and bitten his way free. We walked for a short distance but worried about crocodiles. It's a wild coast.

Fast trade wind sailing scooted us around Cape York and Thursday Island. Safari tents were set up on Cape York and a kiosk sold ice cream. The inhospitable shores didn't tempt us with their rapacious mosquitoes and sandflies, blue ringed octopus, stone fish, sharks, snakes, crocodiles and, not surprisingly, few people.

The 350 mile sail across the Gulf of Carpentaria was rotten, with short steep rough seas and toothache. Gove on the NW corner of the Gulf is the third largest city in the Northern Territory and only has 3,600 people. It's a smart modern town completely owned and administered by Nabalco who scrape up red bauxite with giant diggers. Huge trucks take it to the plant for processing into white alumina for shipping worldwide. After Xrays, a young dentist extracted my tooth with the minimum of discomfort,

Huge trucks take the Bauxite to be processed. Notice the size of the driver

but I didn't feel too good.

There wasn't a road to Gove. Everyone and everything is flown or shipped in. Shops sold buckets of ice cream: Tao was in heaven. A happy town of young people making money with good living conditions and no crime. The Aborigines who own the land are happy too as they get paid a royalty for every ton of bauxite mined.

Clypeus was laid alongside scrubbing off posts

CLYPEUS was tied alongside the beach scrubbing-off posts for anti-fouling. As the lowest tides were at midnight, for two nights we spent four dark hours paddling round her scraping and painting. We were worried about crocs and for the first night shone a torch around every 15 minutes looking for their red eyes. We didn't see anything, but on paying our dues, the club secretary said: "Good job you only took two nights, by the third night the crocs would have sussed you out and been ready for you. They have survived for a million years because they watch the habits of their prey before attacking. Here's your change."

Tao tried out the croc cages for size. Because they are an endangered species and cannot be hunted, they are trapped in

Tao tries it out for size.

Looking for 'The hole in the wall' between the Wessell islands

the cages and taken many miles inland. However they are territorial beasts so eventually find their way back home.

On 11th July 1989 I wrote:

Four days to Darwin. Yet another Strong Wind Warning is keeping us hiding behind the Wessell Islands. Yesterday was really exciting, we sailed through "The Gugari Rip" or "The hole in the Wall": a 60 metre gap between two islands. The Rip runs at up to 9 knots so we had to time our approach carefully for slack high water. We were about half an hour early so had rough overfalls at the entrance and a four knot current against us through the pass.

Nine other yachts, all trying to get to Darwin in time for the race, converged on the Rip within half an hour, so our greatest hazard, as usual, was man made. Those boats at the front we were bucking the strong tide, and those at the back catching up, so that all ten yachts were within 500 metres of each other at one time.

On Wigram Island, Innes on QUALLEE, and I decided to row ashore and look for shells. Ten steps from the rubber dinghy we came to large, fresh, crocodile tracks leading over the top of the beach. Even though I had my camera around my neck we ran straight back to the dinghy too frightened to stop long enough to take a photo.'

'The Top End' Entering the gap (Gulgar rip) up to 9 knots

A large amphibious vehicle told us to "get back on your boat mate' there's 3 metre crocs and sharks here

All that remained of Port Essington, a Victorian settlement that hadn't survived, were the stone chimney walls of the settlers' houses. Conditions had been too harsh. It reminded us of another pioneer settlement that had failed: in Ceduna on the south Australian coast where the whispering shifting sands had buried the houses up to the chimneys.

One last story about crocodiles. Two days before Darwin we anchored in Alcaro Bay, east of Cape Don. It looked a pleasant sandy bay with a small river flowing out between the mangroves. Exploring in the rubber dinghy with the Mercury outboard we entered the river. A large amphibious vehicle with about eight men on board came from the lighthouse direction, crossed the river behind us, and shouted. We couldn't make out what they were saying so just waved and carried on into the mangroves for a couple of hundred yards but decided it seemed ominous. The midges steamed up from the river. Coming back to the river entrance the amphibian was waiting for us and the skipper shouted: "There was a bloody great shark following you, its big fin above the water. They flip inflatables over you know! There are lots of three and four metre crocs in there too mate, I'd get back to your boat if I was you."

We did. They were the lighthouse maintenance crew returning to their large white government vessel anchored in the bay and weren't kidding. They motored over to warn SUTAMON and QUALLEE as well.

At last we anchored off Darwin and actually arrived at the Yacht Club for the Skipper and Navigator's meeting with 20 minutes to spare after a 1,500 mile journey. It seemed amazing to be in a modern, high rise city in the middle of absolutely nowhere. Every road from Darwin leads to the outback for thousands of miles before reaching a major town.

A stack of mail awaited us. Our Taipei commitment was still on and we realised that for the next six weeks each day of our life on CLYPEUS would be even more precious.

Darwin Yacht Club had done an amazing amount of preparation to ensure we all had a hassle free, happy time. It was worth the steep U.S.$400 entrance fee which included all our Indonesian cruising permits otherwise difficult to obtain. Fifty yachts gathered for the Race and the setting, facilities and ambiance of the yacht club were delightful.

Darwin's Town Brass Band played at the farewell party and BAGHEERA's flaming rum punches made even the quarter mile trudge with the dinghies to the far-out tide-line a giggle. Later I was able to write in their visitors' book:

Bubble, bubble toil and trouble
Fire burn and cauldron bubble,
Measure large of sunsoaked rum
In the cauldron mix and turn.
Skin of orange, juice of lime,
Heat it up and bubble fine;
Stir in sugar, mix it up,
Set afire and light the cup.
For a charm or powerful trouble,
Like a hell broth boil and bubble.
Bagheera's brew makes friends worldwide
But sailors, beware of Darwin's falling tide!

-Macbeth Act IV with apologies.

CHAPTER TWENTY FIVE

Indonesia - Bali
July 89 to September 89
Lat 08°45' N Long 115° 14'E

The Darwin to Ambon Race was a great success although we finished near the back of the fleet. A good fast sail, taking four and a half days for the 560 mile course across the Arafura Sea and into the Timor Sea. There were receptions, prize givings, dance displays, choirs and bands, including a group of schoolboys blowing soft melodies on large shells. Jack, a student from Moa island studying at Ambon University, offered to guide us around. He was improving his English and passed on a wealth of information. He said he had no hope of continuing his education because he came from the wrong island and wasn't tall enough!

He guided our minibus around tropical Ambon Island visiting 11th Century Arab Mosques, Portuguese Forts, an 11th Century Dutch Christian Church, and to animist shrines. At a Holy Pool, a keeper hand fed raw eggs to sacred eels. Jack proudly pointed out acres of clove trees, pepper vines and nutmeg trees.

The well-kept War Graves Cemetery was a shock and emotional experience: so many rows of headstones to "An unknown Australian Soldier" aged 18 or 19. Rows and rows of British graves: men who had been taken from Singapore and shipped to Japanese occupied Ambon where they were bombed by the Americans. We were appalled at our ignorance.

White people are a rarity in the Mollucca (Spice) Islands and a crowd gathered wherever we went. Stopping to bargain in the market ensured one half of the crowd helping you and the other half encouraging the stall holder to make as much money as he could. They bargained with great humour and friendliness but no one spoke English, although many had fluent Dutch or Japanese.

We found Indonesia fascinating but very stressful. The winds and tides are strong and unpredictable with heavy overfalls in many of the Straits. On arriving at an anchorage men in dugout canoes often started hassling us before the anchor was down. Going ashore, crowds of eager children gathered round wanting to shake our hands, touch our white skin and shout "Hello Mister". It was mentally and physically tiring.

The village people can be Hindu, Muslim or Christian. Even in the hottest weather long skirts, covered shoulders or trousers must be worn. As usual I took little gifts ashore but wasn't able to give anything away - how do you give one mother out of twenty, all carrying babies, a little gift? How do you sit and talk to one woman with the light dimmed by the heads of twenty others bending over trying to understand

and listen? They unintentionally tore apart my little "proud granny photo album" as the next interested group tugged at it to try and get a glimpse of our home life.

There are 170 million people in Indonesia (5th largest population in the world). In the islands they are really trying, since their Independence in 1945, to live by Pancasila (meaning peaceful co-existence) and thought they were progressing. Jack itemised the principles for me:

1.   Respect the religion of others
2.   Friendly relations with all people.
3.   Unity – all Indonesian people must unite
4.   Democratically elected representatives every five years
5.   Justice for all.

On the beach of remote island of Bone Rate in the Tiger Island Group, Hindu ship builders were building boats of up to 300 tons with only adzes and saws. No metal fastenings, each plank is carved (not bent) to fit the next one. The beach was the workshop, bathroom and toilet for 6,000 villagers and indescribably filthy.

Photo by T Misdom

They build boats of up to 300 tons with just an adze and saw on the beach

At the village well when Sue and I did our washing, we were watched by a hundred or so ladies who inspected and discussed each item as we crouched to scrub it on the stone platform. Little boys wound up buckets of water from the well and the ladies loaned a pink plastic baby bath in which to rinse the clothes. Some ladies had their hair curled in plastic rollers with white face packs on to make their skin whiter (I think it's made of powdered rice and mashed fruit). Beautiful people living on rice, rice and more rice with a little added vegetable, fish or chicken. Some looked under-nourished, but they had happy, eager healthy looking children.

Anna Louise and Howard show us the galley on SINOR JAYA

Three young Australians were living on a big sailing Bugis boat, trying to make their fortune by importing teak into Australia. It had all looked good on paper. They had bargained for fifty tons of teak at $100 a ton hoping to sell it at $1,500 a ton in Australia within six months. However they had been there four months already and only had seventeen tons on board. The heavy teak was being cut by hand on an adjacent island and being carried the three miles to the water's edge on men's shoulders. Meanwhile their creditors in Australia were becoming impatient and unhappy. The two young men and young woman were existing on rice, fish and bananas. The apple and chocolate biscuits we were able to give them brought tears to their eyes.

I had wanted to visit Komodo Island since reading *Sailing All Seas* by Dwight Long, published in 1954 and David Attenborough's Zoo *Quest for a Dragon*, published in 1957. The Island, nor the dragons, disappointed us and we too met hazards.

As we bumpily rowed in the dinghy towards the beach in the strong onshore wind, we were suddenly carried on a crest and unceremoniously dumped in the water, our rubber dinghy flipped over and came down on top of us. We scrabbled up the white sand pulling it behind us. Fortunately as we were both wearing shorts and T shirts it was no problem drying out in the hot wind. At the National Park Office we hired a guide Marko. Armed only with a strong forked stick, he warily led us a mile and a half through scrubby woodland to the fenced enclosure where we could relax and watch, as the dragons roamed free in the countryside. They were impressive creatures: dark brown, scaled, twelve-foot-long lizards, their forked tongues flicking in and out to the dust. They had too much skin, it hung in folds around their necks and their massive tails swung from side to side as they waddled along. They sat on their hind legs with their little forelegs begging and sniffing, then raced out of sight with their mighty tails up in the air like Dino in The Flintstones, making a loud exhaling hissing sound.

About 1,500 of these prehistoric dragons, with a life span of 30 years, live on the island. They have eaten small children and dogs, but now the Wardens feed them once a week and the rest of the time they hunt spasmodically.

Sunday is dinner day when freshly killed goats and chickens are held out on rods. The dragons snarl, growl, hiss and fight, savagely clawing, and climbing over each other to reach the poor animals which they rip apart with their massive jaws. They quickly swallow the limbs whole without chewing and are immediately ready to fight for the next joint. After feeding they lie on the dusty ground in the sun to sleep and digest, often, bizarrely, with one hind leg forward and one back. Incredibly, chickens now peck the ground between them picking up any tasty morsels of their relatives, or perhaps they are just playing 'chicken'.

We returned to the Wardens' office and cafeteria for a leisurely cold beer and nasi goreng. On returning to CLYPEUS we panicked on realising she was aground on the coral, with nine inches of red anti-fouling showing and about to lean over on her side. The anchor had dragged. We rowed to her at top speed, started the motor and as each wave surfed towards us I pushed down the throttle. As the engine screamed and raced, Peter winched in the chain and we gradually ground and bounced back to deep water. Oh! the relief of being safely afloat again to motor into the calm water in the lee of the mountain. In the still air of dawn next morning, as I recorded the muezzin calling the faithful to prayer, and, by the luck of Allah, happened to look over the side to find we were on the edge of a steep sand bank, almost ready to fall. Once again, in panic we motored off a lee shore. The sea dragon is always waiting, ready to devour us.

Komodo was arid and dry. Peter collects shells and star fish

Komodo was relatively dry and arid but we passed verdant islands and smoking volcanoes to get to Lombok Island. The rough anchorage at Ampenan meant we both couldn't leave the boat. A young man came out in a canoe to sell souvenirs and offered to take me on a tour. I spent the day on the back of his motorbike, complete with crash helmet and haversack. We returned having seen palaces, gardens and ornamental lakes, 18th Century Dutch water conduits, Sesak dancing and fighting, and colourful markets. Woven baskets, sarongs, potatoes, pineapples, bananas and beans were all good buys and had to be carried on the back of the bike.

The Sesak stick fighting was really exciting. Young men, evenly matched, in national dress, fight with five-foot-long bamboo rods with only a leather shield to protect themselves. The bouts are for three rounds of three minutes and they really do whack into each other. A gamelan gong and drum band keep up the tempo and excitement. It is a skilled, stylised display of hip-wiggling, strutting, shoulder shaking and nimble-footedness between whams and whops, with

Sesak stick fighting, Lombok

all the panache of fencing. The weekly tournament is only for male spectators, but lady tourists are allowed to watch.

60,000 people starved to death on Lombok in 1966, those that survived did so by eating mice. I don't remember ever hearing about it. 6,000 people died in 1963 on Bali when

Mt. Agung blew. We never realised just how much goes on in the world that we don't hear about. It seems that if television cameras are not there, it hasn't happened.

At last we were in Bali, the cruising sailor's dream harbour; safe and well after riding the surf in through the coral pass. So many different islands, cultures, seas, and weather conditions exist within Indonesia. Each island is like a different country. The brown, smooth skinned people are a blend of Chinese, Malay, Arab, Portuguese and Dutch: Christian, Moslem, Hindu, and Buddhist. They have been trading with the Chinese since 200 BC. and with India and the Arabs since the first century. Young people seem to be free to marry into other sects and make up their own minds which God they will follow. Moslems appeared to be on the increase, but the devotion of Hindus is unbelievable. Christians were generous and friendly and often spoke English.

Tiered temple s within Pura Tanan Ayun

Our VW Safari rented for 3 days a 20,000 Rupis at day $12US a day

Bali offered so much to see, do, buy, watch, listen, smell, and taste and all affordable. We rented a jeep for three days and saw as much as we could cram in - too much - I can't remember the names of all the temples and villages. We saw exquisite wood carving and silver smithing, The Elephant Cave Temple, Monkey Forest. (The monkeys were gentle little things with soft fingers and no scratchy claws.) Rice paddies, Hindu temples, Mt. Agung and the Mother Temples. The Barong and Legong Dancing in Ubud was spectacular.

At Mt. Batur we stayed at a losman (cottage) within the Crater and took a boat across the caldera lake to Bali Aga where the people retain a social code similar to pre-Hindu Bali. Here the dead are not cremated but are simply laid out in a nearby ravine with a bamboo cage over them. It was ghoulish and the guides were mercenary and persistent trying to sell us skulls and femurs. They told us that if a person is old and has had children there is no mourning at death because the soul is still alive and well, only the body is dead. The soul will be reincarnated at whichever of the seven levels it deserves.

Galungan, the Balinese New Year, which occurs every 210 days is celebrated with processions of beautiful girls in single file, carrying towers of delicately arranged offerings on their heads. The younger girls at the front wore long sarongs with golden bodices that covered one shoulder, which denoted they were too young to marry. Older girls with bare shoulders informed the world that they were available for a suitable marriage and following them the married women whose golden bodices had long sleeves and high necklines. A band of pipes, drums and bugles in a cacophony of

CHAPTER TWENTY FIVE

*Girls of marriagble age have both shoulders
bare. Too young, one shoulder is covered.
Already married, both shoulders covered*

*Would you like to buy a turtle?
No thank you*

noise marched to keep bad spirits away from their richly adorned temple.

On the opposite side of the road cock fighting was in progress. Men on their haunches tied spurs to their fighting cocks. Betting was fast and furious when the long legged chickens were held up. So much shouting and gesticulating before the match began and then suddenly the fight was all over. A poor bloodied cockerel lay twitching on the sand while the other crowed its head off as its proud owner held it aloft.

As we sailed north and crossed the Equator again the winds were fickle and it was hot and humid. Sea snakes and porpoises were all we saw in the sea except for the myriads of fishermen, now wearing coolie hats, sailing fast, or rowing their sampans standing up facing forwards with crossed oars.

Borneo (now Kalimantan) deserved an extended visit, but we only visited some coastal villages. Later I took an adventure tour into the interior up the Strang Rive by canoe and spent two nights in a long house with the head-hunting Dayak tribesmen and saw orang utangs and proboscis monkeys.

A mile or so off the jungle coastline, some fishermen approached and offered us a live turtle and didn't seem upset when we declined.

They towed us inshore so that we could visit their home where the skipper's wife with white paste on her face welcomed us inside her one roomed hut and offered boiled water and ikin bilis. These tiny fish/shrimp seemed to be the main (only?) protein to go with their rice.

At night we steered between hundreds of 'glow worms', each of them a one-man fishing prau with a kerosene lamp suspended over the sea. It was difficult to decide where the stars stopped and the fishermen started. Fishing platforms and oil rigs studded the ocean. The fishing platforms, built on reefs and made of bamboo, have a little thatched house on top and a large net suspended beneath. Bright kerosene lamps hang high to attract the fish.

However, the bamboo fish traps suspended from floats and just under the surface are not lit and we had some emergency about-turns. It took 15 days of hard sailing to reach Singapore Strait. A voyage with no hassles, except for one major squall, when we had to take all sail off and lie ahull for a couple of hours. We estimated the wind was sometimes more than 40 knots, which was stronger than any we had met across the big oceans.

Booking out of Indonesia at Tanjung Penang was pleasant as the Harbour Master was extremely friendly and, with his wife, took us out to dinner and to his home. The main course was goat stew but so tough and chewy that we had to discreetly dispose of it into our napkins. Much of Tanjung Penang is built on stilts over the water and it was a long walk along the rickety wooden slats into the market. It was smelly too as all waste is dropped directly under the houses and there were dead rats and cats amongst the general flotsam. Luckily it was spring tides so the area was thoroughly washed out whilst we were there.

We were welcomed by the skipper's wife with white paste on her face

The boat boys in their canoes went to desperate lengths to get trade. They looked like pirhana fish attacking prey as they rushed to surround a ferry or motorised delivery sampan. The front man in each canoe would swarm onto the arriving boat while it was still moving and start lifting out parcels or hassling passengers to taxi them ashore.

The last night of our voyage to Singapore was spent in Indonesian waters anchored in a bay off Batam Island. Skyscrapers glittered in the distance. It seemed unbelievable to be here, anchored in stone-age Indonesia, but looking at one of the most modern cities in the world.

Crisp Singapore Harbour Control messages told us to sail around to Changi Sailing Club on the North East coast in the morning, find a mooring and then travel on public transport into the city to book in. However as soon as we said we had guns on board, we were told that police officers would be there to meet us and take them into custody. We were back in the real world after seven years on the seven seas.

Singapore
October 1989
At 1°16' N Long 103°57' E

CHAPTER TWENTY SIX

A s we approached Singapore so the whole tempo of life speeded up and we could feel worries settling on our shoulders again. Those last days became a blur, smudged under the growing anticipation of a new world and the realisation that we were nearly at the end of a significant phase in our lives.

Anchoring off Change Yacht Club, it was wonderful to be met by old friends Jep and Ted, who had seen us off from the Hamble. They had extended their holiday from England to meet us, and Pat and Kascia who now lived in Singapore. Pat was Manager of the Asia region for the American Company Peter was rejoining.

After completing CLYPEUS's formalities and surrendering our guns, we took our friends sailing for a couple of days and then it was rush, rush, rush applying for visas, international driving licenses, civilised clothes and new passports (all the pages were full although they still had six years before expiring).

We were like children on the top deck of the air-conditioned buses, marvelling at the machine's automatic deduction of fares on our tickets.

A crane hauled CLYPEUS out of the water onto a low loader and trundled to a storage boat yard. Peter bought some small electric fans and connected them to the solar panels to ventilate the cabins to lessen the inevitable mould and bugs. (It worked. After two years the interior was still sweet, clean and dry). We packed, cleaned and polished, put Boric Acid on the food shelves to discourage cockroaches and camphor balls in cupboards. It was hard to leave her, she was part of our life. A boat in which you have sailed thousands of miles and in which you have lived for seven years, becomes as close as your trusted friend. If you fail, you fail together.

Pat and Kascia made us very welcome in their gracious modern apartment. Each day we zoomed in their air-conditioned car, over and under clean flower-banked freeways, between super high-rise hotels and apartment blocks, from their air conditioning into the oppressive steam heat in land-bound CLYPEUS. We tried to adjust to the physical, social and emotional changes. I had come to think civilisation was clean plumbing and higher education. However the most difficult aspect was adjusting to social positions and pecking orders and having to ask people for permission to do things. We had got so used to either doing things ourselves, or going directly to the person from whom we required something. We hadn't realised how, in our cruising life, everybody had been equal, no matter what colour, creed or financial status. If they had the information, we were only too happy to learn from them.

Back to be part of the Mass on Singapore's MRT (Mass) rapid transport system

Re-entry into the modern world was traumatic. It all seemed too fast, too bright, too crowded and too hot. After travelling at four to five miles per hour, the rush and noise of the road traffic overwhelmed us. We felt herded when standing in a pack of people waiting for the signal to allow us to cross the road. In Singapore the MRT (Mass Rapid Transport) was clean and bright, the trains programmed to stop at a precise spot so that the doors open exactly where the glass platform doors slide open. The escalators moved up into the daylight so fast they seemed to spit us out into the bright, burning, sunshine.

The department stores were over-whelming in their choice and variety of goods. So much stuff. Was it really necessary? Of course I enjoyed looking and touching but felt very much a country cousin.

The new Raffles

While Peter went to the office to re-familiarise himself with the Company there was time for a little sightseeing of apparently squeaky-clean Singapore. However the back lanes and temples revealed a life that was fast disappearing. Shop-houses where roller shutters opened onto a stall backed by a ceiling-high jumble of goods and packing cases, or a welding, coffin-making, or woodworking shop. Business men as well as wives and workers fed paper money, cardboard telephones and Mercedes, into pavement or temple incinerators to supply the heavenly needs of departed loved ones. It seemed strange then, but later, when working with children in Taipei, I realised how these traditions helped children, and their parents, deal with grief. They were still doing something positive for their loved ones.

Raffles Hotel was being re-built and tourist shows transferred to The Cockpit Hotel. I watched charming Chinese, Indian and Malay dancing and a snake-charming performance when "vely fliendly snakes" wrapped themselves around tourist volunteers.

After the first seven years on board, our life took on a fairy tale aspect. The Company, whisked us from a hot small boat on the Equator by 'Raffles Class' on Singapore Airlines - champagne before take off and all the trimmings, to live in expensive air conditioned five-star hotels in Taiwan. Our beds for one night cost more than the previous two months' housekeeping. A breakfast bill would have fed us for four days. We enjoyed it of course, but the change in values was hard to justify.

It brought to mind, once again the Babylonian Philosophy

The more I have, the more I want
The more I want, the less I have,
The less I have, the less I want,
The less I want, the more I have....

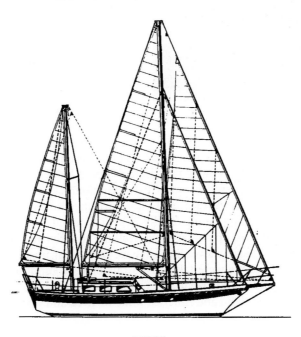

CONCLUSION

What have we learned long term? – To seize the day and make the most of now. To grab opportunities and not to be disappointed if they turnout badly - at least we tried. We learned to survive on our own resources and be content with what we have. Our boat is like a space capsule, the responsibility is ours for keeping our equipment and ourselves in good order with no outside help for months on end. A man and a woman have complementary skills to make a team.

We have had the opportunity to appreciate each other and say "Thank you. I couldn't have done that" and have learned to acknowledge our weaknesses and meld our accomplishments.

We left our family home in October 1982. In October 1989, after seven years on the seven seas, we re-entered the working world, having to conform every day to set timetables and civilisation's social requirements. After 50,000 miles sailing free, we would no longer be in charge of our own destinies.

Peter back in a business suit instructing Japanese engineers

In retrospect, I often wonder who actually has the best life? Idyllic though life in the Pacific looked, the Islanders still had social restrictions, poor health care, scarce fresh water, little variety in their food, few books, no television or refrigeration and a very simple life-style. It was exciting for us now to re-learn to cope with cars, insurance, licences, on-line computers, faxes, email, telephone cards, mobile phones, TVs and VCRs. I enjoyed the luxury of a washing machine and dryer, hot water, and a cooker and table which didn't roll.

The land-life attraction for Peter was returning to a stimulating and creative job. For me, it was being able to telephone and visit our families in the UK, the USA and Australia, as the company provided an annual 'home leave' flight. Having a stable address eased editorial correspondence with international sailing magazines that were publishing my articles. Two years in Taiwan stretched to another three years in Singapore where a training course at the British Council - to teach English as a Second Language - opened up new avenues. Helping children and adult students gave me an insight into the Asian way of life. Then we were off again and sailed CLYPEUS to Europe. In the Red Sea we were taken from our boat at gunpoint and held under house arrest for a month in Eritrea under suspicion of spying. Red Sea Peril was written and published in England and America while we lived and worked in Shanghai for another two year contract.

Now CLYPEUS is hauled out of the Mediterranean each winter and in the summers we slowly sail west to cross our outward track at Ibiza. We are enjoying our prosaic home beside Milford Haven Estuary. A little sailing dinghy sits at the bottom of the garden to use when withdrawal symptoms overcome us, then we putter up-river with a picnic basket and a bottle of wine. Using my BC (before cruising) skills, I started a gentle exercise class: 'Keep Fit for the Gracious Years' and am proud to know the ladies who participate who are making the effort to keep well and graceful. It's good to know I should still be able to dance and exercise to music like them, when I'm 85 too. Joining a Writers' Group, which became an outreach class from the University of Wales, gave me the confidence to apply to study for a Masters Degree in Creative

Writing. It has proved an enjoyable, worthwhile course and I've gained some confidence. We have just celebrated our Golden Wedding and my 70th Birthday. It has been the time of my life partying and swimming with all our family, being twirled around the dance floor by six-foot-plus grandsons and renewing friendships of over sixty years. Three score years and ten was something we expected to fear –I'm enjoying every minute and I hope you will too!

We've learned to value green and pleasant Britain for its stability and moderation and realise how lucky we are to have been born into such a privileged society where clean water is taken for granted. We appreciate the opportunities for everyone to continue their education, read erudite newspapers, listen to Radio 4, and most of all, to realise that a loving family is the greatest of life's gifts.

We have had time. Time together which we will never regret when all the twenty-four hours were ours. There grew a bond of togetherness in that small, small space. We really had forsaken all others when on board and, even now, when we return to our little floating home, we just sit and look at each other and smile. We are at peace in our sanctuary.

Now, in Pembrokeshire, life has never been happier for both of us and if we died tomorrow we would have no regrets:

> "Happy the man, and happy he alone,
> He, who can call today his own;
> He who, secure within, can say,
> Tomorrow do thy worst, for I have lived today.
>
> John Dryden translation from Horace
> Bk III

• •

APPENDIX 1.

Parameters for our Ocean Voyaging Boat:

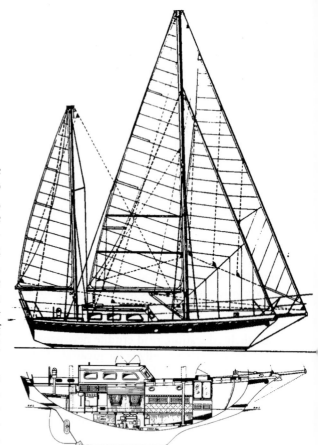

Parameters for the boat were that it be strong, have a deep keel, two masts, small cockpit, and at least two rooms so that we could close a door between us - to sulk if necessary. We also both wanted our own work space. And, no way, did I want to have to make up beds each evening in the main cabin. We are untidy sailors at sea and the bliss of sinking into a tidy, dry bed would be heaven.

A 36' yacht was as large as we felt we could manage both physically and financially. A bigger boat would mean a larger anchor to heave up and down, bigger sails, additional marina charges, higher insurance premiums. Also we wanted to be sure either of us could sail it single-handed in case of accidents or illness. We wanted to do it all on our own, no crew.

Peter also felt simple equipment was safest, to ensure easy ocean maintance and minimal reliance on electricity and batteries: no roller reefing headsails and a manual anchor winch.

A steel hull would have been our first choice, but those within our budget already had rust problems and osmosis threatened the older fibre glass yachts. Wooden hulls need too much maintenance in the tropics and the fate of Robertson's in their 43' Lucette which had sunk in three minutes after being holed by killer whales was fresh in our minds. After twenty years CLYPEUS' ferro cement hull has proved stable, inert and easy to repair but she is relatively slow - a matron amongst sophisticated modern Ms's.

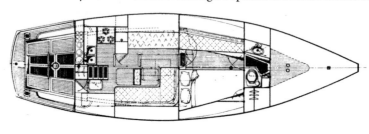

APPENDIX 2

Equipment carried

Engine Perkins 4108M + Paragon
    Gearbox

Bilge pumps:1 Rule 3500 -1 Rule 1500

Main Steering Compass - Sestrel

Aires Self Steering

Ampair Towing/windmill Generator

Autohelm 3000

Ham Radio Kenwod TS430 + Tuner

Icom VHF Radio M57 and VHF
    Antenna

Grundig Satelit Radio

Phillips AP MK8 GPS

SeaFarer Echo Sounder

Compass - Hand Bearing

Binnoculars Tamaya

Sextant Tamaya M833 Univision

Barograph Fischer 207

Anchor winch Simpson Lawrence

CQR Anchor 60lb +

Bruce Anchor 20Kg

Fisherman Anchor 60 lb

18mm Multiplait warp 60m

18mm nylon 3 strand 100m

3/8ths Anchor Chain - galv 10g
    Kg +130 feet

2 Hand Bilge pumps

Lavac Toilet

Mercury 2.2 Outboard Motor

Fibreglass dinghy 8 ft (unsinkable)

Avon 8 Inflatable & accessories

Avon Redcrest Dinghy

2 - Solar Panels 45 watt

Solar Panel 85 watt

Phillips SW Radio D2999

Set of sails:

 2 - Mainsails

 1 - Storm Jib

 2 - Working Jibs

 1 - Storm Trysail

 2 - Staysails

 1 - Genoa

 2 - Mizzens

 1 - Cruising Chute

Hand Searchlight

Pilot Books & Tables

Charts.

Signal Flares

Mini Fridge

Honda Generator 500 watt

Gas cooker Neptune 2000

Sewing Machine

Sony Music Centre

Folding Bicycle (second hand)

Cabin clock Phillips

2 Aluminium Gas Bottles -

1 set Bow and Stern Navigation lights

Masthead Tri-white Navigation light

APPENDIX 3.

Countdown preparations

It took us three years of planning and evening classes to acquire the right boat and gear, First Aid and Yachtmaster certificates. It was traumatic organising the sale of the house, furniture, our faithful Folkboat and our cars. The period between the old life and actually setting sail was difficult; depression and excitement following closely on each other's heels.

This is our final countdown list.

1. HEALTH: See your Doctor and have thorough medical check up. Any problems, minor operations, get them sorted out as soon as possible.

2. READ: every cruising book and magazine you can: Hiscocks, Pardys, Roth, Robertson, Baileys, Annie Hill, Copeland, Coopers. We found Mike Saunders "Walkabouts" particularly inspiring.

3. CONSIDER joining the Cruising Association or other Cruising Club. They have much information to offer you.

4. DECISION MAKING:
a) How long do you want/can you afford to be away?

b) Where do you actually want to go? Around the world? To the Caribbean, to the Med? It will affect your choice of boat.

c) Should you change to a more suitable boat?

d) Should you sell your home, close it up, or let it under management? (If you have no property and are non resident for three years in the UK you may not have to pay Income Tax.)

e) Present employment. Will you take long service/sabbatical leave? Early retirement? Normal retirement or just hand in your notice.

5. CONSULT:

Solicitor - to make wills, sell house? arrange power of attorney.
Accountant - for advice on your tax situation, investments, UK or Offshore?
Bank - Ways of getting cash overseas. It is so much easier with the advent of credit and debit cards. Our Bank automatically paid our Visa card account each month. as well as standing orders etc. Annual subscriptions (do you need them all now?). Banks sometimes hold your mail for you overseas.

Family - provision for parents? provision for children? Will somebody act as your legal agent and write cheques?

6. ADDITIONAL QUALIFICATIONS

First Aid Courses

Yacht/Ocen Masters Course

Celestial Navigation

VHF and Ham Radio Licence

Diesel engine course

Additional language? (We wish we had studied Spanish as well as French)

ONE YEAR BEFORE DEPARTURE

7. DECIDE:

a) on date to leave house and move on board.
b) on date to leave UK

8. ACQUIRE: information and make arrangements for:

a) Visas
b) Inoculations
c) Insurance (boat and personal)
d) Pensions.
e) Dental: check up and treatment.
f) Eyes: check up - new, extra glasses? prescription sun glasses?
g) Passports: check expiry date, start applying for special visas:Galapagos etc.
h) Spares: accumulate and order boat spares and additional equipment.

Collect second hand charts, chandlery catalogues, spare parts manuals, suppliers' email addresses. (USA West Marine Catalogue is a great source of information)

i) Plan stores
j) Medical Kit. Assess familiar medications that suit you. Our Doctor went through my list with suggestions. Then our friendly pharmacist, who, one month before saiing, sold us the items, or lower cost nearest substitute on non-prescription items, and packed them in ziplock bags with dessicants.

SIX MONTHS BEFORE DEPARTURE:

Get as many things as possible finalised now.

9. DECIDE PROBABLE ROUTE and order charts ready for delivery one month before leaving. This includes Pilots, Cruising Guides, Pilot Charts, Light lists.

10. BUY OR MAKE FLAGS and courtesy ensigns (see if your sail maker will give you some spinnaker offcuts for the short stay ensigns. Traditional bunting is best for extended use)

11. START ACQUIRING STORES that won't deteriorate - paper goods, detergents etc. Take advantage of any bargains.

12 DECIDE IF YOU ARE GOING TO CARRY GUNS. Licence? (We decided after seven years that they were more trouble than they were worth).

13. START CLOTHING PILE (if you have a spare room in which to allot corners and space it helps enormously) Thermal wear, sun wear, oilskins, sailing boots, sailing shoes.

14. CHOOSE ENTERTAINMENT books and music you want to have with you

15. START AND COMPLETE INOCULATIONS

16. FINALISE: VISAS, INSURANCE, INVESTMENTS, UK property arrangements. Mail forwarders and mail holders.

ONE MONTH BEFORE DEPARTURE:

17. **DENTIST FINAL CHECK UP.** Ask if he will supply a dental emergency kit. Many dentists are interested and surprisingly happy to do so.

18. **BUY STORES, REMOVE LABELS FROM TINS, VARNISH AND MARK** what is in them and when purchased.

19 **ORGANISE LEAVING PARTY/VISIT RELATIVES**

20. **SEND OUR CHANGE OF ADDRESS INFORMATION.** To family and friends an itinerary and addresses where you can receive mail on your route. (Banks, American Express, Post Restante (often return mail to sender by sea if not claimed after three weeks) specific Marinas 'to be held for arrival' (NOT c/o Port Captain or Harbour Office as security is usually very poor.)

21. **COLLECT CHARTS** and pilot books

22. **COLLECT CURRENCY FROM BANK** (It's always wise to have some American dollars even if you are not going there.)

23. **DO EVERYTHING YOU CAN WHILE YOU STILL HAVE TELEPHONE AND TRANSPORT.** Decide if you want to have an international mobile phone.

ONE WEEK BEFORE DEPARTURE

24. **BUY AND PACK FRESH STORES.**

25. **FINAL ROUND OF GOODBYES.**

26. **DISPOSE OF CAR** at very last minute having negotiated its sale weeks beforehand.

SAIL AWAY to a nearby quiet harbour, collect yourselves and check your final lists. Don't be too proud to go back for those cotter pins your forgot, you could need them the first night out.

Remember to clear Customs.

BON VOYAGE -

the actual sailing seems easy comparted with the preparation, so take heart!

APPENDIX 4

Insurance

No Company would insure just the two of us across the Atlantic, or in the Caribbean. We eventually managed to get a Lloyds Insurance Policy through Lloyds Brokers. But in Tahiti the cost increased to over a third of our income so we continued voyaging uninsured.

Now in the Mediterannean we will reinsure but for third party only.

Health Insurance is also prohibitive once you say you are going to a remote region and not by public transport. Fortunately most crews keep very well away from civilisation.

APPENDIX 5

Liferafts and Panic bags

We prepare two survival boats when ocean crossings.

The half inflated Avon dinghy is always on the foredeck with the pump and oars tucked inside.

A hard unsinkable fibreglass dinghy is carried on top of the doghouse with quick release fastenings. Peter thinks a commercial liferaft is too much of a gamble. Poor reports on the state of rafts and survival packs are discouraging. He prefers to know both dinghies are in good order and that he can sail towards land not just drift around hoping someone else will pick us up.

HARD DINGHY ON CABIN TOP contains: Oars, rowlocks, bailer, mast and sail are tucked inside, together with a 5 gallon waterproof plastic tub which carries:

8 x 1litre plastic bags of pure water

Hand bearing compass

Mirror

Strong knife

Needles, thread, scissors

Plastic mugs, plates,

2 knives (one serrated with a fine point) spoons and forks.

Waterproof First Aid box (including antibiotic powder, pills and cream)

Sea sick pills (Dramamine)

Anti-histamine pills (Piriton)

Space blanket (could also be used as a solar still and for catching water)

2 Long sleeved shirts/ hats/ towelling scarves

Fishing line, hooks, spinners and gaff

Multi Vitamin tablets

Tin of Cumberland Candy.

Tin of lemon drops

Notepad and pencils

Small funnel

Araldite

Travel Chess set

Australian Wine box 'silver' plastic liners (can be inflated as cushions, for storing water, signalling mirror).

IN COCKPIT IN A WATERPROOF CANISTER (ex Army shell container)

Flares, Torch, waterproof matches, candles.

Another small compass and mirror

More fishing line and hooks

Swiss Army knife

Small plastic bottle of Dettol

Plastic bag with tweezers, scissors,
triangular bandage, Elastoplast
Sun cream

IN STRING BAG BY HATCH:

Onions, Oranges, lemons, limes, apples/melon/green papaya (whatever is available)

2 x 1 litre plastic bottles of water

Big sharp knife in sheath

2 x 5 gallon plastic jerry jugs of water are stored in the cockpit, not quite full so that they will float.

APPENDIX 6.

Water

Peter is a design engineer and has adapted many simple ideas to increase our comfort. Our Endurance 35 has capacity for 125 gallons of fresh water in three tanks. The water in the two 50 gallon tanks is electrically pumped to taps in the galley and head. The 25 gallon drinking water tank has a separate hand pump directly to the sink. The faucet on this pump can be swung out over the edge of the sink so that bottles and thermos flasks can be filled.

Initially, to collect water, we hung a bucket at the forward end of the main boom whenever it rained. It wasn't satisfactory, the first two buckets full were usually salty, and whenever the boat heeled most of the water emptied out. Often, when a quick shower passed by, it was all over by the time the bucket was firmly attached to the gooseneck, I would be soaking wet with a teaspoon of water to show for my effort. At other times untying the bucket full of water and staggering down the deck to the tank filler spilt most of it. Then trying to pour what was left into the funnel wasn't easy. The constant battling to and from the mast against the elements soon made us think that there must be a better way.

Our second attempt was a funnel sewn into a central hole in the cockpit awning, with a plastic pipe down to a bucket, or directly into the water tanks. This worked reasonably well, except that as a squall hit the wind blew up underneath the awning and all the precious water cascaded down the lee side into the sea. The funnel with the plastic pipe hanging down the centre of the cockpit was a nuisance and unattractive.

Ten years ago Peter fixed 1" sqare strips of wood along both edges of the cabin roof, to act as a water catchment. A small pipe was fitted each side at the lowest point for a hose to be attached. As soon as it looks like rain we now push plastic hose onto the copper tubes and when the downpour has had time to wash the dinghy and cabin top, pop the hose into the water tank filler and voila! Minimum discomfort, maximum water.

It is wise to take at least two five gallon screwtop plastic containers because even if you have extensive tanks, somewhere along the way you are going to have to walk to a well, or the village water tap, for your water.

Are filters necessary? In our experience; No. The hand pumped drinking water developed a bad taste. We ruined the Freshness Filter sawing it open to examine the inside, but we couldn't see anything wrong, no build up of dirt or mould. The problem turned out to be algae in the clear plastic piping after the filter. Peter replaced it with black Alkathene piping three years ago and we have had no further trouble.

To save your water and extend your cruising range consider the following suggestions:-

Washing clothes in seawater is no problem. Many detergents work well especially the liquid cold water types now on the market. If a conditioner such as Comfort is put in half a bucket of fresh water for the final rinse, smalls first, the clothes dry bright and soft and not salty, sticky and hard.

It does seem unfair that there are so many electronic aids to help the skipper with navigation, steering and such, but the boat girls are still washing as their great grand-mothers did. However, it is more fun stomping the washing in a bucket on deck wearing a bikini, than programming the housebound washing machine. If I use two buckets, one for each foot, I kid myself I've got a "twin tub". Of course going to a store to try on the buckets to make sure they fit your feet, like one of Cinderella's Ugly Sisters, can cause a few raised eyebrows.

Washing dishes for us starts by collecting a bucketful of seawater. A foot pump and seawater tap in the galley would be a great improvement. Liquid detergents work well. Do have a couple of cups of fresh water in a bowl just to rinse in. Salt can make the plates taste and encourage mould and also corrode aluminium pans. Don't use harbour water as even the clearest water will have effluent in it.

Cooking at sea. One cup of seawater has about two rounded teaspoons of salt in it. Boil rice in one part salt water to two parts fresh. For boiling vegetables use one part salt water to three parts fresh. Cook pasta in one part salt water to three parts fresh. Eggs of course can be boiled in all salt water.

Shampooing. I have long hair so everyone thinks I must have a problem - not so. On long ocean passages holding my head above a bucket while Peter pours jugs of cool seawater over it makes a welcome change. The cheaper the shampoo, the better it seems to work in seawater. The `own brand family size' shampoo with a good conditioner is an ideal combination. Lather and rinse your hair twice then rinse again, all in sea water. Apply the conditioner, wait for a few minutes then rinse with a pint jug of fresh water pouring it through your hair again and again. Try having a shampoo whilst swimming, rinsing will never be easier. I carry an aerosol dry shampoo to use when conditions are too difficult.

Personal bathing and showering can be a problem, but a good wash down standing in half a bowl of fresh water and using one of the bath and shower gels takes all the salt away and makes you feel soft and clean.

After a sea water wash or swim a quick spray using a mist spray bottle filled with fresh water makes a good final rinse before towelling dry. It is good to get the salt off your skin every day, as rashes, itches and other skin problems can develop so quickly, especially in the tropics.

For those of you still sailing in cold climes, imagine waking up after a rainy night and finding the dinghy full of soft, warm, fresh water.

Can you just see yourself pouring in the bubble bath, lying in the dinghy in the sun singing "If my friends could see me now."

FOOD AND STORES FOR OCEAN VOYAGING. As you have read, I enjoy my food. There are so many good recipe books to choose from. Marilyn Bailey's 'The Galley Cook' was very easy to use even in the roughest weather. My other standby was The Hamlyn Colour Cook Book.

I'm sure you have your own favourites - there are so many, but choose small ones

APPENDIX 7.

Cyclones

The weatherman announced: "Severe tropical cyclone Aivu, centre pressure 950 mbar, heading SW at 6 knots with winds gusting up to 150 mph, seas very high to phenomenal" and here we were in Townsville's Breakwater Marina directly in its path.

Many precautions have to be taken even when you in a "cyclone proof Marina."

In these days of superior weather forecasting there is time for preparation. We had two whole days between cyclone Aivu's official introduction, and the arrival of gale force winds. Four hourly marine radio reports, plus warnings on local radio and TV, kept us up to date on the exact movement of the storm centre.

The Marina management offered us the following advice, which was most helpful.

1. Double up all mooring lines by running duplicate ropes to alternative bollards, allowing slight slackness to ensure that they are only required to work if the first rope chafes through. We rigged extra springs as well as a line across the double pen to our neighbour.

2. Examine all synthetic ropes very carefully, especially those of polypropylene and polyester fibres in case they have suffered UV degradation.

3. Check deck cleats. Use main structural members, like the mast, as mooring points.

4. Reduce windage by taking down all deck gear:- awnings, dodgers, sails, lifebuoys, spare rope, dan buoy, buckets, water containers; deflate and pack inflatables and stow all inside. As there wasn't sufficient room below to store all the sails we double wrapped and tied the furled sails and covers so that the wind could not tease out any ends and allow flapping to start them shredding.

5. Dinghies and bicycles should be stored ashore if possible. (Some yachts tied their dinghies fore and aft and sank them!)

6. Check cockpit drains, the manual and automatic bilge pumps and close all sea-cocks.

7. Fill the water tanks in case of a long term water problem.

8. Disconnect all shore power and water leads.

9 Pack emergency bags.

10. The Marina management had warned that the power and water might be cut off

and it may not be possible to leave or return to our boats once the cyclone hit.

11. It was relatively easy to decide what emergency food, bedding and clothes should be packed, together with passports, money, bank cards, ship's papers, travelers' cheques and jewelry. But, what about the GPS, ham radio, computer, TV, transistor radio, sextant, barograph and all those photographs and negatives of our journey so far? What was irreplaceable and what was only money?

12 The local radio station gave Emergency Service information and let us know that there would temporary accommodation available in the State and Commonwealth Government offices should it be necessary.

13. Clear up anything lying around on the dock or environs.

By Monday evening all was prepared, and our emergency bags taken to an upstairs room in the Marina Admin Building, which was of steel and concrete construction. However, Aivu had decided to slow down and intensify, so we all decided to go back to our boats to sleep. It would now be another 18 hours before dangerous winds reached the coast.

We slept fitfully with the VHF on Ch.67 and learnt that the central pressure was down to 940 millibars and still heading our way. The wind was strengthening and whistling through the rigging, the rain drummed on the cabin roof. Had we taken out everything important and practical? We would have to leave books, pictures, souvenirs, furnishings, tape recorder and tapes. These two days had the highest Spring tides of the month, and an extra tidal surge of 2-3 metres would float the whole Marina off its piles. It was impossible to imagine what destruction could be caused.

Advice had flown around like: "Make sure you raise a burgee to the top of your main mast so that you can recognize your boat under the water." How likely was it? We just didn't know, but we had seen the ravages and wrecks from so many cyclones on our way across the Pacific.

At 9 a.m. on Tuesday we left our home apprehensively, the wind speed was now 40/50 knots, stronger in gusts, palm trees bent and the rain fell in sheets. The wind pushed us up the pontoon and we fought our way crab-like to the stairs. In the warm, well lit room, the boat children were playing with each other and their toys, making cubby houses, happily enjoying the company. We chatted, sorted out our corner of belongings, had a coffee, another chat, a hot shower and shampoo, just in case the water was cut off later. There was nothing anybody could do except watch the progress of the storm and be prepared for any emergency. The wind strengthened and we watched and waited.

Around mid morning the forecaster announced that the eye would pass to the south east of us and cross the coast about 70 miles away. The wind veered to south and then west, blowing offshore now, so that we were in the lee of the land. It stayed like this through the afternoon, and we became convinced that the centre was well on its way inland destroying homes and crops.

It was the first time we had been through this sort of exercise, and although today it ended in an anticlimax, will it next time? The reports continued to let us know that Aivu was dying, a particularly wet death, drowning the Queensland countryside. A cask of good Australian wine was brought out and we all had a glass or three to celebrate our good fortune.

Though rain and floods continued for several days we were all back on board our boats that evening, grateful and aware of our good luck. Not only had Aivu missed us by 50 miles but also, at the time of the worst wind gusts, it was dead low water and our boats had been well down in the shelter of the Marina basin.

Had we over-reacted? How do boaters in the Tropics manage not to get blasé and complacent when this has happened to them so often? Now there is much clearing up and putting back to do. However, before we do put anything back, what is that depression forming in the Coral Sea now? Is it worth clearing up yet? Could it be another cyclone?

(We have no experience of a cyclone/hurricane/typhoon at sea)

APPENDIX 8

Crocodiles

As more yachts venture around northern Australian waters, more information needs to be available on how to deal with crocodiles. They are becoming a definite hazard having been a protected species since 1971.

Do you know what to do if you are on a beach and a crocodile swims in? Perhaps you are between her and her nest.

Where would you go if a crocodile suddenly appeared over the sand dune between you and your dinghy?

These questions worried us as we cruised north. There were "Beware Crocodiles" and "Estuarine Crocodiles Inhabit this Area" signs on many beaches, but advice on what to do if you met one, was hard to come by.

There are 26 types of crocodile and alligator in the world, but in Australia, there are only two. These are the (salty) estuarine or salt-water crocodile (Crocodylus porosus) and the (freshie) freshwater or Johnston's crocodile (Crocodylus Johnstoni). Salties eat dogs and humans, freshies do not.

Male salties mature at about 16 years of age and can grow to six metres. The females mature at 10, and grow to two or three metres. They nest in the wet season (November to April) laying about 50 eggs in a soil and vegetation mound about half a metre high. The female usually remains close to the nest throughout the three month incubation, assisting the release of the hatchlings when they are fully developed.

To distinguish between salties and freshies, the latter has a narrow snout and a row of four large scales behind the head. Salties have a broader snout and do not have the row of scales.

When travelling inland we did see freshies basking in the sun on the riverbank and it was nice to know which they were.

There were so many 'nasties' in the sea north of Cairns we decided it was safer not to swim. We anticipated this being a great hardship but it didn't prove to be. Entering the water to clear propellers and for underwater maintenance was scary. We always covered as much of our bodies as possible and kept a lookout.

We gathered the following information from locals and nature reserve wardens:

1. Don't swim where salties could be. They are in all northern tidal rivers and around the coast. They penetrate up into the freshwater areas and large numbers are found in freshwater lagoons and swamps.

2. If chased by a crocodile, run in a zig-zag, as crocs cannot change direction quickly. Keep running. Although your pursuer is very fast, he/she tires quickly.

3.Climb a tree or rock if there is one. However, the croc may be more patient than you and sit below licking his lips.

4. Always carry a strong stick and if cornered try to push it down the crocodile's throat. If it approaches your dinghy in the water, jab an oar down its throat, which is very sensitive.

5.Do not keep a regular routine. When anchored for a few days, go ashore at different times. Vary the time when you collect water, oysters or shells, or have your beach barbecue.

6.Take care where and when you clean your fish. Try to clean them while still at sea or save the waste until you are under way again. There's nothing a crocodile likes more than a ready-made meal on the beach and he will be back again tomorrow. Carcasses of dead animal attract crocodiles so be very wary if you find one.

Crocodiles have survived since the dinosaurs because they are careful hunters. They watch their prey, decide on the most advantageous time to attack, wait and then strike.

At night if you shine a torch across the water or mud, you may see their eyes glowing red. Don't rely on it though.

We decided to anti-foul CLYPEUS on the drying piles at Gove Yacht Club. There were no problems except low water was at 2am and there was no moon. "Watch out for crocs!" We thought the members joked as we filled in the booking form. At midnight, with great trepidation, we climbed down the ladder into the ankle deep water, scanning the shoreline and bay with the flashlight every ten minutes looking for red eyes. We continued to scrub, paint and scan; but gave up searching as there didn't seem to be anything out there and we were fighting against time and tide. For two nights we paddled around in the dark between midnight and 4am and actually saw nothing. Afloat again and chatting in the yacht club somebody said "Good job you didn't stay and work another night. The crocs would have sussed you out and been waiting!"

Popular beaches and estuaries have warnings and crocodile traps. The wardens remove the crocs when caught, and release them well away in the bush. However, crocodiles are territorial and eventually find their way back even if it takes months or years. Remote beaches have no warnings. Often there are fresh tracks leading from high tide marks into the scrub. Even in Port Douglas there were slides down into the mangrove swamps and in Cooktown we were told that two large ones had been seen on the foreshore in the last six months. If we could see tracks on the beach, we didn't go ashore. Crocodile tracks are similar to those of turtles but with a heavier tail furrow. When walking near water we looked for slides where the reptiles slid into the water.

We didn't actually see a crocodile. They are an avoidable hazard.

APPENDIX 9

Bibliography

There are those books to read before you set off; those necessary on the voyage; the travel guides and fun recreational books to enjoy on the way. Most cruisers have a plastic bag of paperbacks ready to swap, some do it one for one, others by weight! I have only listed the books we know and enjoy - there are many others.

Reference Books:

Atlas

Australian Fisherman's Companiion

Celestial Navigation - Mary Blewitt

Cruising for Seniors - Paul Keller

Cruising Under Sail - Eric Hiscock

Dangerous Marine Animals - B.Halstead

Dictionaries English,French, Spanish, Indonesian

Field Guide to Seabirds - Capt G.S.Tuck

First Aid Books - Boots

Fitting out Ferro-Cement Hulls - Tucker

Flags - Granada Guides

Hamlyn Guide to Shells of the World

Hamlyn Guide to Minerals, Rocks & Fossils

McMillan & Silk Cut Almanac

McMillan The Weather Handbook - Alan Watts

Metal Corrosion in Boats - Nigel Warren

Ocean Passages for the World

Ocean Routes - Jimmy Cornell

Ocean Sailing - Rod James

Pilots and Charts

12 Volt Doctor's Alternator Book - Beyn

12 Volt Doctor's Practical Handbook - Beyn

Sell up and Sail - Bill & Laurel Cooper

Survive the Savage Sea - Robertson

The Glassfibre Handbook - R.H. Warring

Travellers Guide to Health - Lt.Col Adam

West Marine Catalogue (much info)

Where There is No Doctor

Yachtsman's Handbook-

The Bible and Shakespeare

Cruising Tales:

117 Days Adrift - Maurice & Marilyn Bailey

After 50,000 miles - Hal Roth

Beyond the West Horizon - E. Hiscock

Blown Away - Herb Payson

Cruising in Serrafyn - Lin & Larry Pardey

Cruising in Tropical waters and Coral -A. Lucas

Desperate Voyage - John Caldwell

Magic of the Swatchways - M Griffiths

Once is Enough - M. Smeeton

Riddle of the Sands - Erskine Childers

Sailing Alone Around the World - Slocum

Small Boat Shoal Water   -

Tristan Jones' Adventures (any or all of them)

The Boat That Wouldn't Float -N. Farson

The Walkabouts - Mike Saunders

Three Boys and a Boat -

Two and a Half Ton Dream

You Can't Blow Back Again - Herb Payson

Don't forget the games too: Cards, Scrabble (a timer is essential some people take SO Long) Boggle, Trivial Pursuits, Chess. Crossword books.

Acknowledgements

So many people have helped us on our way, if I have missed your name please forgive me.

Our families deserve our deepest thanks for being generous in letting us go and then being kind enough to welcome us whenever we came back.

Our eternal gratitude for taking care of our parents to Liz Davis and Hilary Gallagher.

We gratefully thank all those listed below:

For help with charts and information:
Basil D'Olivera, Paul Billing, Rod Laver, the Cruising Association.

For medical and dental help:
Dr. Hugh Dodd, Ron Scarborough and GregorJohnston.

For building such a sturdy boat:
Norman Bagshaw & Sons, Fareham.

For supplying our reliable Perkins diesel engine:
Mr Durrant of Golden Arrow Marine, Shoreham.

For help and advice with sails:
Peter Lucas of Lucas Sails, Portsmouth

For welcoming us into their homes whenever we came home:
Paul, Noel and Andrea and their families, Sheila and Tony, Liz, Lois and James Barrell, Trish and Ray Davis, Jep and Ted Norman, Sally and John Spurgeon, Pat and Peter Walsh, Ros and Arthur Webster

For giving us respite from the sea:
In the Canary Islands: Julie and Austin Ballion, Kiki and Bernard Suchard
In Venezuala: Loney and Levine Stoutjesdje, Carmen and Juan Lassi
In the USA: Alice and Paul, Sally Cox, Kathy and Bill Edwards, Jean and Peter Green, Phyllis and Marian Hetrick, Emily and Paul Keller, Else and Phil Landis, Helen and Art Neal, Rose and Bob Selfridge, Kathy and Dick Voeltz, Ruth and Jack Wright,
In New Zealand: Rose and Andrew Offord, Agnes and Michael Offord, Peta and Neil Stubbings, Georgie and Phil Gardiner, and Margaret of Opua Post Office.
In Australia: Hilary and Pat, Ann and Don Roberts, Mandy Brewis, Shelley and Simon Brewis, Beryl and Richard Newell, Clive, Ann and Gordon Toft, Royston in Coff's Post Office.
In Singapore: Kascia and Pat Brown, Ruth and David Hughes, Sue Williams
In Cyprus: Jean and Sam Bearda, Marguerite and Mike Long, Carole and Jim Moore

For friendship along the way: ASHANTI, BAGHEERA, DEMI, DOUBLE M, GLORY B III, GREEN DOLPHIN, HI-FI, HUNTRESS, KULLAROO, LADY KATE, LAZYBONES, LIBERTY, LITTLE SLOOP, MARA, MAIKWAI, MAIRA, MITHRA, NANOOK, NUAGE, OCEAN WINDS, PLACE IN THE SUN, POM POM, QUALLEE OF SYDNEY, RALPH ROVER, RELATIVITY, RICOCHET, ROSE RAMBLER, SAIORSE, SEAWEED V, SHOESTRING, STAR, SUMMER WIND, SUNCHASER, SUTAMON, TARA TWO, TATTLER, TIMSHELL, TUCUMCARI, TUT SWEET, TYCHE, WINDSEEKER,

To our friends for keeping in touch for twenty years in spite of all the different addresses. You don't realise just how much your letters meant to us: Lois and James Barrell, Anna and Cecil Bourchier, Glen Bowker, Shirley and Bob Brown, Sylvia and John Chandler, Denise and Michael Chittock, Marilyn Cunningham, Mary and Derek Diprose, Carole and Peter du Berne, Sheila and Colin Easton, Joy and Graham Gare, Janet and Malcolm Green, Eileen Halliday, Joan and Desmond Heuval, Teen and John Highmoor, Janet and Cliff Hughes, Angrid and Gregor Johnston, Shirleen and Clyde Jones, Sally Juniper, Dorte and Henrik Juul, Marian and Mike Lough, Sheila and John Martin, Ann and Larry McAlister, Paddy and Bill Monger, Sheelagh and David Noakes, Nettie and Mike Palmer, Irene and Graham Palmer, Gill and Brian Pilcher, Mary and Peter Prior, Christine and Brian Pullen, Terry and David Read, Heather and Graeme Redman, Brenda and Geoff Richards, Barbara and Graeme Reid, Gloria and Brian Sayce, Denise and Geoff Serbutt, Heather and Tony Smith, Sally and John Spurgeon.

For reading, editing and making suggestions during the writing of this book: Pat and Frank Harbud, Margaret Llewellyn, Nigel Jenkins, Hazel Cushion, Hilary, Sheila, Gill and Brian Pilcher, Trish Davis and my friends in Pembroke Dock Writers' Group.

For being so helpful in our new life in Wales:
Sandy Benham-Pellowe and Angela Kerr.

My thanks to Fred Barter for his constant encouragement and expertise.

LASTLY, to CLYPEUS our boat and our home, for looking after us and forgiving our mistakes.

Index